Oregon

Byways

Oregon

Byways

75 Scenic Drives in the Cascades and Siskiyous, Canyons and Coast

By ART BERNSTEIN

WILDERNESS PRESS
BERKELEY, CA

FIRST EDITION August 2003

Published by **Wilderness Press**
          1200 5th Street
          Berkeley, CA 94710
          (800) 443-7227; FAX (510) 558-1696
          mail@wildernesspress.com

Contact us for a free catalog
Visit our website at **www.wildernesspress.com**

Front cover photo: Mt. Hood (Drive 2)
Back cover: Approaching Dug Bar on the Snake River (Drive 55)
Frontispiece: Mt. Hood from Cooper Spur Rd. (Drive 2)

Acknowledgments

The author gratefully acknowledges the many outstanding individuals who made this book possible, starting with Tony Huegel, originator of this scenic byways series. I should also thank Wilderness Press (Mike Jones and Jannie Dresser) for their confidence and encouragement. And I thank Don Skillman for recommending me to Tony Huegel and Mike Jones. Michael Dobrin, representing Toyota Public Relations, deserves a nod for supplying the magnificent sport-utility vehicles (SUVs) that made this project infinitely easier and more fun. Among public land management people, Liz Stevenson-Shaw, the information officer for Umpqua National Forest, rose to the surface (as she always does), providing maps and reference material for national forests throughout the entire state. I've come to expect such "above and beyond" efforts from Liz. For information on the roads and recovery process following the 2002 Biscuit Fire, I thank Siskiyou National Forest employees Rene Casteran, Judie McHugh, and Diana Saint Marie. And of course, I am happy to acknowledge Patricia Bernstein, who accompanied me on several of these journeys, even when the going got rough.

And finally, there are the loyal readers and booksellers who have followed my writing career and purchased my books with such enthusiasm over the years. They need to know that they are, in large part, responsible for making my life worth living.

Disclaimer

Oregon Byways helps you enjoy backcountry driving. It assumes that you have a high-clearance vehicle that is properly equipped for backcountry travel on unpaved, sometimes unmaintained and primitive roads. The book is not intended to be an exhaustive, all-encompassing authority on backcountry driving in Oregon, nor is it intended as your only source of information about the subject or about the described drives.

Although the drives herein are all reasonably safe, certain risks and dangers are inevitable when driving off-pavement in remote areas. At any time, the condition of unpaved roads can deteriorate quickly and substantially. Signs get knocked over, turned around, or vandalized. Roads designated herein as unpaved may be improved or paved at any time. Thus, you could encounter conditions considerably different or worse than described here. If you drive the routes in this book, just as with any other backcountry roads, you assume all risks, dangers, and liability that may result. The author and publisher of this book disclaim any and all liability for any injury, loss, or damage that you, your passengers, or your vehicle may incur.

Always exercise the caution and good judgment that visiting the backcountry demands. Bring the proper supplies, and, above all, be prepared to deal with accidents, injuries, breakdowns, and other problems on your own, because help will almost always be far away and a long time coming.

Contents

Preface

A Land of Fire and Renewal:
The 2002 Biscuit Fire

On July 13, 2002, following an unusually dry winter, a rainless lightning storm assailed the mountains of southwest Oregon, touching off dozens of small forest fires. Five significant blazes were set off in the rugged, inaccessible backcountry within and near the 180,000-acre Kalmiopsis Wilderness. One fire took hold in dense old-growth forest a half-mile west of Florence Creek which flows from the Kalmiopsis' northern boundary south into the Illinois River. Another blaze flared up 30 miles south in the pine- and brush-covered hills one mile east of Sourdough Camp (Trip 48), a remote and beautiful spot at the southern tip of the Kalmiopsis. The Florence Fire roared up the creek to Bald Ridge while the Sourdough Fire (later named the Sour-Biscuit Fire) soon incinerated everything between its origin and nearby Biscuit Hill, quickly merging with three other blazes in the vicinity. The Sour-Biscuit Fire eventually converged with the Florence Fire to form the massive and historic Biscuit Fire.

By September 5, when the Biscuit Fire was officially declared contained, over 499,570 acres had burned, making it Oregon's largest forest fire in 150 years in a state known for its many large forest fires. The conflagration dwarfed Oregon's famous Tillamook Burn of the 1940s. Over $154 million dollars were spent to suppress the fire, and the National Guard was called out. At the fire's height, over 7,000 workers manned the lines, heroically averting disaster for the communities of Cave Junction, Selma, Agness, and Brookings.

The fire just about ruined the summer hiking season. As a hiking fanatic, I live for July and August when high country snow is finally cleared and remote wilderness trails open up. In summer 2002, wherever you went in the far west, no matter how deep into the wilderness you hiked, you encountered choking, stifling smoke (there were many, many other forest fires that summer, and the thinly stretched fire-fighting resources partly explained why the Biscuit Fire got so badly out of control).

Biscuit Fire on Eight Dollar Road (Drive 42)

When I was finally able to explore the roads within the Biscuit Fire's perimeter, I was struck more than anything by the apparent lack of an ecological downside. The fire caused severe economic loss, mainly in timber reserves and houses burned. Fish habitat might have been impaired in some areas due to increased siltation, but otherwise the fire may have been more beneficial than destructive in the long run. Those I spoke with in the Forest Service did not counter my assessment.

Roads Affected in *Oregon Byways*

Thirteen of the 75 scenic back road trips in this book are located within the boundaries of the infamous Biscuit Fire. They are Drives 18-23, 39-46, and 48 (those drives are indicated by the ◕ symbol in the Contents). This book was about to go to print when the fires occurred so publication was held up to allow an update concerning possible alteration to roads and scenery. Nearly all of the roads had reopened after autumn and winter rains, although many were under snow in their far reaches or extremely muddy when I checked them out, and therefore undriveable. Where I was unable to re-drive a route, I consulted with Forest Service employees. There were only two sections that had not been re-visited by the Forest Service at the time I updated this book, and they are: (1) the far end of the road to Silver Creek Falls in Drive 6 which is blocked by multiple fallen trees and heavily burned; and, (2) the far end of Little Todd Creek Road, Drive 44, which is gated and was also heavily burned.

All roads are now reopened and their conditions will be equivalent to the way they were before the fire. However, since road signage was poor *before* the fire, *it has gotten worse*. Several years ago, Siskiyou National Forest's road maintenance budget was drastically cut and available funds were dedicated to maintaining roads rather than placing new road signs. With less vegetation to absorb spring runoff, roads may be muddier than usual, with more ruts and washouts. Some bridges and wooden culverts have also been damaged or weakened. And, as a result of numerous fallen and dying trees, there will undoubtedly be more fallen snags blocking the roadway.

A Few Words to the Wise

As recommended for every Drive in this book, you should bring a detailed map. Remember that pathfinding is part of the adventure, and all of these roads are worth driving—even more so since the fire.

INTRODUCTION

top: Turnoff to Crack-in-the-Ground. Note sign—"Cars not recommended"
(Drive 62)
bottom: Road to Succor Creek State Park (Drive 74)

Introduction

First of all, let's get one thing straight: I could easily have included a hundred drives in this book, even a thousand. I could have written an entire book on four-wheel-drive (4WD) roads to fire lookouts alone and still not covered them all. But still, my selection criteria were fairly broad:

1. The roads had to be scenic.
2. At least half of each trip had to follow unpaved roads.
3. The roads had to be at least partly in Oregon.

In my thirty years of exploring and writing about the Oregon backcountry, I've concluded that Oregon is an exceptionally scenic state, with mile after mile of unpaved roads. For this book, my 75 selections were sometimes arbitrary, sometimes intensely personal. They total 1,975 miles, are more or less spread over the entire state, and offer an array of scenery, driving distances, and levels of difficulty. You may disagree with some of my selections but I can guarantee that if you visit every place I describe, you will experience the wonders of Oregon in a way that cannot possibly be duplicated by sticking to the main highways. And you will miss very little worth seeing in Oregon, except perhaps downtown Portland or the Crater Lake rim. If you do tour downtown Portland or the Crater Lake rim, to obtain an altogether deeper level of experience check out Drive 1 (Molalla Canyon, near Portland) and Drive 36 (Sand Creek Pinnacles, near Crater Lake).

My selections are weighted toward the southwest corner of Oregon. I happen to live in that area and I know it best. I also have another legitimate reason: Southwest Oregon contains the most unpaved roads. Northwest Oregon (Portland, Eugene, Salem) has more total roads than southwest Oregon, since it has a larger population, but roads there tend to be paved. As for northeast and southeast Oregon, both areas have many miles of unpaved road but they also have fewer total roads. Central Oregon ranks somewhere between southwest and northwest Oregon in the amount of unpaved roadway. But still, there may have been a little bias.

I otherwise spread my selections evenly around the state. The only areas I had problems with were the north coast, the Portland area (not surprisingly, as I mentioned), Malheur National Forest, Umatilla National Forest, and the Blue Mountains. These are all magnificent regions with breathtaking scenery, but on the north coast and in the Portland area all the good roads are paved, and in the Malheur, Umatilla, and Blue Mountain areas, as scenic as they are, I just couldn't pinpoint a suitable route to a specific destination (although I'm sure residents of those places could enlighten me in a hurry). I did squeeze in a nice little drive along the north fork of the Malheur River (Drive 73). The best road in the Blue Mountains, to Anthony Lakes, is paved.

I also tried to include unusual places, places about which people might be curious. Like the top of the Abert Rim (Drive 64), where established roads go only along the rim's bottom. Or the bottom of Hells Canyon (Drive 55), where the most popular road goes only along the top. I did not, alas, succeed in some of these quests. According to the Bureau of Land Management's (BLM's) Vale District map, a very long (about 40 miles), very primitive road takes off near the Oregon–Nevada line and eventually passes the spot where Oregon, Nevada, and Idaho intersect. I could not find this road.

But I have included dozens of knockout trips in the central and south coast areas, the Siskiyou Mountains, the Mt. Hood area, and the northern, central and southern Cascades. Close-up views of all the state's highest peaks are here, plus a couple of drives in the Ochoco Mountains, several in the John Day and Wallowa-Hells Canyon areas, a bunch in the central Oregon lava country, and a bunch more in the southeast desert and Steens Mountain areas. One trip crosses the Idaho line and four cross the California line.

And not once did I get lost or stuck (although in Drive 48 it was only because at a junction some thoughtful soul had left directions, marked on a plastic milk jug).

A conclusion I drew from my travels: every region of Oregon is gorgeous and has its own unique appeal. It was hard to go wrong. As I said, I could have covered a thousand roads here. The fact is, you can throw a dart at an Oregon map and it will invariably land within a millimeter of a scenic wonder worthy of your time (have you seen the Rome Pillars, near Jordan Valley? Check out Drive 75). Considering Oregon's size (it is the tenth-largest state, covering 96,000 square miles), that's a lot of scenic bang for the buck.

I used a four-wheel-drive vehicle for about half the drives. Since my primary criteria were the quality of the scenery and of the destination, not the road surface, I do not consider this a 4WD book. Except in the very worst weather, nearly every trip described herein could probably be covered in a two-wheel-drive vehicle, although high clearance, front-wheel drive, and good shock absorbers (especially these) are essential on the majority of the roads.

Of the 75 drives, the following are rated "difficult" and 4WD is highly recommended: Badger Lake (Drive 3), Elk Lake (Drive 9), Klamath Canyon (Drive 37), Chetco Pass (Drive 40), Tennessee Lookout (Drive 43), Sourdough Camp (Drive 48), and Abert Rim (Drive 64). The Rock Lakes Road (Drive 4), High Rock Road (Drive 5), Skyline Road (Drive 7), Quartz Mountain Road (Drive 31), Hershberger Lookout (Drive 33), Pelican Butte (Drive 35), Lower Imnaha Canyon (Drive 58) and Leslie Gulch (Drive 74) drives are "moderate-to-difficult" and may require some driving skill. Many of the "side trips," listed at the end of each drive, are also best visited with 4WD.

How to use Oregon Byways

The following information is provided for each of the 75 drives:

LOCATION. This section tells the general region where the drive is located so the reader will know where to look on an Oregon road map (see also "LOCATOR MAP" at the beginning of the "Drive" sections). Locations may be expressed as a section of the state (northeast, central, southwest), the nearest city or major town ("east of Roseburg"), or a mountain range or geographic region (Harney Basin, Northern Cascades).

HIGHLIGHTS. This section gives a brief summary of the drive's main attractions. Bear in mind that drives are selected primarily for scenic quality, not driving challenge.

DIFFICULTY. This is a fairly subjective heading. In general, "Easy" means the road is pretty much smooth sailing. "Moderate" means there are substantial stretches that are bumpy, rutted, steep, narrow, very curvy, sometimes muddy and on which (unless you are crazy) you will be going less than 30 mph and might consider shifting into 4WD. A "Difficult" road is narrower, bumpier, steeper and more challenging than a "Moderate" road and you will definitely want to shift into 4WD. Avoid drives designated as "Difficult" if you don't have 4WD. The section also briefly describes the overall road conditions on each trip (there is usually a variety).

DISTANCE. This heading gives the distance in miles for each drive, and the drive's starting and finishing points. If the drive is a loop, the beginning and end points will be identical. A starting point given as "Highway 101" (for example), refers to the spot where the initial turnoff from Highway 101, as described under "Getting There," leaves the highway. Similarly, an ending point given as "Highway 101," refers to where the last described road meets Highway 101. Because driving styles, and time spent out of the car, vary greatly, driving times are not given.

HIGH ELEVATION. I was originally going to include a heading called "Best Season" but weather in Oregon (rain and snow), is so variable year to year that generalizing about it borders on folly. The best single piece of information by which to estimate whether a road is likely to be opened and passable or blocked by snow, is the road's highest elevation, expressed in feet above sea level. By knowing a drive's highest elevation, you can estimate your chances of getting through based on current weather conditions and snow pack. Secondary and unpaved roads are virtually never plowed in winter.

By and large, unplowed roads above 5,000 feet become passable by mid-June in Oregon but may become passable as early as mid-May or as late as early July, depending on the snowfall the previous winter. Roads under 3,000 feet are generally snow-free year round, except during low-elevation snowstorms, which might occur two or three times during an average Oregon winter.

Mud on the road, and swollen creeks running across the road, can present a problem during the rainy season, and during the spring snow melt, no matter what the elevation. Oregon's rainy season is winter. When it snows at higher elevations, it rains at lower elevations. If a road is especially prone to muddying up, flash floods or high water, that is discussed under "Special Information."

Elevations were obtained from United States Geological Survey topographic maps, which are public-domain. Most elevations are estimates only, arrived at by interpolating between the map's contour lines. The elevation difference (or "interval") between contour lines may be as much as 400 feet. Elevations arrived at in this manner are expressed to the nearest 100 feet and may be off by as much as 200 feet. Occasionally, USGS maps give a benchmark showing the precise elevation, in which case that was the figured used.

MAPS. This section tells the name of the United States Geological Survey 7.5-minute topographic map(s) on which the described drive appears. These maps offer outstanding detail but don't cover much area, only about 10 miles by 10 miles. United States Department of Agriculture (USDA) Forest Service National Forest maps, and United States Bureau of Land Management (BLM) District maps, cover much larger areas and are strongly recommend. National Forest maps applicable to this book include Deschutes, Fremont, Mt. Hood, Ochoco, Rogue River, Siskiyou, Siuslaw, Umpqua, Wallow-Whitman, Willamette, and Winema. BLM District maps include Burns, Coos Bay, North and South Lakeview, Medford, Prineville, Salem, and North and South Vale. Many of the drives are shown on highway maps of Oregon but with little detail. See the "Administration" section for each trip to determine which map(s) you will need.

ADMINISTRATION. This section lists the primary administering agencies of the described roads or the adjacent land around the roads. Most roads are administered either by the Forest Service or the BLM. See "Addresses" at the end of the book.

GETTING THERE. This section explains how to get to the beginning of the described drive (and sometimes the end) and includes major roads, turns, distances between turns and road surfaces (paved, gravel, dirt) during the actual drive. It also includes detailed descriptions of junctions that when you get there are poorly marked or don't match the map.

Do not, I repeat, *do not*, attempt to navigate solely by the description in this section or by the accompanying map inset. Obtain the appropriate state highway, National Forest or BLM map, plan your route beforehand and bring the map with you. Your route may differ from the described route if you approach from a different direction, combine two or more drives or take side trips.

The road numbers and names shown on published maps are frequently not posted on the ground, especially on dirt roads (current Forest Service policy is to post fewer road signs than previously). My descriptions attempt to stick to what's visible on the ground so you won't look for road numbers that may not exist.

Most distances in this section are rounded to the nearest 0.2 of a mile and are based on either mileposts alongside the road, mileage posted on road signs or the odometer in the author's car (which may not agree with your car's odometer). To avoid confusion, where a distance was indicated on a posted road sign, that is the figure used. Posted signs nearly always give distances in whole miles. If the posted distance differed significantly from the mileage shown on my odometer, that is noted in the text. Where a more precise distance is essential to locating a turnoff, it is given to the nearest 0.1 of a mile.

"Mileposts" are small signs located at one-mile intervals alongside a road, indicating the distance from the road's beginning. In the text, this is abbreviated as "MP." Remember that a turnoff located 0.2 of a mile beyond MP 58 (for example), heading west, will be 0.8 of a mile past MP 59 if you are heading in the opposite direction.

Roads may be either (1) paved four-lane Interstate freeways (designated as "I" in "Getting There"), (2) four-lane or two-lane paved U.S. or state or highways (designated as "Highway" or "Hwy."), (3) two-lane paved county roads (designated as "CR"), (4) two-lane paved, one-lane paved, gravel or dirt Forest Service or BLM roads (designated as "FR" for "Forest Road"), or (5) spur roads, which are low-quality gravel or dirt roads branching from a Forest Road (designated as "Spur").

Above all, remember that things change. Road signs can vanish, new signs get posted and roads deteriorate or become closed-off, rerouted or resurfaced. So don't be shocked if what you see differs from what the author describes. Consider it part of the adventure.

REST STOPS. This section provides information on where to find things like toilets, picnic sites, campgrounds, convenience stores and gas stations.

SPECIAL INFORMATION. This section contains pertinent information not provided elsewhere. Included are such things as whether a trip could be done in the reverse direction (sometimes one direction is far preferable, sometimes it doesn't matter), entrance fees, construction delays, seasonally locked gates, road washouts and proneness to flash floods.

Note: I was caught in a flash flood while researching this book, on Highway 140 in Warner Canyon on the way to Drive 66. Following an intense summer thunderstorm, including three inches of hail accumulation on the road, water began pouring down the hillsides and across the pavement in dozens of places, carrying tons of mud and rock with it. On the way back, two hours later, everything had returned to normal, with the impressive help of the Oregon Highway Department.

THE DRIVE. This section is the main narrative, the "story"of each trip. It describes in detail what you will be seeing and provides background information on the natural and human history as well as occasional personal anecdotes. Only rarely are road conditions, distances and junctions described in this section because that information is provided in other sections (see "Difficulty" and "Getting There").

SIDE TRIPS. This section contains alternate routes, variations on main routes, nearby attractions, etc. This section may include routes covered in other chapters as main drives or side trips. Although some side trips are described in as much detail as the main drive, there is usually a good reason why it is a side trip and not a main drive. This is usually explained in the text. A few short side routes are included as part of the main drive because the drives are pretty much pointless without them. These include Bagby Hot Springs (Drive 11), Summit Lake (Drive 26), Fairview Lookout (Drive 29) and Quartz Mountain (Drive 31).

MAP INSET. The map inset for each chapter is based on a number of public-domain map sources. Insets are intended for trip planning only and you are strongly urged to bring a more detailed Forest Service, BLM, state or commercial road map on the actual trip.

Mountaintop elevations shown on map insets are based primarily on National Forest maps, secondarily on BLM maps (if not shown on a National Forest map), and tertiarily on the official Oregon State Highway Department road map (if not shown on a National Forest or BLM map). If no elevation is shown on the inset, it means that none was given on any of the above sources. Readers should be aware that mountaintop elevation figures, on maps from different sources, rarely agree.

ICONS. See page 22 for icon key.

Lake Abert, Abert Rim (Drive 64)

White River Falls (Drive 52)

Lower Deschutes River (Drive 52)

Land of Rivers, Volcanoes, and Wonder

"From great Hells Canyon to Wizard Island,
From the Doug-fir forest to Cape Blanco's waters,
Oregon was made for you and me."

(Apologies to Woody Guthrie)

The beauty and abundance of Oregon have been cherished by human beings for 25,000 years, beginning with a group of nomadic hunters and gatherers who settled in the lower Rogue Canyon, near what is today the town of Marial. To find out for yourself what the big attraction in Marial was 25,000 years ago, see Drive 38.

From that tenuous beginning, tribes sprang up all over the region. Principal groups were the Takelmas and Tututnis in the Rogue Valley, the Umpquas in the Umpqua Valley, the Modocs and Klamaths in the Klamath Basin and the Umatillas in eastern Oregon. Tribes east of the Cascade Mountains put up with little rainfall (10 to 15 inches annually) and a colder climate in exchange for rivers full of salmon and wetlands that featured some of the continent's most productive waterfowl breeding areas. Tribes west of the Cascades enjoyed plenty of rain (over 100 inches a year in some places), abundant game and edible plants (huckleberries in particular), and more than abundant salmon, along with a pleasant, moderate climate.

The Pacific Northwest coastal tribes, from Oregon into southeast Alaska, were considered North America's most culturally advanced nonagricultural groups. Because the surfeit of salmon easily met most survival needs, they were able to devote an increased amount of time to strictly cultural matters. (See Drive 52 for directions to a Native American scaffolding that was built over a river rapid for the purpose of snagging salmon.)

Beginning with the Lewis and Clark expedition in the early 1800's (although explorers like Francis Drake and George Vancouver visited the Oregon coast prior to Lewis and Clark), Europeans began trickling into the region. (See Drive 75 for an interesting Lewis and Clark landmark.) By the 1830's, following trails blazed by settlers like Peter Skene Ogden and Peter Applegate, the trickle had become a deluge. Enduring many hardships, pioneers made the cross-country trip by ox-drawn wagon. They settled in what began as a Hudson's Bay Company fiefdom and later became a United States Territory, with the Hudson's Bay Company's John McLoughlin as first territorial governor. The "Oregon Country" originally included what are now the states of Oregon, Washington, and Idaho, as well as part of British Columbia. In western valleys, such as the Willamette and Umpqua, pioneers discovered what the native tribes had encountered eons earlier: some of the world's richest farmland, with abundant rain, a mild climate, and lots and lots of fish. (At the time, California was considered to be a remote backwater, too hot and arid to bother with. To grow crops in California, you had to irrigate.)

Everything changed for Oregon in the late 1840's when gold was discovered at Sutter's Mill, near Auburn, California. The great California Gold Rush extended into southern Oregon's Siskiyou Mountains, especially Jackson, Josephine, Douglas, and Curry counties. (To visit some early gold mining areas, see Drives 29, 43 and 49.) As a result of population growth spurred by the Gold Rush, the Oregon Territory became three states of the United States in 1859 (Oregon, Washington, and Idaho). Despite the partition into three states, Oregon still ended up as the tenth largest state in the country, covering 96,000 square miles.

To accommodate the population explosion, native groups were subjugated—tragic chapter in Oregon's early history. Southern Oregon's Rogue tribes fought particularly hard and bravely against overwhelming odds. And the Modocs of the Klamath Basin made history in 1875 when Modoc chief Captain Jack and a band of 100 of his people held off the U.S. Army for six months, at what is now Lava Beds National Monument in northern California. (See Drives 56 and 57 for landmarks associated with Chief Joseph of the Nez Perce, and his heartbreaking attempt, in the face of colonization, simply to move his tribe to Canada.)

Following the (non-native) discovery of Crater Lake in 1886, this scenic landmark became, in 1902, America's fourth national park (after Yellowstone, Yosemite, and Mt. Rainier), predating the 1916 establishment of the National Park Service. Crater Lake was also the world's fourth national park, since there were no other countries with national parks in 1916. Crater Lake remains one of the National Park Service's more popular units, with two million visitors annually. Visitors are drawn to the lake's impossibly blue waters, its cliff-enclosed shoreline, and the fact that it is North America's deepest lake, at nearly 2,000 feet (although most of the lake's 17,000 acres are not nearly that deep). For an unusual perspective on Oregon's only national park, which is today extremely automobile-oriented, see Drive 36. See the geology section, below, for more on Crater Lake.

Until the late 1970's, the basis of the Oregon economy was timber products. Trees were initially cut down with two-man whipsaws. Logs were then yarded out of the woods by motorized winches called "steam donkeys" (and sometimes by real donkeys), and floated down rivers to local sawmills, with the finished lumber shipped off by train. "Wigwam" chip burners, associated with small sawmills, dotted the rural landscape for decades. Logging accelerated after World War II with the advent of the chainsaw and the log truck, but the pace proved unsustainable, especially given the rising environmental movement. By the start of the twenty-first century, Oregon's economy had greatly diversified. Drive 13 presents an interesting slice of Oregon's colorful logging history.

Geography, Geology, and Ecology

Geographically, Oregon can be divided into many regions. The most obvious are:

1. The *Columbia River Gorge*, which forms Oregon's northern border, is a spectacular region where a major river, on its way to the Pacific Ocean, knifes cleanly and abruptly through the Cascade Mountain range. The cliffs of basaltic lava are breathtaking, the many high waterfalls are stunning (including Multnomah Falls, at 580 feet the highest in the United States outside Yosemite), and even the immense dams are impressive. It is fascinating to drive along the gorge and observe the transition from a coastal forest of shore pine and Sitka spruce to an inland rain forest of Douglas-fir, western hemlock, and western redcedar, to ponderosa pine country, to grassland covered only with sagebrush and a few junipers. See Drive 52 for an interesting view of the Columbia Gorge.

2. The *Willamette and Umpqua valleys* were the destination of the early settlers. These are flat river basins with deep soils and lush farmland

Owyhee Canyon (Drive 75)

between the Cascades and the coastal ranges. Originally, vast expanses of Douglas-fir forest covered the valleys, except where frequent fires created openings. The Willamette Valley is home to Oregon's four largest cities, Portland, Eugene, Salem, and Gresham.

3. The *Coastal Ranges*, along the Pacific coast, are much lower than the inland Cascades, Siskiyous, or Wallowas, rarely rising above 4,000 feet. Unlike the inland ranges, the coastal ranges are composed mostly of sandstone. Since the coastal ranges get the brunt of the frequent and intense winter storms blowing in off the Pacific, trees in the forests are immense, rivers are fast and wild, and the canyons are deep and rocky. This is prime logging and Douglas-fir country. Drive 14 offers an excellent tour of a coastal river canyon that opens on to the ocean.

4. The *Rogue / Siskiyou Region* of southwest Oregon contains the state's oldest rock and two of its most spectacular white-water canyons, the lower Rogue and Illinois rivers (Drives 39 and 45). Geologically, the Siskiyous are a "pluton," a large chunk of granite (and metamorphosed lava) that extends 150 miles into California. The formation, called the "Klamath system," includes California's Trinity Alps and Marble Mountains as well as the Siskiyous. The highest peak in the Oregon Siskiyous is Mt. Ashland (7,495 feet), visited in Drive 51. The highest peak in the Klamath system is Mt. Eddy (9,050 feet), near Mt. Shasta.

The Siskiyou region is famous for its botanical diversity. It occupies an overlap zone between the Pacific Northwest, California Sierra, and coastal range forest regions. It is the only mountain bridge between the coastal ranges and the inland Cascades, it contains many out-of-place species left over from the last ice age, and it contains large areas of serpentinite soils, which are home to many unusual plant species.* See Drive 42 for a good botanical tour of the Siskiyous.

5. The *Cascade Mountains*, a string of dormant and recently active volcanoes, run north-south down the middle of Oregon and divide the state into two distinct regions. The barrier begins at northern California's Lassen Peak,

* The ice age moved the natural ranges of many species due to the climate change. After the ice age, the species resumed their former ranges, except in isolated spots, many in the Siskiyous.

which last erupted in 1917, and ends at Mt. Garibaldi in British Columbia. It includes two peaks that exceed 14,000 feet, Mts. Shasta and Rainier, neither of which is in Oregon. The highest Oregon peak in the Cascades is Mt. Hood, topping out at 11,249 feet (see Drives 2 and 6). The Three Sisters (Drive 28) and Mt. Jefferson (Drive 7), also in Oregon, all exceed 10,000 feet elevation. The highway passes between the major Cascade peaks are fairly low, at around 5,000 feet, compared to the passes in the California Sierra Nevada, some of which exceed 9,000 feet.

The Cascades consist of the High Cascades and the much older Western Cascades. The Western Cascades lie slightly west of the High Cascades, but the two systems intermingle. The High Cascades reach their maximum extent in southern Oregon, in the vast lava country around Bend and Crater Lake (Drives 34, 37, and several others). They are characterized by immense, composite volcanoes, lava fields, cinder cones, and recent volcanic activity. The Western Cascades are mostly in Washington. They are much more eroded and are characterized by less distinct landforms, by exposed volcanic plugs at the cores of ancient volcanoes, and by a distinct and universal 18-degree tilt to their bedded lava flows. See Drive 32 and others.

The climax of the southern High Cascades is Crater Lake, which until 7,000 years ago was a 12,000-foot, glaciated peak, subsequently named Mt. Mazama. After a major eruption sent a plume of ash around the world, the peak caved in on itself and the resulting caldera filled with rainwater and formed this magnificent lake. There are two other similar formations nearby, Newberry Caldera (Drive 25) near Bend, and the Mountain Lakes Basin near Klamath Falls, which may be viewed from atop Pelican Butte (Drive 35). There is another such formation in northern California, the Medicine Lake Highland, just east of Mt. Shasta.

6. The *Wallowa Mountains*, and the adjacent Blue Mountains, in Oregon's extreme northeast corner, are the only segments of the Rocky Mountains in Oregon. The Seven Devils Mountains, just over the Idaho state line, are also part of the Rockies. Several Rocky Mountain tree species occur in Oregon only in the Wallowas, including Rocky Mountain juniper.

Called the "Alps of North America," the Wallowa Mountains and Eagle Cap Wilderness are considered by many to be the most beautiful mountains

Abert Rim, Abert Lake from top of rim (Drive 64)

Klamath Canyon in California (Drive 37)

anywhere. The white granite peaks and vast floral meadows rise to over 9,000 feet in many places, with dozens of immense glacial valleys and gemlike cirque lakes dotting the region. See Drive 56 for a close-up tour of a Wallowa glacial valley, and Drives 55 and 57 for a look at Hells Canyon, North America's deepest gorge, which separates the Wallowas from the Seven Devils. All this scenery is unparalleled anywhere else in Oregon.

7. What I've called the *Desert Plateau* is actually an "everything else" category of high desert, semi-arid ranch land, fault-block mountain ranges, and mighty river canyons. In Washington, the region is called the Inland Empire. In Oregon it is called, variously, Central Oregon, Southeast Oregon, the Lava Plateau, or simply "the desert." This vast and lonely area includes not only miles and miles of barren desert but the Steens Mountains (9,700 feet), the North Warner Mountains (8,500 feet), and the Ochoco Mountains (8,200 feet). To tour the Steens, Warners, and Ochocos, see Drives 67, 64, and 53.

The region boasts several interesting features. One is the aforementioned Lava Plateau, a mysterious area of layered lava flows covering thousands of square miles with no obvious source. Many of the region's benches, rimrock, and canyon walls are made of plateau lava. See Drives 24, 52, and 62 for examples of bedded lava. See Drives 61 and 71 for tours of high-desert volcanic formations.

An interesting feature that significantly overlaps southeast Oregon is the Great Basin, an immense, multistate region with no drainage to the ocean and many dry sinks and lake beds. Geologically, this is basin-and-range (or "*horst* and *graben*") country, where the land is being pulled apart rather than pushed together, forming alternating lineal valleys and fault-block mountain uplifts. See Drives 64 and 65 for spectacular examples of basin-and-range formations.

Major river canyons of the region include the John Day, Deschutes, Crooked, Owyhee, and Snake. See Drives 24, 52, 54, 59, 60, 74, and 75.

Ecologically, the dominant plant of the desert plateau is sagebrush, followed by more sagebrush, and still more sagebrush. Other dominant species include grass, bitterbrush, rabbitbrush, western Juniper, and sagebrush, with pockets, in the moister mountain areas, of ponderosa pine, lodgepole pine, Douglas-fir, quaking aspen, Englemann spruce, noble fir, and western Larch.

Back-road Driving

by Tony Huegel
Creator of Backcountry Byways

ADVENTURING IN YOUR 4WD. *Oregon Byways* is intended to introduce backcountry touring to people who travel in factory-stock, high-clearance vehicles, particularly SUVs, equipped for possibly rough off-highway conditions. Since relatively few people who drive SUVs take advantage of all their vehicle's features, I'll assume that most readers' experience is limited. My hope is to help you have a safe and enjoyable experience while protecting the natural environment.

    KNOW YOUR VEHICLE. Some automakers, eager to tap into the motoring public's yen for at least the appearance of adventure, have begun to apply the label "sport-utility" to just about anything with wheels. Don't be fooled. Know what you're driving, and drive within the vehicle's limits, as well as your own.

    Familiarize yourself with your vehicle's four-wheel drive system. Is it full-time, part-time, or automatic? In a full-time, or permanent, 4WD system, all four wheels are continuously engaged as driving wheels; there is no two-wheel drive (2WD) mode. (A multimode system, however, will include a 2WD mode.) Full-time 4WD uses either a center differential or viscous coupling to allow the front and rear axles to turn independently for typical daily driving. Some systems allow the driver to "lock" the center differential so that, in poor conditions, both axles will turn together for greater traction. A part-time system uses only the rear wheels as driving wheels until the driver engages 4WD. A part-time system must be disengaged from 4WD on pavement to avoid excessive drive train stress. An automatic system is designed to sense on its own when 4WD should be engaged. All-wheel-drive (AWD) systems, such as those used in some passenger cars and vans, provide power to all four wheels much as full-time 4WD systems do. But AWD vehicles are usually designed for all-weather, not all-terrain use.

    Does your vehicle have a transfer case? More than any other feature, a transfer case identifies a vehicle suited to all-terrain travel. It sends power to the front axles as well as the rear axles, and, acting as an auxiliary transmission, it provides a wider range of gear ratios for a wider range of driving conditions. Use high-range 2WD for everyday driving in normal conditions, both on pavement and off. Use high-range 4WD when added traction is helpful or necessary on loose or slick surfaces, but when conditions are not difficult. Use low-range 4WD in difficult low-speed conditions when maximum traction and power are needed, and to keep engine revs high while moving slowly through rough or steep terrain.

    Does the vehicle have all-season highway tires or all-terrain tires? Tires take a terrible beating in off-highway conditions, for which all-terrain tires are designed.

    Find out where the engine's air intake is, and how high it is. This is important to avoid the devastating consequences of sucking water into the engine through the air intake while fording waterways.

    Does the vehicle have steel "skid plates" protecting undercarriage components like the engine oil pan, transfer case and transmission? Skid plates are essential to avoiding the expensive and inconvenient damage that obstacles, particularly roadbed rocks, can inflict.

    WEATHER AND WHEN TO GO. Rainfall in Oregon varies from a couple inches a year in the southeast desert to hundreds of inches a year in the coastal rain forest. Visitors to the Cascades can count on violent summertime thunderstorms, snow by late October, and, above 4,000 feet, a winter pack that closes most back roads. Summer nights in the Cascades are wonderful. The desert is usually snow-free in winter but it is subject to occasional driving blizzards. In summer, the desert is usually a little cooler and less humid than the western valleys because of higher elevation. Winter rain near the coast can be terrifying.

In spring, streams swell with runoff, but the desert lands east of the Cascades often contain a pallet of wildflowers. Lower forest roads can be muddy through June or early July. A road that is clear for miles can remain blocked as late as mid-July by a slow-melting, late-season snowdrift lingering in a single spot of shade.

Pay attention to the sky, even the distant sky, in case a storm is brewing. Stay out of washes and narrow canyons if a storm seems likely. When it rains, many dirt roads can become dangerously slick. Some may become impassable, even with a 4WD. But danger aside, driving on muddy roads leaves tracks that can erode into major ruts, so avoid doing it simply for that reason.

I particularly enjoy September and early October. Daytime temperatures are mild, the aspens are turning color, and the sunlight is taking on its golden autumn hue. But, remember, the days by then are growing shorter, and you do not want to drive at night.

GOING ALONE. There is security in having more than one vehicle, and more than one source of ideas and of labor if things go awry. In rough terrain, it's also fun to be with other people. But when on vacation, or venturing off for a few hours, a day, or a weekend, you and yours will probably go alone, in a single vehicle. And that's OK, so long as your vehicle is reliable and you're prepared to handle emergencies alone.

You won't always have the road to yourself. On the contrary, Oregonians love their back roads. Tourists do, too. Exploring backcountry roads is becoming an increasingly popular form of recreation. While the more remote roads may provide genuine solitude, you will almost certainly be sharing other roads with all sorts of users, from mountain bikers and hikers to all-terrain vehicle riders, ranchers, and loggers. Be alert, and be considerate.

RULES OF THE ROAD. Even where no one will be watching, there are rules to follow, and practices that help keep you safe, that keep your vehicle operating reliably, and that preserve natural and historic areas. Misconduct and bad mistakes can result in personal injury, damage to your vehicle, areas being closed, and perhaps even legal penalties.

Here are some things to keep in mind:

1. Drive only on established roads where motor vehicles are permitted. Mechanized travel of any kind, including motorcycles and mountain bikes, is not allowed in designated wilderness areas unless a legal corridor exists. Never go "off-road," make a new route, or follow the tracks of someone who did.

2. Do not disturb archaeological or historic sites or artifacts. They are not replaceable, and they are protected by federal laws. Do not touch Native American rock art. Have the utmost respect and care for historic structures, and treat them like the important relics of bygone times that they are.

3. Do not use archaeological or historic sites for picnics or camping unless they are developed for those purposes.

4. Your vehicle must be street-legal to take these drives. Obey traffic laws and regulatory signs, wear your seat belt, and keep the kids buckled up.

5. If you get lost or stuck, stay with your vehicle unless you are certain help is nearby.

6. Some of the places you will visit remain honeycombed with old mines that can pose many dangers. View these places only from a distance.

7. Dangerous blind curves are common. Round them carefully.

8. If you camp, use minimum-impact practices and leave no trace of your stay. Camp only at established campsites or in areas that show previous use. Bring your own water (many developed campgrounds are dry), and camp at least 300 feet from the banks of streams, ponds and lakes to avoid damage and pollution, and to allow access by wildlife. Clean up your campsite before you leave and take your trash with you.

9. Never camp in desert washes or narrow canyons, especially in summer when the desert's inability to absorb sudden downpours creates flash floods that can instantly sweep you and your vehicle away.

10. Leave gates as you find them. Don't disturb livestock.

11. Don't drink directly from streams, which can be contaminated by that longtime bane of backpackers, the parasite giardia.

12. Avoid parking on grass because hot exhaust systems can ignite fires.

13. Avoid driving on steep hillsides, stream banks, or in boggy areas.

WHAT TO BRING. Things can and will go wrong. Be prepared to handle problems alone, perhaps even to spend a night or two. Here's a basic checklist of some things to bring:

1. A topped-off fuel tank. Fill up before every backcountry drive, every time. You will use your vehicle's low gears much of the time, which will mean higher fuel consumption than during highway driving. It shouldn't be necessary to carry extra fuel.

2. A shovel. Mine has been a life-saver, and is the single most useful tool I carry.

3. A first-aid kit, food, drinks, and clothing for inclement weather.

4. Good all-terrain tires, a properly inflated spare, a jack, a small board to support the jack on dirt, a couple of cans of pressurized tire sealant (available at department stores), a small electric air compressor (the kind that plugs into the cigarette lighter, also available at department stores), a tire pressure gauge, and tire chains. Warning: Old mine sites and ghost towns are often littered with old, rusty nails.

5. Basic tools, including a folding saw for removing deadfall, jumper cables, duct tape, electrical tape, baling wire, spare fuses, a multipurpose knife, a high-strength tow strap, a fire extinguisher, and a plastic sheet to put on the ground. An assortment of screws, washers, nuts, and such could come in handy as well, especially if you're driving an older or modified (meaning trouble-prone) vehicle.

6. Maps, a compass, extra eyeglasses, and keys, binoculars, trash bags, a flashlight or a head lamp with extra batteries, matches, a watch, hats, sunscreen, and insect repellent.

7. Except for the food, I keep much of this stuff ready to go in a large plastic storage container. It's important to tie it all down so it doesn't get tossed about on the rough roads.

8. These days, a cellular telephone can be handy, though they often don't work in remote areas.

OFF-HIGHWAY DRIVING. Most of the time, simply driving more slowly and cautiously than you do on paved roads will get you where you want to go. Here are some tips for those inevitable times when the going gets rough.

1. Uphill traffic has the right of way, if that is practical, because it's usually easier and safer to, on your way down a hill, back up to a pullout using gravity as a brake than it is to back down a slope while fighting the pull of gravity.

South Fork John Day River (Drive 60)

2. Think ahead. If you have a part-time 4WD system, engage it before you absolutely need it to stay out of trouble.

3. When in doubt, scout. If the road ahead seems dicey, walk it and see.

4. Air down (let air out of your tires) in sand, deep mud, and rocky terrain. While standard tire pressure will nearly always suffice, deep mud and soft, dry sand may require temporarily airing down to 15–18 pounds per square inch (PSI) or even lower to expand the tire's "footprint" for greater flotation. Dampening dry sand with water can firm the sand up. On rocky terrain, airing down will soften the ride and lessen the punishment the roadbed inflicts on the suspension. On especially rocky and steep terrain, airing down will also allow the tires to conform to the rocks so they can grip better. (On the other hand, shallow mud may have firm ground just beneath it, so normal tire inflation or even over-inflation can help tires penetrate to terra firma.) Remember to re-inflate the tires (using your electric air compressor) before driving at speed or on pavement.

5. Maintain steady forward momentum in sand, mud, and snow. Stopping can often be the worst thing to do, so go as slow as you can, but as fast as you must. Higher gears can be more effective than lower gears.

6. Because of the problems that driving in mud poses—roadbed damage, vehicle damage, the possibility of transporting biological organisms from one ecosystem to another—it is best to avoid it.

7. If you begin to lose traction in mud, turn the steering wheel rapidly one way and then the other, back and forth. That can help the tires get a grip. If you do get stuck, dig out the sides of the tires to relieve suction. Then pack debris around the tires for traction.

8. Dust storms and flash floods are dangerous. Blinding dust, rain, or hail storms can kick up suddenly in the desert. Do not attempt to drive through one. Instead, pull over to a safe place, turn off the engine to avoid clogging the air filter, and wait it out, keeping windows and doors closed.

9. In spring, and during and after summer storms, you are likely to encounter flooded roads.

10. In spring, check the depth and speed of the water before fording. If it's fast and deep, stay out and come back in a few weeks if you can.

11. Stick to the high points in the road. When the going gets rough, shift into low range, go slowly, and keep the tires on the high spots in the road and keep the undercarriage away from obstacles. Do not let large rocks pass directly beneath the vehicle.

12. Keep your thumbs on top of the steering wheel. They can be badly injured if a front tire suddenly jerked in an unexpected direction. If the steering wheel is being rocked back and forth by the terrain, keep your hands loose on the wheel, at 10 and 2 o'clock.

13. Lean forward in rough conditions, keeping your back away from the seat back. That way you won't be tossed around as much.

14. Straddle ruts, letting them pass beneath the vehicle. If you must cross a rut, do so at an angle, easing over one tire at a time. Do the same for depressions, dips, ledges, and waterbars.

15. If you get stuck, raise the vehicle with a good jack (not the bumper-mounted kind) and fill in the space beneath and around the affected wheels with dirt and debris until you've created a ramp (make it high enough so that the wheel is on a downslope).

16. To get over a ledge, either use the rock ramp that will most likely already be there, or build one using a few nearby rocks. You may need to put one wheel over at a time.

17. If you build a rudimentary ramp to get over an obstacle or out of a rut, put the dirt and rocks back where you found them. Don't leave an excavation site behind.

18. Be prepared to remove deadfall from the roadway. If you must drive over a fallen tree or limb, approach at an angle and put one wheel over it at a time. If you carry a folding saw, cut the deadfall away. If the obstacle is too large to cut or move by hand, consider using your tow strap to pull it out of the way.

19. Have someone act as a spotter to help you maneuver through difficult places, and use low range and a low gear for better control.

20. Try not to spin your tires, which tears up the road and can get you stuck, or stuck worse than you already may be. Some SUVs have sophisticated four-wheel electronic traction-control systems that are intended to eliminate wheel spin by instantly transferring power from spinning wheels to wheels that have traction. A few SUVs, such as Toyota's Four-Runner and Land Cruiser, can be purchased with locking differentials, aka "lockers." These vastly improve your ability to get through nasty situations by equalizing power to the driving wheels and eliminating the differential's tendency to transfer power to the wheel with the least traction.

21. If your vehicle gets high-centered, that is, the undercarriage is hung atop an object like a rock, jack the vehicle up and see if the obstacle can be removed. Or build small ramps, using dirt and rocks, beneath the tires so you can drive off of the obstacle.

22. Before climbing over a steep, blind hilltop, learn what's up there and on the other side. Depending on how steep it is, shift into first or second gear or low range. Keep moving as you climb, then slow down as you near the top.

23. If the engine stalls on a hill, stop and immediately set the parking brake and restart the engine. If you have a manual transmission, you'll have to work the clutch, hand brake, and accelerator simultaneously to get going again without rolling backward.

24. If you can't make it up a hill, don't try to turn around. Stop and put the transmission in reverse or low range. Tilt the exterior mirrors, if you can, so that you can see what the rear tires are doing. Then slowly back straight down. Never descend in neutral, because you will be in free fall and run the

risk of overheating your brakes. If you must apply the brakes, do so lightly and steadily to avoid losing traction and going into a slide.

25. Avoid traversing a side-sloped road or hill. Occasionally, low quality mountain roads will tilt the vehicle "off-camber," which is almost always unnerving, especially if the road has become wet and perhaps a bit slick. Lean heavily toward caution (pun intended) under such circumstances. You might remove cargo from the roof to lower your vehicle's already-high center of gravity. Then go slowly. If you decide not to continue, do not attempt to turn around. Tilt the exterior mirrors so you can watch the rear tires, shift into reverse or low range for greater low-speed control, and slowly back up until you reach a safe spot.

26. Avoid crossing waterways. Fording streams and shallow rivers is fun but many living things reside in or depend on undisturbed streams, and they can be harmed by stirred-up sediment and eroded stream banks. If you must cross, use an established crossing point. Check the depth with a stick if you're unsure about it, measuring the depth against the height of your vehicle. Or walk across the stream first. Don't cross in your vehicle if the current is fast and deep. Never enter a desert wash if it's flooding. Check for deep holes. Often, a somewhat fast-moving perennial stream will be safer to cross than a sluggish one because continuously moving water prevents sediments from settling, keeping the bed rocky and firm. Slow-moving or still water lets sediment and mud build up.

27. A slow, steady crossing will stir up less sediment, and will make less of a bow wake, thus minimizing stream-bank erosion and the impact on plants and wildlife. (In particularly deep water, however, a bow wake can create a beneficial air pocket for the engine.)

28. Be aware of where your engine's air intake is. It may not be high enough to ford deep water.

29. No stream crossings in this book are more than a few inches deep, except during winter storms and floods. If you encounter such a stream, turn back. Which brings us to my last bit of advice. . .

30. When in doubt—turn about. No destination is worth risking a wrecked vehicle, serious injury, or worse.

4WD ACCESSORIES. Properly equipped SUVs are built to take people to places that sedans, vans, and station wagons either cannot go, or

Illinois River crossing—low-water bridge (submerged)—Chetco Pass Rd. (Drive 40)

Muddy Topsy Road above Klamath Canyon (Drive 37)

shouldn't. Despite their comforts, they are rugged and reliable transport in backcountry or frontcountry. They can go from the showroom straight into the hills without modification.

Manual transmissions have advantages. They are more responsive and provide slightly better fuel mileage. They are better at engine braking on steep terrain. But many clutch-equipped vehicles require the driver to fully depress the clutch pedal when starting the engine, which can be a problem if you're stalled on a steep hill. However, on a steep incline you can put the transmission in first gear or low range and let the starter motor start the engine while it simultaneously pulls the vehicle forward. It's also possible to compression-start (or roll-start) the engine if the starter or battery dies. Automatic transmissions are easier to use when the going is rough, where a manual transmission can require three feet: one for the brake, one for the clutch and one for the accelerator, all working pretty much simultaneously. Not to mention a free hand for constant shifting.

I've learned to appreciate options I once dismissed as unnecessary. Easily adjusted electric side mirrors, for example, will pay for themselves the first time you have to back up a narrow shelf road with a killer drop-off. In narrow, high-walled canyons, a sunroof is a handy option indeed.

There is a huge four-wheel-drive accessory market. Are those add-ons necessary? It depends on how much and what type of adventure motoring you plan to do. Serious four-wheeling on technically challenging routes differs from backcountry touring. The former can require extensive vehicle modifications, which can degrade on-highway performance and reliability. The latter does not. Still, if you enjoy traveling the west's vast network of backcountry roads, there can be real benefits to extra lights, beefier tires, a more versatile roof carrier, heavier skid plates, perhaps even an after-market locking differential, or a winch.

Maintenance is essential. Backcountry roads are hard on all vehicles, so follow the recommendations in your owner's manual for dusty, wet, and muddy conditions. Check the tires often because no part of your vehicle will take a greater beating. Wash your vehicle, when you return to town, to prevent rust and corrosion. You also don't want to carry home the mud, dirt, and debris that has collected underneath your vehicle, because transporting spores, insects, and other organisms to disparate geographic regions via off-highway vehicles can spread pests and diseases.

Finally, as you travel and afterwards, tell us what you've found, or let us know of drives and tips you'd like to see added to future editions. Write to Wilderness Press, 1200 Fifth St., Berkeley, California, 94710.

Author's Favorites

COOPER SPUR, MT. HOOD (DRIVE 2). Mt. Hood's highest and most beautiful road ends at a lovely campground, and includes an overlook of the Eliot Glacier, a visit to an old lodge, and the entrance to a spectacular trail system.

GOLDEN AND SILVER FALLS (DRIVE 16). This pair of waterfalls near Coos Bay underscores the facts that no two waterfalls are alike and that the beauty of waterfalls is infinite in its variety. No waterfall anywhere is more beautiful or unusual than Golden Falls—except maybe Silver Falls, a quarter mile away. You'll see. The Millicoma River Valley isn't bad, either.

FISH CREEK VALLEY (DRIVE 32). This gem of a road plunges 4 miles into the Rogue–Umpqua Divide Wilderness, with the Wilderness boundary on both sides of the road. It ends in an enchanted valley of green meadows, jutting summits (including Fish Mountain, highest in the wilderness), fantastic rock formations, and many trailheads.

ILLINOIS RIVER CANYON (DRIVE 39). Oregon's most impressive river canyon is accessed by a challenging, 21-mile dirt road that ends at the Kalmiopsis Wilderness boundary. Amid towering orange mountains, the road passes by brilliant blue pools, whitewater rapids, bizarre ecosystems, and dozens of endangered plant species.

HAT POINT, HELLS CANYON (DRIVE 57). Hells Canyon, on the Snake River between Oregon and Idaho, is North America's deepest gorge, 2,000 feet deeper than the Grand Canyon. A challenging, 24-mile unpaved road ends at the only automobile-accessible viewing point of the deepest part of Hells Canyon. Beyond Hat Point, the road is even more challenging.

STEENS MOUNTAIN LOOP (DRIVE 67). Oregon's highest road is a 54-mile loop cresting at 9,700 feet. Immediately southwest of the road's highest point, the mountains plunge 4,000 feet over the course of 5 miles to the Alvord Desert. The Steens are a barren and breathtaking land of aspen groves, immense glacial valleys, cirque lakes, and incredible vistas. Look for mustang herds lower down.

SUCCOR CREEK, LESLIE GULCH (DRIVE 74). This route should be a national monument instead of a seldom visited dirt road. Succor Creek is a splendid canyon with immense yellow monolithic cliffs rising on either side. There is an amazing view of a desert summit when the road rises out of the canyon. Leslie Gulch is a narrow, winding canyon lined with red-rock spires that jut hundreds of feet skyward.

Author's All-Time Number One Favorite

LOWER IMNAHA CANYON (DRIVE 55). This 30-mile drive down the Lower Imnaha Canyon is far superior to the other 74 drives in this book, including the fabulous Steens Mountain Loop and Hat Point Road. This precarious route not only surpasses the others in sheer scenic spectacle, but the road remains largely unimproved so that reaching historic Dug Bar, at the bottom of Hells Canyon, is truly an adventure.

Map Symbols

DRIVE ROUTE:

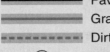 Paved road

Gravel road

Dirt road

 Start

 Finish

 Travel direction

Paved road

Gravel road

Dirt road

River

Trail

Coast

State line

Wilderness, park or natural area

 U.S. Highway

All other roads

 Campground

 Point of interest

 Trailhead

 Town

 Pass

 Mountain

 Ski area

 Lake

 Dam or gate

Mine

North indicator

Guide To Tour Highlight Icons

Photo opportunity

Camping

Picnicking

Hiking

Historic sites

Bird/Wildlife viewing

Geological/ Botanical

Boating

Fishing

Whitewater Rafting

Wilderness Access

4WD Road

Rock Climbing

Mountain biking

Fire

Locator Map

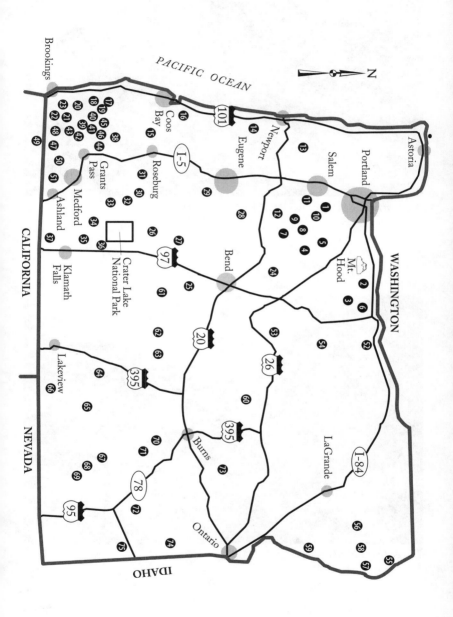

Approaching Dug Bar on Snake River (Drive 55)

Lower Imnaha River Road (Drive 55)

THE DRIVES

Molalla Canyon, Table Rock

LOCATION. Near Salem, east of Woodburn.

HIGHLIGHTS. Molalla River Recreation Area and Table Rock. Until recently, Table Rock was Oregon's only Wilderness Area managed entirely by the BLM.

DIFFICULTY. Easy. A mostly level, wide gravel road along a river. But the road is steep, slow, and winding toward the end.

DISTANCE. 22 miles from Glen Avon to Table Rock Trailhead.

HIGH ELEVATION. 3,200 feet.

MAPS. Fernwood; Gawley Peak; Rooster Rock.

ADMINISTRATION. BLM Salem District

GETTING THERE. Leave I-5 at Woodburn, Exit 271, for Highway 214/Woodburn. Proceed east, through Woodburn, to Highway 211. Follow 211 east to Mathias Road, just past Molalla. Turn right (south) on Mathias, left (east) on S. Feyrer Park Road, then right on S. Dickey Prairie Road. Follow S. Dickey Prairie to the bridge at Glen Avon, which is the start of gravel S. Molalla Road (6-3E-6) and the Molalla River Recreation Area. Follow S. Molalla Road 13 miles to the end, at the junction of Middle Fork and Copper Creek roads. Bear left (east) on Middle Fork Road (7-3E-14) and continue 4.5 miles to Table Rock Road (7-4E-7). It's 4.5 miles (right, south) up Table Rock Road to the trailhead near the road end.

REST STOPS. There are numerous recreational sites along the Molalla River.

THE DRIVE. Finding the road for this trip (the nearest one, in this book, to Portland) can be a challenge because of all the back roads and turns. But the trip is lovely throughout, with charming paved roads through picturesque farmland near Glen Avon.

The Molalla River Recreation Area, south of Glen Avon, consists of a narrow canyon with a gravel road running along it and many turnoffs to swimming holes and picnic sites. Beyond the turnoff up the Middle Fork Road, the canyon gets even narrower and the road becomes a little more primitive, though it stays easily driveable. The well-marked Table Rock Road leads steeply uphill to the Table Rock Trailhead and passes several beautiful creeks, meadows, and vistas. Table Rock is a large volcanic plug, the core of an ancient volcano in the Western Cascade Mountains that has mostly eroded. Table Rock (which isn't quite flat on top) can be seen from I-5 near Woodburn. A fairly steep 2-mile trail leads to the top, but the bottom is also quite nice.

SIDE TRIPS. If you continue on Copper Creek Road instead of turning up Middle Fork Road, a series of more challenging dirt roads will take you to the top of Table Rock's south end, by Pechuck Lookout and Rooster Rock. On the other hand, if you continue up Middle Fork Road past the Table Rock turnoff, you'll end up at Nohorn Butte summit, from which you can drop down into the Clackamas River area. (See Drive 11.)

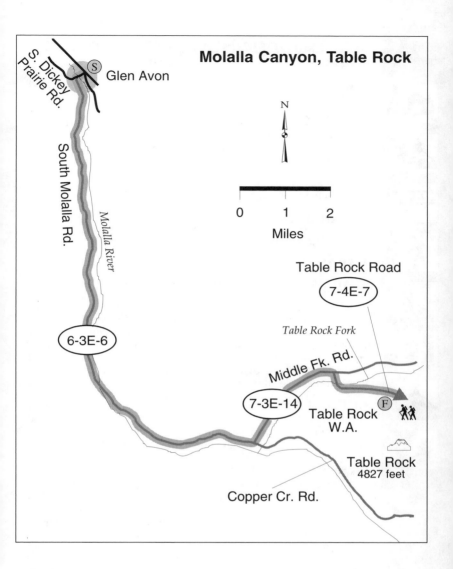

Molalla Canyon, Table Rock

Glen Avon

S. Dickey Prairie Rd.

South Molalla Rd.

Molalla River

N

0   1   2
Miles

Table Rock Road

7-4E-7

6-3E-6

Table Rock Fork

Middle Fk. Rd.

7-3E-14

Table Rock W.A.

Table Rock
4827 feet

Copper Cr. Rd.

Cooper Spur, Mt. Hood

LOCATION. On the east side of Mt. Hood. Northeast of Government Camp and south of the Hood River.

HIGHLIGHTS. This road leads to the highest hiking trail on Mt. Hood, Oregon's highest peak. It also features two campgrounds, an old lodge, many other trailheads, and a close-up view of the Eliot Glacier.

DIFFICULTY. Moderate. A wide, slow, steep gravel road with many switchbacks—a few rough spots.

DISTANCE. 13.5 miles from Highway 35 to Cloudcap.

HIGH ELEVATION. 5,700 feet.

MAP. Mt. Hood North.

ADMINISTRATION. Mt. Hood National Forest.

SPECIAL INFORMATION. When I first drove this road, in 1992, the surface was so badly washboarded it nearly shook my teeth out of my mouth. In 2001, however, I encountered little washboarding and, overall, the situation had very much improved, though it's still a fairly rough road. The trailhead at Cloudcap can get crowded, but if you go midday or mid-week there won't be as much traffic.

GETTING THERE. Take Highway 26 from Portland past Government Camp to Highway 35, which is the road to Hood River. Turn left (north) on Highway 35, then left again (northwest) 9 miles later, at the junction with Forest Road 3510 (paved), also called Cooper Spur or Cloudcap Road. Proceed 2.5 miles to Cooper Spur turnoff (FR 3512). Turn left (west) and follow signs past the Cooper Spur ski area to Cloudcap, 11 miles away. The road is paved to the ski area, which will be at mile 1.5. A 1-mile side spur left (south) at mile 10 leads to the Tilly Jane Campground. Go straight for the final mile to the Cloudcap trailhead area. Be careful, road numbers are not posted on FR 3510 or FR 3512.

REST STOPS. Cooper Spur ski area; Tilly Jane Campground; Cloudcap.

THE DRIVE. The paved roads leading to Cooper Spur Road are probably more scenic than Cooper Spur Road itself, until you approach the end. In fact, the paved highway between Government Camp and the Hood River, which skirts the base of Oregon's highest and most beautiful mountain, 11,236-foot Mt. Hood and travels through the lovely Hood River Valley, ranks among the state's premiere scenic routes.

But the last mile of the Cooper Spur Road has them all beat as far as scenic spectacle. While most of the route is steep, slow, and a little bouncy, with few vistas points and only forest views, there's a certain mystique in just knowing that you're driving straight up the side of a volcano. And there are a couple of excel-

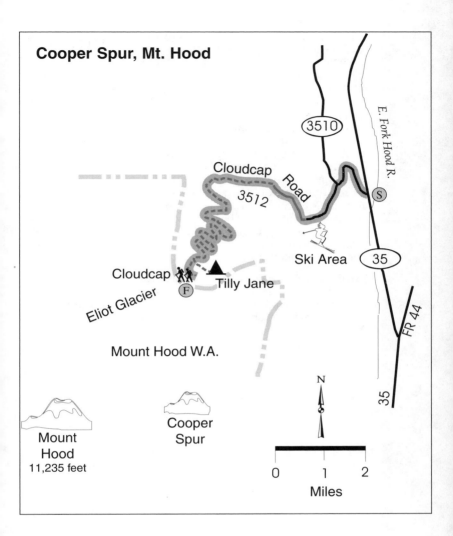

Cooper Spur, Mt. Hood

Cloudcap Road
3510
3512
E. Fork Hood R.
S
Ski Area
35
Cloudcap
Tilly Jane
F
Eliot Glacier
Mount Hood W.A.
FR 44
35
N
Mount
Hood
11,235 feet
Cooper
Spur

0   1   2
Miles

lent vista spots on the way up, one of which affords a dramatic panorama of the Hood River Valley.

Tilly Jane campground (elevation 5,700 feet) is as lovely as its name, with subalpine forests, meadows, and a huge canyon nearby. A very steep, exhausting, and incredibly beautiful 3-mile hike from Tilly Jane leads to the 8,514-foot summit of Cooper Spur, the highest established trail on Mt. Hood.

Cloudcap campground is even more magnificent than Tilly Jane, with a stunning view of the summit's eastern face, as well as of the Eliot Glacier, which begins about 2 miles away. From Cloudcap, Cooper Spur is the barren sub-peak to the left (southeast) of Mt. Hood. The best vista is from behind the lodge, from the top of the rock outcrop above the road. From there, you can also see Mts. St. Helens, Rainier and Adams. The old lodge is very pretty on the outside but rather spartan inside, where you will find some couches, a large fireplace, and a bunch of cots. Trails from Cloudcap Saddle tie in with the Cooper Spur and Mt. Hood Loop Trails, and they also access the Eliot Glacier.

SIDE TRIPS. The route to the Cooper Spur turnoff from Hood River, south on Highway 35 from I-5, is a little longer than the route east and north from Government Camp. The views of Mt. Hood are inspiring on the Hood River route, as are the views of the broad Hood River Valley with its famous apple orchards.

Badger Lake

LOCATION. Badger Creek Wilderness, immediately east of Mt. Hood.

HIGHLIGHTS. A primitive road, with wilderness on either side, leading to a gorgeous glacial cirque lake. Many trails and side trips.

DIFFICULTY. The last 6 miles are narrow, very slow, and contain multiple rocks and ruts; the very last mile is quite steep. I'd rate the road as difficult.

DISTANCE. 27.3 miles from Highway 35 to Badger Lake.

HIGH ELEVATION. 5,385 feet.

MAP. Badger Lake.

ADMINISTRATION. Mt. Hood National Forest.

GETTING THERE. From U.S. 26, 1.5 miles beyond Government Camp, go north on Highway 35, toward Hood River. At mile 5 on Highway 35, look for the White River Sno-Park East, on the right (east). A sign there says ROCK CREEK RESERVOIR. No posted sign tells you that the sno-park is the turnoff to Forest Road 48, but it is. Follow FR 48 for 16 miles to FR 4860. You will pass two other roads that lead to Badger Lake. Follow 4860 for 7.5 miles to Spur 140. Follow Spur 140 for 3.8 miles to Badger Lake.

SPECIAL INFORMATION. Don't be fooled by the long, downhill approach to the Badger Lake turnoff on Forest Road 48, by the high surrounding peaks, or by the fact that FR 4860 seems to have little uphill climb. In fact, FR 4860 reaches an elevation of 5,385 feet at mile 6 and retains snow until fairly late in the season, even after snow has melted at higher elevations.

REST STOPS. Barlow Crossing Campground (on FR 43, just off FR 48); Badger Lake Campground.

THE DRIVE. Forest Road 48 is a fast, two-lane paved downhill road that leads out of the Cascade Mountains and into the broad, low-lying, semi-desert, lava plateau to the east. The first few miles pass some beautiful peaks that are adjacent to Mt. Hood. On the way back from Badger Lake, driving in the opposite direction, the views of Mt. Hood from FR 48 are quite impressive. But this area offers impressive views of Mt. Hood from just about anywhere.

Turning from FR 48 onto FR 4860, there is gravel for a couple of hundred feet, but it soon becomes one-lane blacktop. At mile 3, the surface returns to gravel, the road narrows, and the road quality, with lots of ruts and jutting rock, markedly declines. You then emerge from the forest and are treated to an impressive view of Mt. Hood above Boulder Creek Canyon. At mile 6, the road traverses its high point, which does not feel like a high point but rather like a long level stretch. From there on, the surface is dirt, the road quality deteriorates even further, and the route eventually enters a dense forest. You may run in to snow patches, but console yourself that, between here and Badger Lake (with a few ups and downs), the road loses 1,000 feet in elevation.

You will eventually reach the Spur 140 turnoff at mile 8.5. Go right (north) for Badger Lake and straight for the Camp Windy Campground. The final 3.5 miles on Spur 140 will be about the same as the previous 2.5 miles on FR 4860, as the road proceeds to penetrate the heart of the Wilderness, inscribing a wide loop around the flank of Badger Butte (5,981 feet). After contouring high above the headwaters of Pine Creek, the road rounds a point, contours for another mile, and then begins a steep 1.25-mile descent to Badger Lake, over the course of which it loses 700 feet in elevation. This final segment is very narrow, with many rock outcrops and precarious drop-offs into Badger Creek.

Eventually, the road arrives at its true highlight, 45-acre Badger Lake (elevation 4,472 feet), which is nestled in the woods below an immense glacial cirque. The lake is augmented by a 22-foot-high dam that was built in 1920, and that man-made structure may be why the spot was omitted from the Wilderness. There is a campground at the base of the dam and another at the edge of the lake above the dam. Lake and creek offer great scenic beauty, excellent trout fishing, and many trails, including the popular Badger Creek Trail to Lookout Mountain and Flag Point.

SIDE TRIPS. If you stay on FR 4860 instead of turning onto Spur 140, after 2.5 miles you will arrive at Camp Windy. There's not much there but it's a wonderfully isolated spot.

On the way to the FR 4860 turnoff on FR 48, the FR 4890 and 4880 junctions also access roads that lead to Badger Lake, in 12 miles and 14 miles, respectively. Both take you there via FR 4891 and Camp Windy. FR 4880 also leads to the Boulder Lake trailhead, which features a 0.5-mile path to one of the prettier glacial cirque lakes.

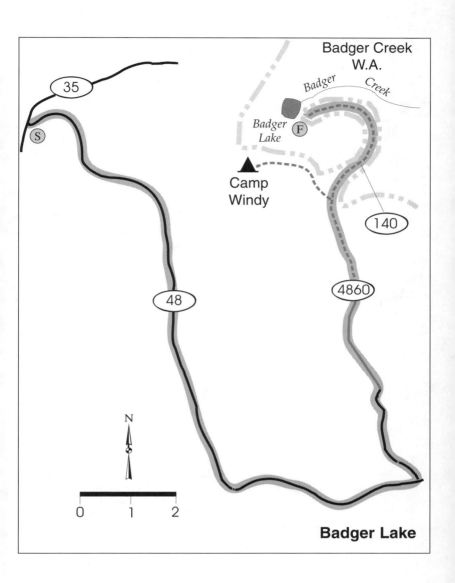

Badger Lake

Rock Lakes, Frazier Turnaround

LOCATION. Forest roads south of Mt. Hood and south of the Salmon-Huckleberry Wilderness.

HIGHLIGHTS. High Rock, an impressive outcrop. Frazier Turnaround, while difficult to reach, is very pretty and very remote. There is a short trail to beautiful Middle Rock Lake.

DIFFICULTY. Moderate to difficult. The road is very narrow and primitive, with some steep drop-offs and muddy spots in spring and fall.

DISTANCE. 5.3 miles from Forest Road 58 to Frazier Turnaround.

HIGH ELEVATION. 4,300 feet.

MAP. High Rock.

ADMINISTRATION. Mt. Hood National Forest.

REST SPOTS. High Rock; Frazier Turnaround Campground; Frazier Fork Campground.

GETTING THERE. Coming from Government Camp, leave Highway 26 just prior to Blue Box Pass and turn onto Forest Road 2660 (first 7 miles gravel, last mile blacktop). When FR 2660 ends, turn right onto FR 58 and proceed 9 miles to the High Rock turnoff, FR 4610, which is paved for 1.5 miles. Watch carefully for Spur 240, to Frazier Turnaround, on the left when FR 4610 crests. If you hit the end of the blacktop, you've gone too far on 4610. It's 3.8 bumpy but level miles down Spur 240 to the Rock Lake Trailhead. Take a right onto the high road at mile 3.6 for the Frazier Fork Campground or continue straight for the Frazier Turnaround Campground (not as big or as nice as Frazier Fork) and for both ends of the Rock Lakes Loop Trail. Both trailheads and the campground are less than 0.5 miles from the junction at mile 3.6. (The road up from Hideaway Lake, shown on the Mt. Hood National Forest map, does not connect to Spur 240.)

THE DRIVE. Before heading out to Spur 240, be sure to drive the short distance to the base of High Rock for a terrific view down Linney Creek into the Salmon-Huckleberry Wilderness. It's possible to climb High Rock (elevation 4,953 feet).

The 3.8-mile Frazier Turnaround Road is fun and challenging. It begins with views north into the canyon of Roaring River, passes a couple of narrow, rocky spots with excellent views south, and ends up at one of the most magnificent, eerie old-growth forests ever. From the Frazier Turnaround Campground, it's a 0.5-mile downhill hike from the right-hand trailhead through the old-growth forest to Middle Rock Lake, a 15-acre pool set in an immense, rocky, glacial cirque.

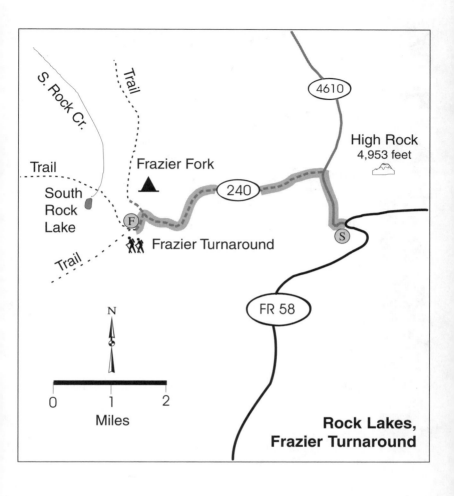

**Rock Lakes,
Frazier Turnaround**

SIDE TRIPS. Serene Lake lies 2.5 miles farther down the trail from Middle Rock Lake. It is similar to Middle Rock Lake but covers 20 acres. The loop's return leg follows the ridge over forests, rock outcrops, and meadows.

High Rock is also the far end of Drive 5, High Rock Road. To link to the end of Drive 5, continue on FR 4610 for 1 mile past High Rock, where the road becomes much narrower and veers off the left. This is a very long, slow, difficult road.

High Rock Road

LOCATION. Southeast of Portland, near Estacada, off the Clackamas River.

HIGHLIGHTS. A beautiful drive along the mountain crest that lies between the North Fork Clackamas River and the Roaring River. The road skirts the southern boundary of the Salmon-Huckleberry Wilderness before it turns south to end at High Rock.

DIFFICULTY. Easy to moderate until the gravel ends, then moderate to difficult. The section near the Wilderness contains some narrow spots and can be muddy in spring and fall.

DISTANCE. 25.8 miles from Highway 224 to Forest Road 58.

HIGH ELEVATION. 4,300 feet.

MAPS. High Rock; Three Lynx.

ADMINISTRATION. Mt. Hood National Forest.

GETTING THERE. From Highway 26 at Sandy, east of Portland, take Highway 211 south to Estacada, then 224 southeast to Promontory Park, 8 miles beyond Estacada. Turn left there, onto Forest Road 4610, which is gravel for 17 miles and dirt for 8.8 miles. FR 4610 ends at FR 58.

REST STOPS. Promontory Park; Squaw Meadow; High Rock.

THE DRIVE. The paved route along the Clackamas River from Estacada to the Ripplebrook Guard Station ranks among the state's prettier drives. You will add a little adventure when you head up FR 4610, which goes through old-growth forest and provides vistas of the North Fork Clackamas and Roaring Rivers. At mile 15, you arrive at a switchback at Squaw Meadow, which contains two little lakes at its center. A steep south-facing drop-off from the meadow produces a great view.

The gravel ends 2 miles past Squaw Meadow, where the road begins to skirt the Wilderness boundary. This segment, though level, can be rough and may be impassible in wet weather. But it's a lot of fun and the views into the canyon of the Roaring River are splendid. The final 4 miles take you around the Roaring River headwaters to High Rock, a massive rock spire. The last mile to FR 58, beyond High Rock, is paved.

Somewhere along FR 4610, according to the map, a trail takes off north and climbs Salmon Butte (elevation 4,677), then drops down to the Salmon River on the Wilderness area's far side. It sounds like a great path but I've never been able to locate the trailhead.

SIDE TRIPS. Spur 240 begins just past where the pavement starts near the end of FR 4610, and it is on the right. This is the Frazier Turnaround Road (Drive 4).

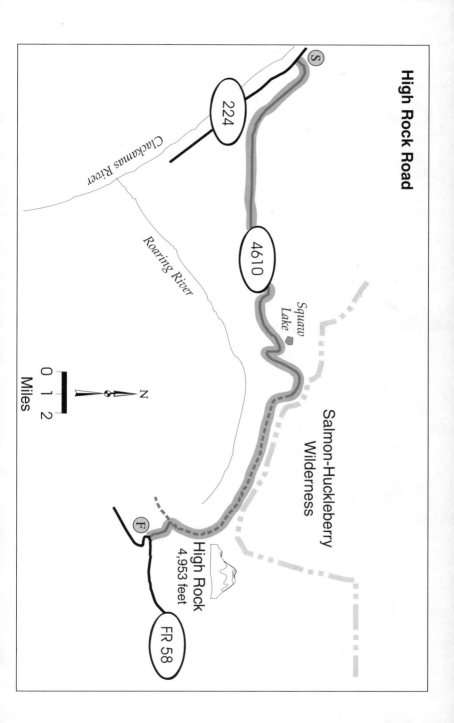

Flag Point

LOCATION. Immediately east of Mt. Hood, on the northern edge of the Badger Creek Wilderness.

HIGHLIGHTS. Awe-inspiring views, from a lookout tower, of Mt. Hood, Mt. Adams, the lava plateau east of the Cascade crest, Badger Creek Canyon, and everything in between. Excellent views leading up to the lookout as well.

DIFFICULTY. Easy to the Spur 200 turnoff. Then, for the last 3.5 miles, moderate to difficult as you ascend a steep, narrow dirt road with lots of ruts and rocks.

DISTANCE. 15.8 miles from Highway 35 to lookout gate.

HIGH ELEVATION. 5,651 feet.

MAP. Flag Point.

ADMINISTRATION. Mt. Hood National Forest.

GETTING THERE. From Highway 35, east of Mt. Hood, take Forest Road 44, which has two lanes and is paved, toward Dufur. At mile 7.3, turn right onto FR 4420, where the sign says FLAG POINT LOOKOUT–7 (it's actually 8 miles). FR 4420 is one-lane blacktop. After 2 miles, at the High Prairie Junction, FR 4420 veers right and FR 2730, also one-lane blacktop, continues straight. Take FR 2730. After 3.5 miles, Spur 200 takes off right, where a small sign says FLAG POINT LOOKOUT–3.5. Spur 200 then ends after 3 miles, at a locked gate, 0.25 miles before the lookout.

REST STOPS. Robinhood and Sherwood Campgrounds on Highway 35; Pebble Ford Campground on FR 44, just past the FR 4420 turnoff; Fifteen Mile Creek Campground on FR 2730.

THE DRIVE. Forest Road 44 winds through lodgepole pine forests and dry, grassy openings until it reaches FR 4420. If you look behind you (or ahead on the way back), FR 44 offers excellent views of Mt. Hood. FR 4420 and FR 2730 follow a ridge that breaks sharply east, with a panorama of the lava plateau ranchlands around The Dalles. The view is much better from the lookout, though. A highlight on FR 2730 is Fifteen Mile Creek, an exceptionally pretty cascading stream with a small campground. This is a great place to stop for lunch.

Things get really interesting after the turnoff to Spur 200. The narrow dirt road meanders steeply uphill through a forest of noble fir, mountain hemlock, and a few larch trees. There are many jutting rocks and a few ruts, though this is not this book's worst road segment, by any means. At mile 2.5 on Spur 200, the road levels off and you arrive at a trailhead (the beginning of a 6-mile hike to Badger Lake) where you may enjoy a panorama of the Badger Creek Canyon, Badger Butte (5,981 feet), and a view of a narrow slice of Mt. Hood peering around Lookout Mountain.

The road ends at a locked gate, 0.25 miles from Flag Point Lookout. The wooden lookout tower at Flag Point offers breathtaking views in all directions, the most spectacular being the

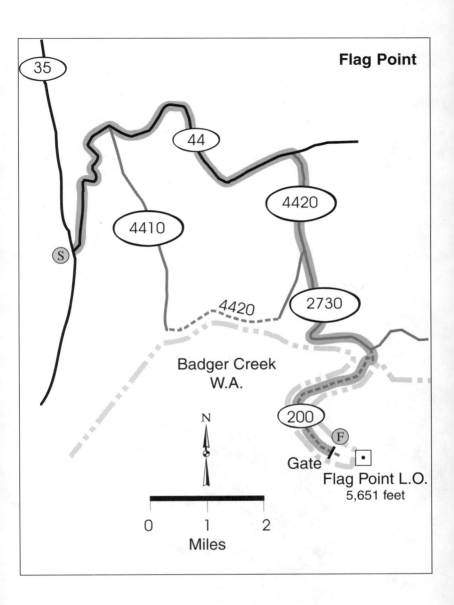

Flag Point

35

44

4420

4410

4420

2730

Badger Creek
W.A.

S

200

F

Gate

Flag Point L.O.
5,651 feet

N

0   1   2

Miles

39

Columbia Gorge and Mt. Adams to the north. It's quite a climb to the top, though, which is about 4 stories up.

SIDE TRIPS. For a more scenic but slightly longer drive, with less blacktop, at mile 4 on FR 44, turn right (north) onto FR 4410, where the sign says HIGH PRAIRIE–4. Unlike the Flag Point Road, which offers views to the east, the gravel road to High Prairie looks westward, from meadow and rimrock, to the looming summit of Mt. Hood, 5 miles away. (This is one of the best views of Mt. Hood.) FR 4410 ends at a "T" junction at High Prairie. For Flag Point, go left (east) for 3.5 miles on the dirt road, which happens to be the upper end of FR 4420. High Prairie itself is an immense meadow, with still more views of Mt. Hood. At the "T" junction, look for a closed-off dirt road heading south. This dirt road is a hiking trail that will take you to the top of Lookout Mountain after 1 mile. Lookout Mountain is a flat-top mesa, covered with small lodgepole and whitebark pines, with a rimrock ledge dropping down toward Badger Lake and Mt. Hood. You can walk along the level summit, at the edge of the rim, for a half mile.

Flag Point Lookout

Skyline Road, Breitenbush Lake

LOCATION. East of Salem, near Detroit, on the pass just north of Mt. Jefferson.

HIGHLIGHTS. A very challenging road with a magnificent trailhead area for the Pacific Crest Trail, which leads north into the Olallie Lakes area and south to Mt. Jefferson, Oregon's second highest peak. Terrific views of Mt. Jefferson from the road. The road also leads to Breitenbush Lake on the Warm Springs Indian Reservation.

DIFFICULTY. Moderate to difficult. Very narrow, slow, and bumpy. Much traffic on weekends, some of it hauling boats.

DISTANCE. 7.25 miles from Forest Road 46 to Breitenbush Lake.

HIGH ELEVATION. 5,600 feet.

MAPS. Breitenbush Hot Springs; Olallie Butte.

ADMINISTRATION. Mt. Hood National Forest.

GETTING THERE. Take Highway 22 east from Salem for 52 miles to Detroit. At the east end of Detroit Lake, bear left on Forest Road 46, which is paved. Proceed for 15 miles to FR 4220, also known as the Skyline Road. It's 7 miles of gravel and dirt to the Pacific Crest Trail (PCT) Trailhead. Bear right at the PCT crossing to reach a 50-car parking lot. Continue another 0.25 miles on FR 4220 to Breitenbush Lake, which has a campground and many facilities.

REST STOPS. PCT Trailhead; Breitenbush Gorge; Breitenbush Lake.

THE DRIVE. This challenging but heavily trafficked trip offers outstanding close-up views of Mt. Jefferson, and a beautiful lake and resort on the western end of the Warm Springs Indian Reservation. Turning off the pavement and onto the Skyline Road, the route is wide and gravelled for the first mile, then becomes surfaced with rough aggregate rock for 2 miles. The rest of the way is very slow and bumpy, with a few narrow spots. According to the road signs, the Skyline Road is unmaintained, but that is obviously not the case. As you approach the PCT crossing, the road exposes steep drop-offs to the south, with views of alpine meadows and of the towering volcanic flanks of Mt. Jefferson and its associated peaks.

The PCT crossing is lovely even if you don't hike the trails. The area boasts a small, unnamed lake, beautiful meadows, and many varieties of huckleberry. Look for Alaska cedar near the trailhead. It's a 1-mile hike south to the turnoff for Pyramid Butte, a 6,096-foot cinder cone. A very steep, 1-mile side trail takes you to the Pyramid Butte summit. Sixty-acre Breitenbush Lake lies in the woods 0.25 mile past the PCT crossing, just over the boundary of the Warm Springs Indian Reservation. There's a campground and a little resort and store here.

SIDE TRIP. FR 46, an easy, paved drive from Detroit all the way to Olallie Lakes, passes Breitenbush Hot Springs and Breitenbush Gorge, both well worth a peek. If you continue on FR 4220, you'll end up at the far end of Drive 8 and the Olallie Lakes area. Beyond Breitenbush Lake, however, FR 4220 is not passable for all vehicles and may be closed. The recommended route to Olallie Lakes is to go back to FR 46 and follow the directions in Drive 8.

Lower Lake, Olallie Lake scenic area

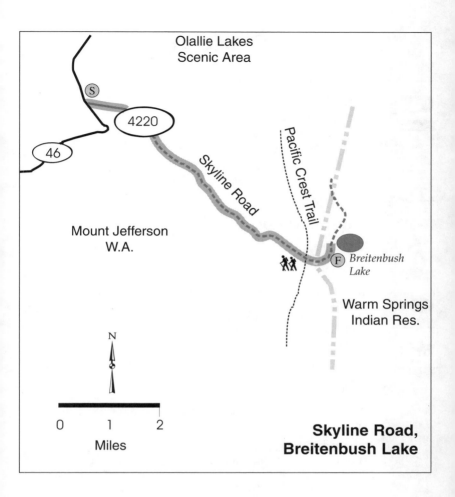

Olallie Lakes
Scenic Area

(S)

4220

46

Skyline Road

Pacific Crest Trail

Mount Jefferson
W.A.

(F) *Breitenbush
Lake*

Warm Springs
Indian Res.

N

0   1   2
Miles

**Skyline Road,
Breitenbush Lake**

Olallie Lakes

LOCATION. East of Salem, near Detroit, just north of Mt. Jefferson.

HIGHLIGHTS. Many large beautiful lakes (some accessible by car, some by trail) in a resort area on the edge of the Warm Springs Indian Reservation. Close-up views of Olallie Butte.

DIFFICULTY. Easy, wide, level gravel road. The last 2 miles are exceedingly rough and may not be passable for all vehicles.

DISTANCE. 13.2 miles from Forest Road 46 to Olallie Lake.

HIGH ELEVATION. 5,000 feet.

MAP. Olallie Butte.

ADMINISTRATION. Mt. Hood National Forest.

GETTING THERE. Take Highway 22 from Salem to Detroit. Continue past Detroit on paved Forest Road 46 for 22 miles to FR 4690, which is blacktopped for all of its 7.2 miles. Where FR 4690 meets FR 4220, turn south onto the gravel and continue to Olallie Lake, 6 miles away.

REST STOPS. There's a campground near Brook Lake at Olallie Meadow; there are multiple campgrounds, picnic sites, and a store at Olallie Lake.

SPECIAL INFORMATION. You can reach Olallie Lake from either FR 46 or from the Skyline Road described in Drive 7.

THE DRIVE. The outstanding scenery of this drive starts with Brook Lake at Olallie Meadow, 2 miles past the junction of FR 4690 with FR 4220. From Olallie Meadow, it's 4 miles to 240-acre Olallie Lake, where there are wonderful views of Olallie Butte, a 7,222-foot cinder cone rising immediately east. Multiple trailheads in the vicinity lead to the butte, as well as numerous lakes of all sizes. Fifteen-acre Lower Lake, reached via a half-mile path from the Lower Lake Campground, offers the shortest and prettiest trail.

South of Olallie Lake the road passes Monon Lake (91 acres), then deteriorates in quality and becomes very steep and winding. The final 2 miles pass Horseshoe Lake (10 acres) and Spoon Lake (5 acres) before emerging at Breitenbush Lake (see Drive 7). The last 2 miles may not be passable for all vehicles. Turn around if you get uncomfortable.

SIDE TRIPS. FR 4691, which is off FR 4690, leads to the far end of the Lower Lake Trail. It's a 0.5-mile hike from a meadow where the trailhead is located to Surprise Lake (5 acres), with another 0.5 miles to Fish Lake (24 acres), and yet another 0.5 miles to Lower Lake. Fish Lake is the prettiest.

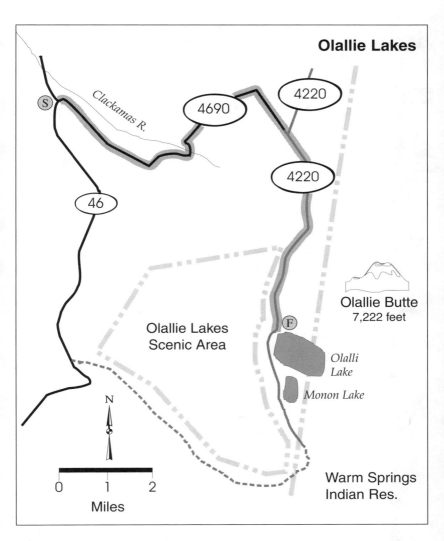

Olallie Lakes

Clackamas R.

S

4690

4220

4220

46

Olallie Butte
7,222 feet

Olallie Lakes
Scenic Area

F

Olalli Lake

Monon Lake

N

Warm Springs
Indian Res.

0   1   2

Miles

Lower Lake, Olallie Lake scenic area

Elk Lake

LOCATION. East of Salem, north of Detroit, at the edge of the Bull of the Woods Wilderness.

HIGHLIGHTS. A challenging road, a lovely lake, and trailheads into one of Oregon's most underrated wilderness areas.

DIFFICULTY. Moderate to difficult. The Elk Lake Road is purposely kept to a low standard of maintenance to discourage overuse. Elk Lake otherwise might get a great deal of visitor spillover from the popular Detroit Lake resort area.

DISTANCE. 7.4 miles from Forest Road 46 to Elk Lake.

HIGH ELEVATION. 4,000 feet.

MAP. Mother Lode Mountain.

ADMINISTRATION. Willamette National Forest.

GETTING THERE. Leave I-5 at Highway 22 east, in Salem, and proceed 52 miles to Detroit. From Detroit, take Forest Road 46 east for 4 miles to FR 4696 and go left (north). It's 1 mile on FR 4696 to FR 4697, where you should go left (west), for a final 6.4 miles to Elk Lake.

REST STOPS. Elk Lake.

THE DRIVE. The first 5 miles of FR 4697 are steep and washboarded as the road climbs through a dense, deep woods. There is a tight switchback at mile 3. The final 2 miles to Elk Lake are extremely rough (very large aggregate gravel), though level. Once at the lake, the road improves considerably. The approximately 100-acre lake is surrounded by meadows and mountains, with many places to pull off and a lovely campground. For the campground, go left at the junction at the lake's far end. If you continue going straight after you reach the junction, you'll end up at the Twin Lakes Trailhead. It's a 4.5 mile walk to the Twin Lakes, which are in the Bull of the Woods Wilderness. Just past the Twin Lakes Trailhead, on the extremely rough road to Beachie Saddle, a very winding 2-mile trail takes off to the summit of Battle Axe Mountain (5,558 feet), which is the source of Battle Axe Creek (or "Babbleax," as we used to say when we were kids).

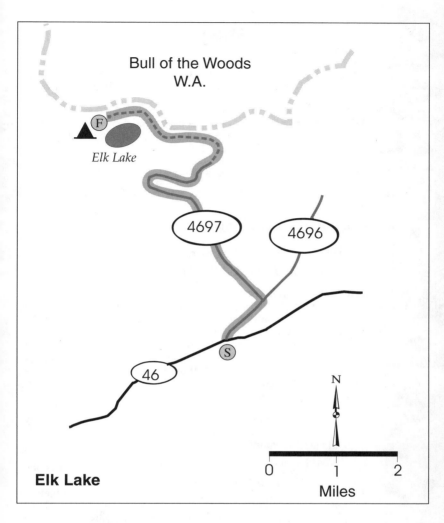

Elk Lake

Elk Lake from Twin Lakes Trail

DRIVE
10

Pansy Basin

LOCATION. East of Portland, south of Estacada, off the Clackamas River on the north side of the Bull of the Woods Wilderness.

HIGHLIGHTS. Vistas of the glacier-carved peaks and valleys of the Bull of the Woods Wilderness, with interesting ecology and great views of Mts. Hood and Jefferson.

DIFFICULTY. Mostly easy gravel roads. Slow and winding.

DISTANCE. 19 miles from Forest Road 46 to Pansy Lake Trailhead.

HIGH ELEVATION. 3,400 feet.

MAP. Bull of the Woods.

ADMINISTRATION. Mt. Hood National Forest.

GETTING THERE. From Highway 26 at Sandy, east of Portland, take Highway 211 south to Estacada. Continue south on Highway 224, which becomes Forest Road 46 one mile past the Ripplebrook Guard Station, at a very complex junction. After 4.5 miles on FR 46, at River Ford Campground, turn right onto FR 63 and follow the pavement for 5.7 miles. Turn right again, onto FR 6340, and follow the gravel for 9 miles, then turn right yet again onto FR 6341, then turn right yet again. A final 4.3 miles of dirt road takes you to the mouth of the Pansy Basin.

REST STOPS. There are numerous campgrounds on Highway 224, FR 46 and FR 63, all along the Clackamas River. There's also a beautiful campsite at the Pansy Basin Trailhead.

THE DRIVE. The paved drive along the Clackamas River is one of Oregon's more pleasant outings. Turning off the Clackamas River onto FR 6340, the route wends its way to a ridgetop, reached after 5 miles. Look for vistas into the Hot Springs Fork Valley (see Drive 11), which is capped by Mts. Hood and Jefferson on the horizon.

The route traverses many logging clearcuts. If you hate clearcuts, you might find yourself somewhat ambivalent in this case since these clearcuts are all overgrown with rhododendron and beargrass, two of the world's showiest wildflowers. Look for glimpses into the craggy peaks of the 35,000-acre Bull of the Woods Wilderness as you approach the junction with FR 6341, where you will turn right.

One mile beyond the junction, FR 6341 begins a long descent into the Pansy Basin, an immense valley of glacial origin that sweeps down from the rocky peaks. These are low but very rugged mountains. The highest, Bull of the Woods Mountain, reaches only 5,523 feet.

The trip ends in the woods at the Pansy Lake Trailhead, where the road crosses Pansy Creek. An easy 1-mile hike takes you to 7-acre, 4-foot-deep Pansy Lake, which is at the base of Bull of the Woods Mountain in the middle of a large meadow.

PORTLAND/NORTHERN CASCADES

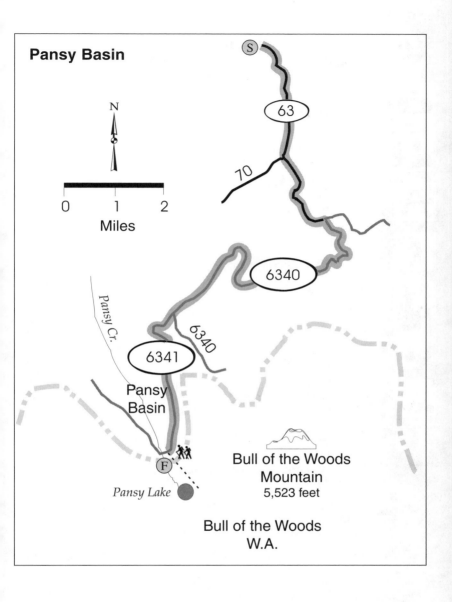

Pansy Basin

N

0   1   2
Miles

63

70

6340

6340

6341

Pansy Cr.

Pansy
Basin

Pansy Lake

Bull of the Woods
Mountain
5,523 feet

Bull of the Woods
W.A.

SIDE TRIPS. If you stay on FR 6340 instead of turning onto FR 6341, you can continue for 3 miles, going near the Wilderness boundary and glimpsing outstanding views of the beautiful Dickey Creek Basin. The road ends at the Bull of the Woods Mountain Trailhead.

Nohorn Butte, Bagby Hot Springs

LOCATION. Southeast of Portland, south of Estacada, off the Clackamas River Road.

HIGHLIGHTS. A fun drive that leads to an impressive little pass and a hot springs by a beautiful creek. What more could anyone want?

DIFFICULTY. Forest Road 70 is wide, level, and easy. Forest Road 7010 winds a lot but is also fairly easy.

DISTANCE. 5.7 miles from Forest Road 63 to Bagby Hot Springs; 15.5 miles to Nohorn summit.

HIGH ELEVATION. 3,600 feet.

MAP. Bagby Hot Springs.

ADMINISTRATION. Mt. Hood National Forest.

GETTING THERE. From Highway 26 at Sandy, east of Portland, take Highway 211 south to Estacada. Continue south on 224, which becomes Forest Road 46 one mile past the Ripplebrook Guard Station, at a very complex junction. After 4.5 miles on 46, at River Ford Campground, turn right onto FR 63, follow the pavement for 4 miles to FR 70, then turn right again. FR 70 leads to the FR 7010 junction to Nohorn Butte (right) after 3.5 miles and, staying on FR 70, to the Bagby Hot Springs Trailhead after 2.2 more miles. It's 12 miles up FR 7010 to Nohorn Butte summit.

REST STOPS. Kingfisher Campground; Bagby Hot Springs Trailhead.

SPECIAL INFORMATION. The trip is somewhat less steep and a little harder to get lost on if you go in the direction I describe. But the opposite direction also works.

THE DRIVE. As noted in Drive 10, it is worth leaving home just for the paved drive along the Clackamas River. Likewise for the gravel drive on FR 70, up the Hot Springs Fork of the Clackamas River. If you continue straight on FR 70 at the junction with FR 7010, the very easy (though sometimes heavily trafficked) drive makes its way to the Bagby Hot Springs Trailhead. A 1.5-mile hike along the creek and over a large footbridge takes you to the hot springs, which contains several historical bath houses and lovely grounds. The trailhead area itself is also rather nice. Most interesting are the sometimes un-hiker-looking hikers, who are often smoking cigarettes and carrying coolers full of beer.

The gravel drive up FR 7010 to Nohorn Butte summit is fun. The view from the pass is fantastic, especially westward, into the Table Rock Creek drainage. This is, in fact, the best view there is of Table Rock.

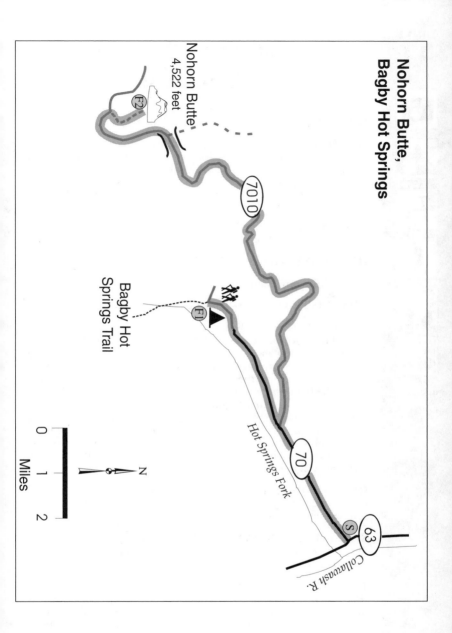

Nohorn Butte,
Bagby Hot Springs

Nohorn Butte,
4,522 feet

Bagby Hot
Springs Trail

Hot Springs Fork

Collawash R.

N

Miles
0   1   2

SIDE TRIPS. A right turn at Nohorn Butte summit will tie you
into Table Rock Road and the Molalla River Canyon Recreation
Area, eventually picking up I-5 at Woodburn (see Drive 1).

Little North Santiam, Opal Lake

LOCATION. East of Salem, north of Highway 22.

HIGHLIGHTS. One of Oregon's most consistently surprising scenic roads, with incredibly beautiful streams, waterfalls, lakes, mountain meadows, trailheads, and alpine vistas.

DIFFICULTY. Easy to moderate gravel road. A little steep as the road approaches the pass.

DISTANCE. 37.2 miles from Highway 22 just east of Stayton to Highway 22 at Detroit.

HIGH ELEVATION. 4,817 feet.

MAPS. Elkhorn; Battle Axe.

ADMINISTRATION. Willamette National Forest.

GETTING THERE. From Highway 22 east, out of Salem toward Detroit Lake, go to the North Fork Road turnoff at mile 23 (between Stayton and Mill City), where a sign says LITTLE NORTH SANTIAM RECREATION AREA. The pavement on North Fork Road ends at mile 16, at the Willamette National Forest boundary, where the road becomes Forest Road 2207. After 1.4 more miles, turn right (south), to continue on FR 2207 (if you go straight, you'll be on FR 2209). From the 2207/2209 junction, follow FR 2207 over the river and past Opal Lake for 16 miles to the junction with FR 2223. Turn left (south) on FR 2223, which is French Creek Road, a one-lane blacktop. It's 3.8 more miles back to Highway 22, at Detroit.

REST STOPS. Canyon Creek; Bear Creek; Elkhorn Valley; Pearl Creek and Shady Cove Campgrounds; not to mention seven campgrounds around Detroit Lake.

SPECIAL INFORMATION. The steep north slope just before the pass retains snow much later than one might expect for this elevation.

THE DRIVE. I repeat, this is one of Oregon's most surprisingly beautiful drives. If (as some claim) the unroaded Opal Creek is the state's most beautiful stream, then Cedar Creek, just one creek west with FR 2207 running along it, is a close second. At the pass, the rock formations, glacial cirques, and floral meadows above Opal Lake feel much higher in elevation than they actually are, especially when you run into snow in June. Actually, none of the peaks rise much over 5,000 feet, if that, and the pass is only 4,817 feet. See Side Trips for more information on Opal Creek.

The 16-mile drive along the Little North Santiam is mostly paved, with many views of farmland and of the river. There is a highlight at mile 14, at Salmon Falls, where you will find impressive rock formations (seen from a bridge) along the river, as well as views of the huge cliffs on the south face of Henline Mountain (4,616 feet) in the distance.

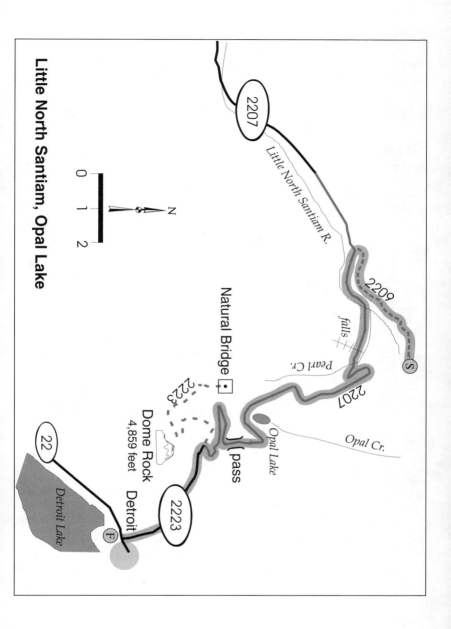

Little North Santiam, Opal Lake

Near the junction with FR 2207, the gravel road passes picnic sites, campgrounds, and swimming holes (and lots of people) to another bridge. The next 3 miles follow Cedar Creek, a narrow, boulder-lined stream with many beautiful pools. Sullivan Creek Falls is a highlight. This waterfall is particularly elegant and the clear blue pool at the base looks like it is maintained by the YMCA.

After the road crosses Sullivan Creek and cuts away from Cedar Creek, it winds around in the woods for a couple of miles and then emerges high above Cedar Creek, with a tremendous view of the immense canyon framing Henline Mountain directly north. Rocky black crags of Dome Rock (highest peak in the area at 4,859 feet), to the south, form the canyon head.

The Opal Lake Trailhead is passed on FR 2207 at mile 12. Here the road runs along a narrow saddle between Opal Creek and Cedar Creek. Beautiful Opal Lake is readily visible below the road, in the woods half a mile away.

Beyond the trailhead, the road crosses to the Opal Creek side of the ridge, with more views of the lake and the Opal Creek canyon. The route then climbs the rocks and meadows to a narrow pass. After that, it's back into the woods as the route rapidly descends to the junction with FR 2223. Many features in the summit area can be accessed by turning right onto FR 2223 instead of left. See Side Trips below. A left on FR 2223 follows French Creek for 4 miles before emerging on Highway 22 just before the bridge, at Detroit Lake. The town of Detroit lies just across the bridge.

SIDE TRIPS. If you continue straight on FR 2209 instead of turning onto FR 2207, the road follows the river for 2 more miles before dead-ending at a locked gate. The Henline Lookout trail begins 1 mile past the FR 2209 and FR 2207 junction, on the north side of the road in the middle of a huge road cut, which is a very unusual place for a trailhead. This very, very steep, switchback-laden path arrives at Henline Lookout in 2.5 miles, where you can enjoy spectacular views of the Little North Santiam and Cedar Creek drainages from the top of the immense bluffs.

From the gate at mile 2 on FR 2209, continue up the road on foot and you'll arrive at the mouth of Opal Creek after 4.5 miles. A path on the river's south side (the closed road is on the north side), leads to the Opal Creek Trail, which arrives at Opal Lake, 10 miles from the gate. This is reported to be one of Oregon's most beautiful hikes. In the 1980s, the Opal Creek drainage and the upper Little North Fork drainage were the center of a hard-fought conservation battle to preserve the old-growth forests. The conservationists won. It's possible to make a day-hike out of Opal Creek by parking one car at the trailhead at Opal Lake on FR 2207, and another at the gate on FR 2209, then doing the path one-way downhill.

If you turn right instead of left on FR 2223 from FR 2207, various gravel and dirt roads lead to Dome Rock, Needle Rock, Tumble Lake, Elephant Rock, and Phantom Natural Bridge. A 1-mile trail leads to Tumble Lake and a 0.5-mile path accesses Phantom Natural Bridge.

Valsetz

LOCATION. Southwest of Salem, near Monmouth, Dallas, and Falls City.

HIGHLIGHTS. An interesting and pleasant drive, mostly through intensively managed industrial forest land. The drive includes a visit to the site of an abandoned town and a defunct reservoir in a wide valley on the South Fork Siletz River.

DIFFICULTY. Easy. Wide gravel road.

DISTANCE. 10 miles from Falls City to the town site.

HIGH ELEVATION. 2,300 feet.

MAP. Valsetz.

ADMINISTRATION. State and private.

GETTING THERE. From Dallas, take Highway 223 (Washington Street) south toward Falls City. It's 6 miles to the Falls City turnoff. Turn right (west) on Falls City Road and continue 5 miles to Falls City. Valsetz Road, which leads to the abandoned town of Valsetz, from Falls City is unmarked but easy to find. Just follow the main road through town and across the bridge (over Little Luckiamute River). Keep going after the pavement ends. It's 10 miles from Falls City to the gate near the Valsetz town site.

REST STOPS. See Side Trips.

SPECIAL INFORMATION. Do not trespass on private lands. As always, obey the posted signs and respect the rights of private property owners.

THE DRIVE. The story of Valsetz is fascinating but sad. The town was founded around 1920 by the Valley and Siletz Railroad to provide housing and services for workers in a lumber mill owned by the two companies. The name of the town is a contraction of "Valley" and "Siletz." The town's main feature was Valsetz Lake, a several-hundred-acre reservoir in the beautiful, flat-bottomed valley of the Siletz River's South Fork.

In its heyday, the town boasted a thousand residents and a K–12 school, which won the state high school football championship for its division in 1984, the same year the town was officially abandoned because of the mill's diminishing profitability. In 1986, the town and mill were razed, the lake was drained, and the reservoir dam was removed.

A mile past Falls City on the Valsetz Road you come to a sign announcing that you are on private property. The next several miles are an interesting lesson in intensive forest management. Tracts range from recent clearcuts to young reproduction to beautiful, fully stocked, well tended older second growth. The trees are almost entirely Douglas-fir since this is the heart of Douglas-fir country.

After 4 miles you leave the private land, wind over a low summit (2,300 feet), then make your way gradually down into the wide, flat valley of the South Siletz (1,500 feet). At mile 8, you come to the upper end of where the Valsetz lake used to be.

At mile 10, you reach a gated road with a large sign, posted by the timber company, that prohibits trespassing even if the gate is open, and even for those on foot. In light of current antilogging activism, this security measure is probably justified. The town site is supposedly a short way up this road, but it has been completely razed and reforested. The only remaining Valsetz building is supposed to be a warehouse, also up this road.

SIDE TRIPS. If you continue on Valsetz Road, turning left just before the gate, you'll cross the South Siletz after a few hundred feet. Across the river, there is a triple fork, all unmarked roads. The wide gravel road to the right should lead to the main Siletz River Road after 15 miles (near the Siletz Indian Reservation), the town of Siletz after 20 miles, and Lincoln City, on the coast, after 45 miles. But I cannot vouch for the 15 miles of back road between Valsetz and the Indian reservation. I started up all three roads out of Valsetz but none coincided with any of the other roads indicated on my map.

There's a nice little county park on the Little Luckiamute, 2 miles from Falls City on the Black Rock Road. To get there, go straight, through Falls City, instead of crossing the river.

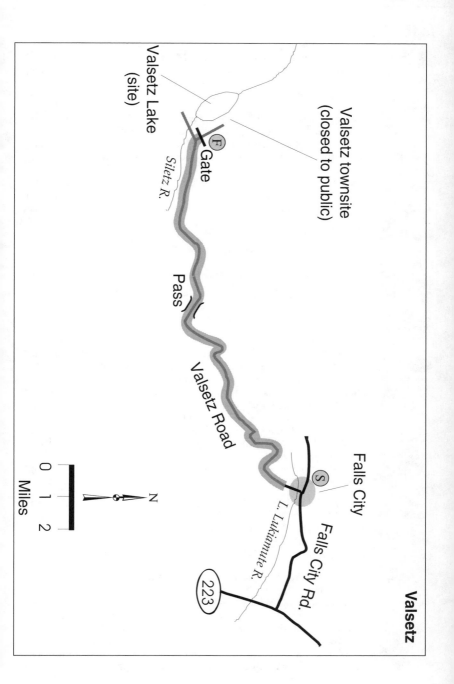

Valsetz

Valsetz townsite
(closed to public)

Valsetz Lake
(site)

F Gate

Siletz R.

Pass

Valsetz Road

Falls City

S

Falls City Rd.

L. Luckiamute R.

223

N

0 1 2
Miles

North Siuslaw River

LOCATION. Near the coast, between Florence and Yachats.

HIGHLIGHTS. A beautiful drive along the North Fork of the Siuslaw River tidal flats, then up a densely forested mountain and along a ridge that runs above the Rock Creek Wilderness. The road emerges on the coast just south of Cape Perpetua.

This is a pretty, pleasant little route that will instantly whisk you away from the crowds on Highway 101. With just a little effort, you can stick your toe into one of the smallest and most charming wilderness areas in the federal system.

DIFFICULTY. One-lane blacktop and easy, wide gravel roads.

DISTANCE. 36.5 miles from Highway 126 to U.S. 101.

HIGH ELEVATION. 2,000 feet.

MAPS. Tiernan; Cummins Peak; Heceta Head.

ADMINISTRATION. Siuslaw National Forest.

GETTING THERE. From Florence, take Highway 126 east toward Eugene. Proceed 1 mile to the North Siuslaw Road and turn left (north). The North Siuslaw Road is two-lane blacktop for 15 miles, then narrows to one-lane blacktop. At mile 23, on a curve that crosses the ridge between the North Fork Siuslaw River and Big Creek, two unpaved roads take off left (west). The road with the orange sign that says TO HIGHWAY 101, is the upper end of Big Creek Road (see Side Trips). After 1.5 more miles (at mile 24.5) on the North Siuslaw Road, gravel Fairview Mountain Road takes off left (west). Signs say ROAD 1055 AND U.S. 101—12 MILES. Turn left on Fairview Mountain Road and proceed to Highway 101.

REST STOPS. Bender Landing County Park is at mile 3 on the North Siuslaw Road. The North Siuslaw Campground is at mile 12. Highway 101 is full of campgrounds and day-use areas, especially around Cape Perpetua on U.S. 101 just north of where Fairview Ridge Road hits U.S. 101.

THE DRIVE. The road starts at a wide riparian tidal flat that occasionally fills with salt water. The flat consists of a grassy expanse with the wide, curvy river meandering through the middle. Bender Landing County Park, 3 miles up, offers the best view of this portion of the river. As you progress, the valley gradually narrows. At mile 11, a side road leads to Highway 36 and Mapleton. At mile 15, the pavement narrows to a winding one-lane blacktop. At mile 20, the road leaves the streamside and starts climbing.

At mile 23, you lose the pavement and cross out of the North Fork drainage and into the Big Creek drainage, passing the upper end of Big Creek Road. One mile later, you pass the main trailhead into the Rock Creek Wilderness. A half-mile after that, you arrive at the upper end of Fairview Mountain Road.

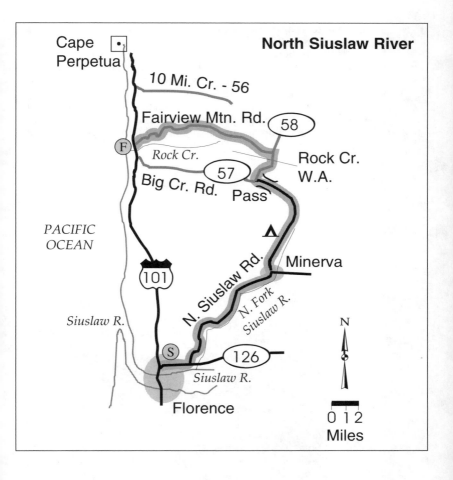

The gravel Fairview Mountain Road follows a ridgetop through a dense woods of Douglas-fir, Sitka spruce, and western redcedar, and overlooks the immense forested canyon of Rock Creek to the south (left), and the equally impressive valley of Tenmile Creek to the north (right). While the views are spectacular, there are no real vista points, just glimpses. At mile 11 on Fairview Mountain Road, the ocean comes dramatically into view below you, like a parting curtain. The final mile peers down over the beach and ocean. And then you are on U.S. 101, back in the crowds.

SIDE TRIPS. You may choose to take Big Creek Road back to U.S. 101. It is narrow and curvy but well maintained, and it mostly follows a creek instead of a ridgetop, though the creek is narrow and brushy and isn't seen all that often. Still, it's a nice drive.

Cape Perpetua is the area's scenic highlight. I'm always irritated, however, by the fact that Cape Perpetua is not a cape. A cape juts out into the ocean. Cape Perpetua is a prominent cliff, very visible from the ocean, but it does not jut. Cape Perpetua boasts a visitor center, a campground, and several short, impressive nature trails. Look for the road to the "Observation Point" for an easy 2-mile drive to the cliff top.

The map shows Tenmile Creek Road, which hits U.S. 101 two miles north of the lower end of Fairview Mountain Road, as connecting with the upper end of the North Siuslaw Road after 10 miles. It does not (as of May, 2001).

Old Town Florence is the area's main tourist hangout and well worth a visit. Nearby Dunes City and Siltcoos Lake offer all manner of fishing, camping, and hiking opportunities. Yachats is also extremely nice.

Coos Bay Wagon Road

Coos Bay Wagon Road

LOCATION. Between Coos Bay and Roseburg.

HIGHLIGHTS. Beautiful gravel road along the East Fork of the Coquille River. Waterfalls, and remote, isolated farmland. Hilltop view of Coos Bay.

DIFFICULTY. Easy and leisurely.

DISTANCE. 52.5 miles from Highway 42 at Tenmile to Highway 101 south of Coos Bay.

HIGH ELEVATION. 1,500 feet.

MAPS. McKinley; Coos Bay; Mt. Gurney; Sitkum; Dora.

ADMINISTRATION. BLM Coos Bay District.

GETTING THERE. Leave I-5 south of Roseburg, at Exit 119, Winston. Take Highway 99 west to the middle of Winston, then head west on Highway 42 towards Coos Bay. At the town of Tenmile (10 miles from Winston), turn right (north) onto Reston Road. After 5 miles, you arrive at Coos Bay Wagon Road. Turn left (west). The pavement ends after 6 miles and begins again 11 miles further on in Sitkum, where you should turn left (still west) and go 5.5 miles to Dora, following signs to Myrtle Point. Two miles past Dora, turn right (north) onto Lone Pine Lane. (Lone Pine Lane is not marked on any map. These roads are all numbered, though most numbers are not posted.) Continue 10 miles to Fairview. At Fairview, turn left (west) onto Forest Road 59, Sumner-Fairview Road, toward Sumner. Two miles later, there is a 3-mile stretch of no pavement. It's 13 miles from Fairview to Highway 101, just south of Coos Bay.

REST STOPS. Tenmile; Iverson Park (near Reston); store in Dora; Frona City Park (in Dora); Cherry Creek Park; store in Fairview; store in Sumner.

THE DRIVE. Even though there's a very scenic paved highway between Roseburg and Coos Bay, it's nice to know this old road is still there. When you first pick up the Coos Bay Wagon Road, 5 miles up Reston Road from Highway 42, the blacktop slowly snakes its way up and over a low, heavily forested mountain and emerges on the east fork of the Coquille River at Brewster Canyon. There you are suddenly catapulted back in time as you travel along a very old, unpaved, leisurely road.

The unpaved segment, through Brewster Canyon, only lasts 11 miles and the river is really just an alder-lined creek. The two waterfalls you pass half way through the canyon aren't particularly high but they are enchanting. One tumbles 20 feet into an emerald pool formed by a large crack in the surrounding bedrock which forces the river into a right-angle turn. The other is 40 feet high and very busy, with water tumbling every direction but up. It's a lovely effect.

As you approach Sitkum, the road skirts several acres of level farmland that is bounded by forested mountains on both sides.

COASTAL

(Sitkum boasts a population of less than 100, a few houses, and some nice farms, but no services.) Back on the blacktop, after more farmland, you arrive at Dora, which has a little store. From Dora, you can either return to Highway 42 and reach Coos Bay via Myrtle Point, or you can take the Sumner Road to Coos Bay. For the latter, follow Lone Pine Lane, which 2 miles past Dora bears uphill to the right, then turn right at the store and gas station in Fairview. If you continue straight at Fairview, you'll come out on Highway 42 at Coquille.

Sumner Road, which loses the pavement for 3 miles, winds through farmland, up and over forested hills, and around shaded draws. Sumner (population less than 200) has a little store but no gas. The highlight of the Sumner Road is a hilltop overlook with Coos Bay far in the distance.

SIDE TRIPS. The area is rife with paved and unpaved back roads. The most scenic of these follows the Middle Fork of the Coquille River northward between Dora and Fairview to a small, minimally developed state park. LaVerne Falls County Park, 5 miles north of Fairview on the Coquille-Fairview Road, is also worth a look for waterfall connoisseurs.

Falls on East Fork of the Coquille River, Coos Bay Wagon Road

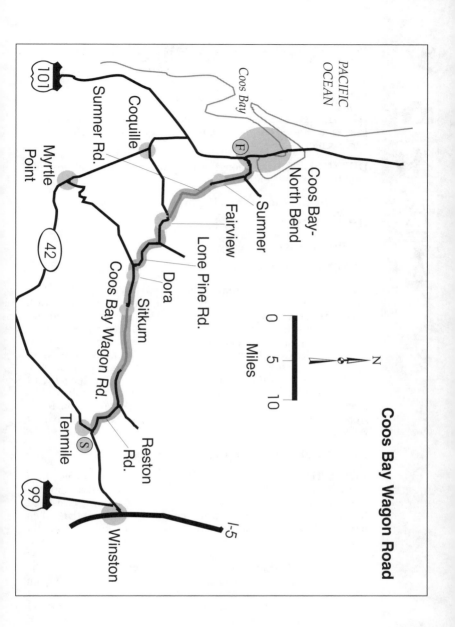

Coos Bay Wagon Road

Golden and Silver Falls

LOCATION. Northwest of Coos Bay.

HIGHLIGHTS. Two of the most beautiful, unusual waterfalls on Heaven or Earth. The drive up the Millicoma River Valley is also very scenic.

DIFFICULTY. Easy, though a little washboarded and possibly muddy toward the end.

DISTANCE. 24 miles from Highway 101 to the falls.

HIGH ELEVATION. 800 feet.

MAPS. Coos Bay; Allegany.

ADMINISTRATION. State and private.

GETTING THERE. From Highway 101, near the Coos Bay southern city limits, turn east at a sign that says COOS RIVER–ALLEGANY. Following signs to Allegany, you immediately crosses a bridge over Isthmus Slough and then makes several turns through an urban area in the town of Eastside before heading out to the Coos River Road. Two miles later, the Coos River is crossed via a bridge (you are still following signs to Allegany), and the route picks up the Millicoma River Road. In Allegany, 14 miles from Coos Bay, signs direct you to Golden and Silver Falls State Park, 10 miles away via the East Fork Millicoma River Road, and then Glen Creek Road. The pavement ends shortly past Allegany.

REST STOPS. Allegany; Golden and Silver Falls.

THE DRIVE. This delightful drive begins by following, then crossing, the immense Coos River. After the river crossing the road gradually makes its way into the enchanting, farm-lined Millicoma River Valley, with its meandering stream, flat, green pastures, hay fields, and densely forested peaks jutting abruptly upward. You lose the pavement shortly beyond the tiny village of Allegany. Eventually, you also lose the Millicoma River. At Nesika Park, the East Fork Millicoma River Road veers to the right and the route to Golden and Silver Falls becomes Glenn Creek Road, but you probably won't notice.

The road ends at a small parking and picnic area (technically a state natural area, not a state park), in a grove of Douglas-fir, bigleaf maple, red alder, and Oregon myrtlewood (known in California as California bay laurel). If you hike up the trail to the right (east), it's a level, 0.25-mile walk along Golden Creek to Golden Falls, which tumble 100 feet over a huge, "V" shaped sandstone outcrop. This is an easy walk to a magnificent waterfall, but the next walk to Silver Falls is even more magnificent.

The closed road straight ahead (north) from the parking area, is a slightly uphill 0.25-mile hike that goes high above Silver Creek and leads to Silver Falls, which also drops 100 feet. (Golden Creek and Silver Creek join to form Glenn Creek a mile below the falls.) Silver Falls fans out over an undercut sandstone

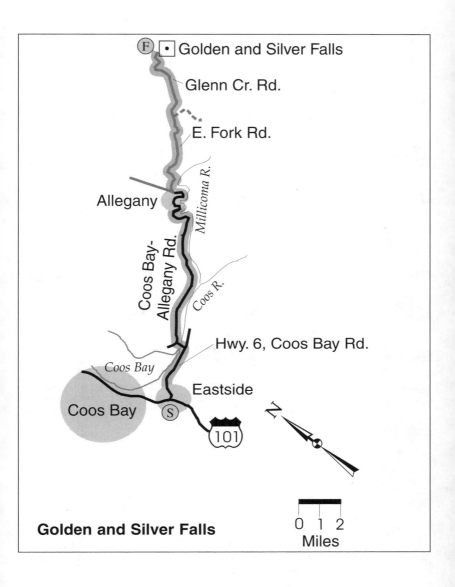

Golden and Silver Falls

dome and is amazing in its unique beauty. A series of cascades flow from the base of the falls to the creek bed. On the opposite side of the creek, another hiking path to Silver Falls branches off at the beginning of the Golden Falls Trail. A side trail (right) on this path leads to the top of Golden Falls.

Agness, Powers, Coquille Falls

LOCATION. The coastal mountains between Gold Beach and Coos Bay.

HIGHLIGHTS. This route explores the famous lower Rogue River canyon from the Oregon coast end, then heads over the mountains to the waterfall-lined South Fork Coquille River.

DIFFICULTY. Long, winding, and slow. Mostly two- and one-lane blacktop, with 12 miles of gravel. Easy to moderate.

DISTANCE. 59 miles from Highway 101 to Powers.

HIGH ELEVATION. 2,300 feet.

MAPS. Gold Beach; Signal Butte; Quosatana Butte; Soldier Camp Mountain; Agness; Illahe; China Flat; Powers.

ADMINISTRATION. Siskiyou National Forest.

GETTING THERE. From Highway 101, follow paved South Bank Road 33, at the north end of Gold Beach, for 31 miles to the bridge over the Rogue River. Just across the bridge, a paved 3-mile side road (left, west) leads to Agness. Beyond the Agness turnoff, Forest Road 33 becomes winding one-lane gravel. It crosses Agness Pass at mile 10 beyond the Agness turnoff, where it regains the pavement. The road emerges from the back country at Powers after 28 miles. Seven two-lane miles later you will arrive at Highway 42 (the Roseburg-Coos Bay Road) near Myrtle Point. A gravel side road right (FR 3348), 13 miles past the Agness turnoff, leads to the Coquille Falls Trailhead.

REST STOPS. Cougar Lane; Agness; Foster Bar and Illahe Campgrounds; Coquille Falls; Coquille Myrtle Grove State Park; and several small campgrounds along the South Fork Coquille River.

THE DRIVE. This is a basic backcountry drive that everyone takes when they first move to the Rogue River country. The trip from Gold Beach, on the coast, to Agness, 30 miles up the Rogue, is a fine, paved route. The mouth of the Illinois River, near Agness, is spectacular, but there's not much to see in Agness itself. Lots of people take the jet boat to Agness from Gold Beach. It's lots of fun and offers a unique perspective on the river, but in my opinion, is very commercial and intrusive.

FR 33 out of Agness, up and over the mountains, reveals a colossal panorama of the Rogue River canyon. On the other side of Agness Pass, the road begins following the South Fork Coquille River, which is much smaller than the Rogue but extremely pretty. Where FR 33 hits bottom, 6 miles beyond Agness Pass, hang a hard right (east) onto the gravel road to Glendale and go for about 1 mile to the Coquille Falls Trailhead. It's a 0.5-mile walk to a multitiered waterfall and natural area.

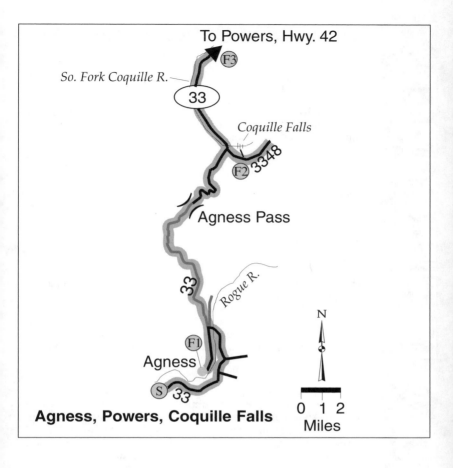

To Powers, Hwy. 42

So. Fork Coquille R.

33

Coquille Falls

3348

Agness Pass

33

Rogue R.

Agness

S 33

N

0 1 2
Miles

Agness, Powers, Coquille Falls

Returning to FR 33 and continuing north, the area is rife with fascinating side roads (such as the road to Barklow Mountain Lookout). If you drive FR 33 in winter after a hard rain, you'll pass a series of cliffs that will most likely have dozens of ephemeral waterfalls, along with a few permanent ones. The myrtle groves aren't bad either. (By the way, do not be fooled by the postcards; Oregon myrtle is not even remotely related to any tree in the Middle East. It isn't even in the Myrtle family, it's in the Laurel family. In California it's called California bay laurel.)

SIDE TRIPS. Be sure to check out Foster Bar near Agness, where river rafters, who put in 41 miles upstream on Grave Creek, end their journey. To reach Foster Bar from FR 33, turn right (east) on FR 3730, at the same junction where you turn left for Agness. Proceed for 3 miles. Also, if you continue up FR 3348, past Coquille Falls, the scenery becomes exquisite in aptly named Eden Valley. Highlights are the Hanging Rock Trail and the Mount Bolivar Trail in the Wild Rogue Wilderness, both about 1 mile long. See Drive 38.

Quosatana Butte, Game Lake

LOCATION. East of Gold Beach and south of the Rogue River, beginning 15 miles from the coast.

HIGHLIGHTS. A scenic drive up the lower Rogue River canyon, then into the mountains past Quosatana Butte, Collier Butte, Big Craggies, Game Lake, and many trailheads.

DIFFICULTY. Moderate, with long, sometimes steep gravel and dirt roads. In spring, a little muddy toward the end.

DISTANCE. 22 miles from Forest Road 33 to Game Lake.

HIGH ELEVATION. 4,000 feet.

MAPS. Quosatana Butte; Horse Sign Butte.

ADMINISTRATION. Siskiyou National Forest.

GETTING THERE. From Gold Beach, take Forest Road 33, South Bank Road, 15 miles to FR 3313, then turn right (south). Eight miles later, at Quosatana Butte, turn left (east) onto FR 3680 and follow it 18 miles to the end, bearing right at all ambiguous-looking junctions. The gravel ends after 4 miles. FR 3680 becomes Spur 400 and continues another 6 miles to Game Lake.

REST STOPS. Quosatana Campground; Game Lake.

THE DRIVE. First of all, Quosatana Campground, on the Rogue River, is one of the prettiest campgrounds you'll ever see, with a fantastic swimming hole. And that's just the start of the trip. Climbing steeply into the rugged coastal mountains, FR 3313 crests at the jutting black outcrop of Quosatana Butte. Turning left onto FR 3680, a number of panoramas come into view, mostly to the south, as the road traverses rocky areas and eerie coastal old-growth. The best vistas are of the Big Craggies (an extremely rocky botanical area containing many endangered species but with no road or trail access), Collier Butte (a barren, ice-cream-cone summit), and the Game Lake (about 8 acres) area, with its lake, campground, and beautiful meadows. A short hike up the Pupps Camp Trail from Game Lake affords an outstanding panorama of green meadows, canyons and rocky summits.

SIDE TRIPS. FR 3680 right (west) instead of left (east), at Quosatana Butte, makes a nice alternate route back to Gold Beach but is longer and less scenic than FR 33. Spur 550, to the right off of FR 3680, accesses Snow Camp Lookout and ties in with the Windy Valley Road (FR 1375) (see Drive 20). And FR 3318, left off of FR 3680, ties in to Wildhorse Prairie and Drive 19.

2002 FIRE. Forest roads 3313 and 3680 remain the same until the junction with FR 3318. From that point there are numerous burned areas, although the road and signs are not affected. Near Collier and Lawson buttes, the route offers a spectacular view northeast into the Lawson Creek drainage—Lawson Creek may have been the most thoroughly burned drainage of the entire Biscuit Fire. The destruction is nearly total as far as the eye can

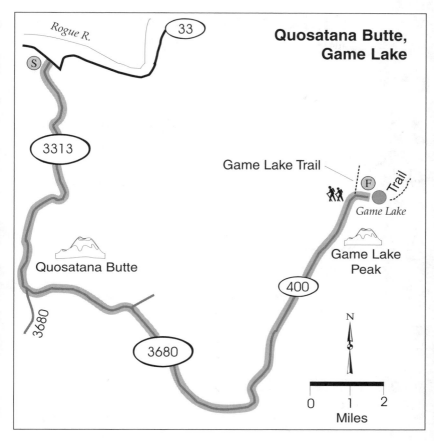

Quosatana Butte, Game Lake

Rogue R.

33

S

3313

Game Lake Trail

F

Trail

Game Lake

Quosatana Butte

Game Lake Peak

3680

400

3680

N

0   1   2

Miles

see. Storm damage had created some narrow spots on FR 3680 near MP 22 but these may have been repaired by now. The last mile to Game Lake was somewhat improved, but nearly two-thirds of the lake's perimeter was burned.

Game Lake

Wildhorse Prairie, Pebble Hill

LOCATION. East of Gold Beach and south of the Rogue River, beginning 20 miles from the coast.

HIGHLIGHTS. A scenic drive up the lower Rogue River canyon, then into the mountains to a magnificent vista point. Lots of old-growth forest and numerous fields of rhododendron in spring. Side trip to Pebble Hill geological site.

DIFFICULTY. Easy, wide, slightly steep, mostly gravel roads.

DISTANCE. 9.5 miles from Forest Road 33 to Wildhorse Prairie.

HIGH ELEVATION. 3,600 feet.

MAP. Horse Sign Butte.

ADMINISTRATION. Siskiyou National Forest.

GETTING THERE. From Gold Beach, take paved, two-lane Forest Road 33, South Bank/Jerrys Flat Road, 20 miles to gravel FR 3318, and turn right. At mile 5, take the dirt side road (Spur 120, left) to Pebble Hill. If you stay on FR 3318, Wildhorse Prairie turns up 4.5 miles later.

REST STOPS. Wildhorse Prairie campsite.

THE DRIVE. This trip begins with the world-class drive up the Rogue River from Gold Beach, then heads up FR 3318, which winds far into the mountains through old-growth forest, new-growth forest, and recent logging sites. If you go in spring, clearcuts that are overgrown with rhododendron produce an impressive display.

At mile 5 on FR 3318, a side road leads 0.25 miles to the Pine Grove Trailhead (1170). The path's first 0.75 miles run beneath coastal old-growth and a beautiful meadow before skirting the north flank of Pebble Hill. The interesting thing about Pebble Hill is the piles of what look like beach pebbles that have been smoothed and rounded by wave action. It's odd to find such deposits so high in the mountains, so far from a beach. Beyond Pebble Hill, the trail becomes a serious hike, dropping 3,000 feet in 3 miles to the Illinois River, on the side without road access.

But the real payoff of the drive, back on FR 3318, is Wildhorse Prairie, an immense grassy knoll looking out across the Rogue River canyon. You can't quite see the river but you can see tier after tier of mountains stretching to the horizon. A short side road just before the prairie, across from the campground, leads to a superb mountaintop vista point.

SIDE TRIPS. If you keep going on FR 3318, you'll end up on FR 3680, the road to Game Lake. See Drive 18.

2002 FIRE. Forest road 338 is in excellent condition with unaffected road signs. The segment from MP 6, where the pavement ends near the Pine Grove Trailhead, to FR 3680, was a main fire line in the Biscuit Fire. Many burned areas lie to the east and none

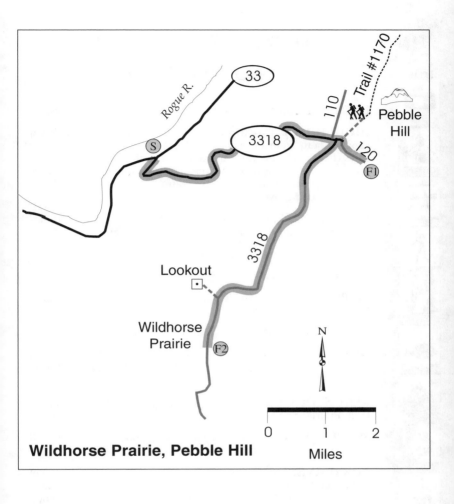

Wildhorse Prairie, Pebble Hill

to the west. The area around Wildhorse Lookout (MP 10) did not burn. A beautiful old "clearcut-turned-rhododendron" field at MP 13 is gone.

Upper Chetco River, Big Craggies

LOCATION. Southern coastal mountains, east of Brookings.

HIGHLIGHTS. This trip explores the immense Chetco River canyon, both from the ocean's edge and high up the canyon's sides. It's the closest you can get by car to the roadless and trail-less Big Craggies Botanical Area. The drive also features Snow Camp Lookout, many side roads and trailheads, and the northern-most redwood grove.

DIFFICULTY. Easy to moderate, mostly gravel. Steep and narrow at the tie-in to Forest Road 3680, at the far end.

DISTANCE. 35 miles from Highway 101 to FR 3680.

HIGH ELEVATION. 2,400 feet.

MAPS. Brookings; Mt. Emily; Bosley Butte; Quail Prairie Mountain; Big Craggies.

ADMINISTRATION. Siskiyou National Forest.

GETTING THERE. From Brookings, take North Bank Road (Forest Road 784, which becomes FR 1376) left and north, for 35 miles to the junction with FR 3680.

REST STOPS. Loeb State Park; Little Redwood Campground; High Prairie; Snow Camp Mountain.

SPECIAL INFORMATION. The drive can be done just as well in the opposite direction.

THE DRIVE. The drive up the Chetco is impressive. It is level and paved for the first 21 miles, to the bridge over the river. Loeb State Park, at mile 7, has a nature trail through a myrtlewood grove and connects to a Forest Service trail through the northern-most redwood grove in the United States. Redwoods are exceed-ingly rare in Oregon (Drive 22 visits another grove). Little Redwood Campground, 5 miles beyond Loeb Park, is also home to a few little redwoods.

After crossing the Chetco, the road steepens somewhat as it climbs into the mountains. The best view back into the canyon comes at High Prairie, at mile 26. Four miles later, a spectacular view of the Big Craggies Botanical Area unfolds. This impressive cluster of gabbro (dark granite) peaks is home to many endan-gered plant species. The only access to the Big Craggies is a trail that ends at the Botanical Area boundary after a steep 4-mile hike (See Side Trips, below).

Beyond the Big Craggies, still on FR 1376, the forest thins out and the way becomes narrow and steep as it ascends to the Rogue–Chetco divide. Snow Camp lookout, 1 mile before the junction with FR 3680, is well worth the 0.5-mile walk up the gated road. The lookout can be rented from the Forest Service like a motel room.

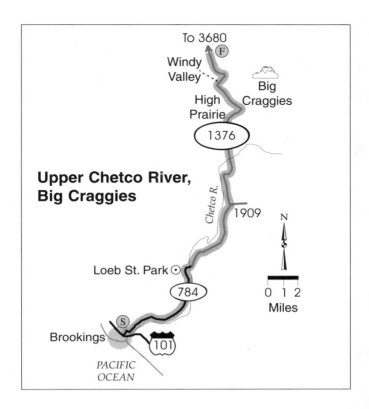

Upper Chetco River, Big Craggies

SIDE TRIPS. FR 1909, right (south) at mile 17, winds for 13 miles to Red Mountain Prairie, and to Vulcan Peak at the edge of the Kalmiopsis Wilderness. An easy 1.5-mile hike leads to beautiful and unusual Vulcan Lake, with its red serpentinite rock. (See Drive 21.) FR 1917, right (east) at mile 18, runs for 10 miles to the Long Ridge Campground and Quail Prairie Mountain Lookout. Spur 360, right (east) just past High Prairie, is a dirt road that drops steeply down to the trailhead for the Tincup and Mislatnah trails. The latter ends at the edge of the Big Craggies Botanical Area. At mile 29, on the left on FR 1376, the 1.5-mile Windy Valley Trail is worth a look, both for the valley and for the vista westward, down the Pistol River, after 0.5 mile of hiking.

2002 FIRE. Forest road 1376 is in decent condition as it passes through several burned areas in the upper reaches. A wet-season Port Orford cedar gate* was recently installed above Brookings, just past the road crossing of the Chetco River where it begins to climb. There is also a new Port Orford cedar gate at the road's far end, near the junction with FR 3680.

---

* *Port Orford cedar gate closures.* Port Orford cedar, a beautiful tree native to southwest Oregon, is susceptible to a lethal fungus called Port Orford cedar root-rot. The fungal spores are spread by cars driving through mud and standing water in wet weather. To combat the disease, the Forest Service in southwest Oregon has recently erected numerous road gates, with signs to identify them as part of the Port Orford cedar root-rot control program. Gates are closed and locked from November 1 to June 1. The gates are kept closed and unlocked throughout the rest of the year, and drivers may pass through but must immediately close the gate behind them.

Vulcan Peak

LOCATION. In the mountains east of Brookings, at the edge of the Kalmiopsis Wilderness.

HIGHLIGHTS. A long, winding road up the Chetco goes high into the mountains through coastal old-growth forest, and ends at a beautiful, barren red peak with a view of the ocean.

DIFFICULTY. Easy to moderate. Easy gravel to Red Mountain Prairie, and a little rough and rocky beyond.

DISTANCE. 16.25 miles from Chetco River Road to Vulcan Peak Trailhead.

HIGH ELEVATION. 3,600 feet.

MAP. Quail Prairie Mountain.

ADMINISTRATION. Siskiyou National Forest.

GETTING THERE. From Brookings, go inland and east on Chetco River Road (County Road 784, which becomes Forest Road 1376). After 18 miles, at the South Fork Campground, turn right onto FR 1909. Follow 1909 for 16 miles before turning onto the 0.25-mile spur to the Vulcan Peak Trailhead.

REST STOPS. Loeb State Park; Little Redwood Campground (beautiful swimming hole); South Fork Campground; Red Mountain Prairie.

THE DRIVE. This is one of those long, leisurely, mostly easy, drives everybody on the south coast should do at least once. It begins with the drive up the Chetco, past Loeb State Park and Little Redwood Campground. Loeb State Park has a nature trail through a myrtlewood grove and another trail through the north-ernmost redwood grove in the United States, one of a few red-wood groves in Oregon.

At South Fork Campground, you leave the blacktop and follow a curvy gravel road into the mountains, eventually winding up on Devil's Backbone and around Polliwog Butte. There's not much to see, except miles of dense Douglas-fir forest and side creeks.

Things change dramatically at Red Mountain Prairie, near the turnoff to Spur 250, which is on the right. Red Mountain Prairie is a grassy opening with a view of forested ridges that plunge into deep canyons. Beyond Red Mountain Prairie, Vulcan Peak, a bar-ren, orange serpentinite outcrop, comes into view. A steep, 1-mile hiking trail at the end of the short spur road takes you from a rocky flat to the 4,655-foot summit. From the aerie on top, you can see Vulcan Lake, the entire Kalmiopsis Wilderness, every mountain within 100 miles, including Preston Peak in California, and the Pacific Ocean. I was struck by the contrast between the desert-like barrenness of the serpentinite and the near rain forest that stretches to the ocean.

SIDE TRIPS. One mile of driving on FR 1909, from the Vulcan Peak turnoff to the Vulcan Lake Trailhead, takes you over a fair-ly rough road. The hike to the strange and beautiful Vulcan Lake

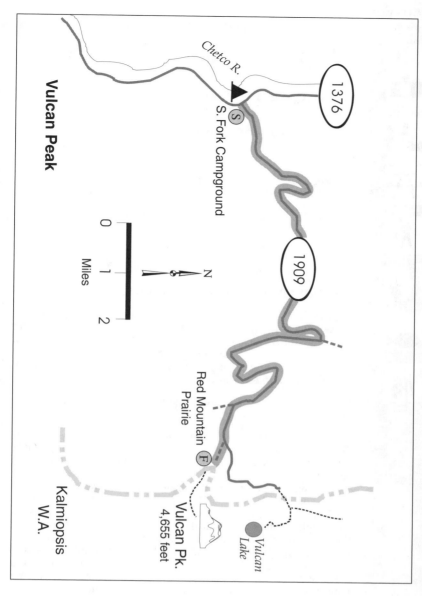

Vulcan Peak

lasts for 1.5 miles, with lots of stunted, serpentinite-adapted plants to see, such as California coffeeberry, Jeffrey pine, and Sadler oak.

2002 FIRE. Forest road 1909 was burned over in several places at its upper end and is in generally poor condition, with many snags and much ravel (loose, fallen rock). The Forest Service had a spring 2003 clean-up planned, but call first to check on the road's current condition. There is a new Port Orford cedar gate* on this road.

* See note at Drive 20.

Winchuck River, Packsaddle Mountain

LOCATION. East of Brookings on the south coast. The route ends at the edge of the Kalmiopsis Wilderness.

HIGHLIGHTS. A beautiful drive along a river and then into the mountains for a view of the ocean from 18 miles away and 2,707 feet up.

DIFFICULTY. Easy. The route is paved to the Winchuck Campground and is wide with gravel to the Packsaddle Trailhead.

DISTANCE. 18.75 miles from Highway 101 to Sourdough Trailhead.

HIGH ELEVATION. 2,707 feet.

MAP. Fourth of July Creek.

ADMINISTRATION. Siskiyou National Forest.

GETTING THERE. One mile north of the California line, take the Winchuck River Road, County Road 896, east and away from the ocean. It's 8 miles of pavement to the Winchuck Campground. Continue east beyond the campground on gravel FR 1107 for 10 miles to the turnoff right (east) onto Spur 220, an easy, gravel, 0.75-mile road to the Sourdough Trailhead.

REST STOPS. Winchuck Campground; Pallady Spring; Sourdough Trailhead.

THE DRIVE. The drive along Oregon's southernmost river is picturesque and paved for the initial 8 miles, with lots of little farms. Winchuck Campground is full of trees, nature trails, and beautiful picnic spots.

The pavement ends at the bridge over the Winchuck River, just beyond the Winchuck Campground, at the beginning of FR 1107. The first couple of miles are curvy and a little steep, with some tight switchbacks, but the road is gravel and pleasant. As you climb the ridge, there's not much to see because of the dense forest. At mile 9, you arrive at Pallady Spring, a little picnic site with a steep, 0.5-mile trail down into a rocky fern gully with a creek at the bottom. Beyond Pallady Spring, you start passing long vistas and rock outcrops. But they're nothing like the ones you'll shortly see on Spur 220, at mile 10.

During it's short, easily-driven existence, Spur 220 provides an incredible view of the densely-forested canyon of the Smith River's North Fork, with the orange upwellings of Red Mountain and Vulcan Peak (see Drive 21) in the distance to the north. Everything east of the North Fork inside Kalmiopsis Wilderness.

The Sourdough Trailhead is located near the summit of Packsaddle Mountain, at a saddle with a vista north on one side and south on the other. Walk up the path a couple of hundred feet for a stunning view of the mouth of the Winchuck River and of the Pacific ocean. The trail leads to Sourdough Camp in 3.5 miles (see Drive 48).

COASTAL

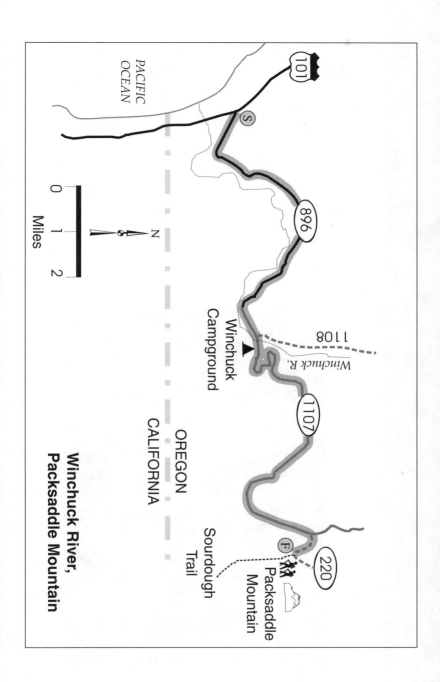

Winchuck River,
Packsaddle Mountain

SIDE TRIPS. At the Winchuck Campground, go left (north) for 1.5 miles on FR 1108 for Ludlum House, another fine spot along the Winchuck. Ludlum House is a county recreational facility that can be rented for special occasions. If you continue past Spur 220 on FR 1107 and turn left onto FR 1205, you'll end up at the Wheeler Creek Natural Area (Drive 23) after 14 miles.

2002 FIRE. This area and roads FR1107 and 220 were unaffected.

Road near Packsaddle Mountain

Wheeler Creek Natural Area

LOCATION. Near the south coast, in the mountains southeast of Brookings.

HIGHLIGHTS. Tours one of four natural redwood groves in Oregon, and what is possibly the most atypical redwood grove in the world. One mile away by trail is the only spot on the United States mainland that was bombed during World War II.

DIFFICULTY. Moderate. The road is a little narrow, somewhat steep in spots, and slow and curvy. The gravel surface is well-groomed.

DISTANCE. 19.5 miles from Highway 101 to Wheeler Creek Natural Area.

HIGH ELEVATION. 2,400 feet.

MAP. Mt. Emily.

ADMINISTRATION. Siskiyou National Forest.

GETTING THERE. From the town of Harbor, on Highway 101 just south of Brookings, take South Bank Road, County Road 808, the first road heading inland up the Chetco River and south of the Chetco River bridge. Follow the pavement 6 miles to Mt. Emily Road (FR 1205), a narrow gravel route uphill to the right. (If you come to Mill Creek, you've gone too far.) Stay on FR 1205 for 13.5 miles to the Wheeler Creek Natural Area, following signs to the Bomb Site Trailhead.

REST STOPS. Harbor; Wheeler Creek Natural Area.

THE DRIVE. The typical habitat of California redwoods is sheltered bottomlands with rich, deep soil, in river canyons near the Pacific coast. The species ventures inland and up mountainsides only in the center of its geographic range, where the habitat is ideal. At the fringes of this range, redwood sticks to the tried and true canyon bottoms. The northernmost redwood grove, near Oregon's Loeb State Park, on the Chetco River out of Brookings, is located in just such an ideal canyon (see Drive 20).

This brings us to the Wheeler Creek Natural Area, a redwood grove at the very edge of the species' range, located on a mountain-top, a site where redwood is the last thing you would expect to find.

The drive begins with a pleasant, paved excursion up the Chetco River, with Mt. Emily (elevation 2,926 feet), rising dead ahead. Turning onto Mt. Emily Road (which takes off left after 2 miles, though you remain on FR 1205), the route becomes narrow and curvy, with lots of side creeks that plunge down steep gullies lined with ferns and moss-covered alders and maples. Eventually, the road meets Wheeler Creek, which it follows for 2 miles before again steeply climbing.

At the turnout to the Wheeler Creek Natural Area, nature begins playing her tricks. This second-most northern redwood grove sits on a thinly soiled, rocky mountain top, 10 miles inland.

COASTAL

And the redwoods grow alongside Douglas-fir rather than Western hemlock and tanoak (an unusual occurrence, but not unheard of). Rather than towering giants, however, these redwoods are stunted little trees, which is to be expected at the fringe of a plant's geographic range. Since their presence is so unusual, and since this site is so unsuited for redwoods, it's a mystery that these trees did not die out eons ago. The natural area is accessed by a pretty little side road on the left. There is a parking area after a couple of hundred feet.

Across FR 1205 from the Natural Area turnout, on the right, you will find the Bomb Site Trailhead. Park at the natural area or along the shoulder. It's a 1-mile hike to what seems like a random spot in the forest, of no special scenic value. But in the summer of 1943 a Japanese bomber tried to set the woods on fire (not that hard to do in summer) by dropping bombs here. The idea was to create domestic chaos in the United States and thus divert American attention from the war with Japan. It didn't work.

SIDE TRIPS. If you continue on FR 1205, then turn right onto FR 1107, you'll end up at the Sourdough Trailhead on Packsaddle Mountain (Drive 22) after 14 miles.

2002 FIRE. This area and roads CR 808 and 1205 were unaffected.

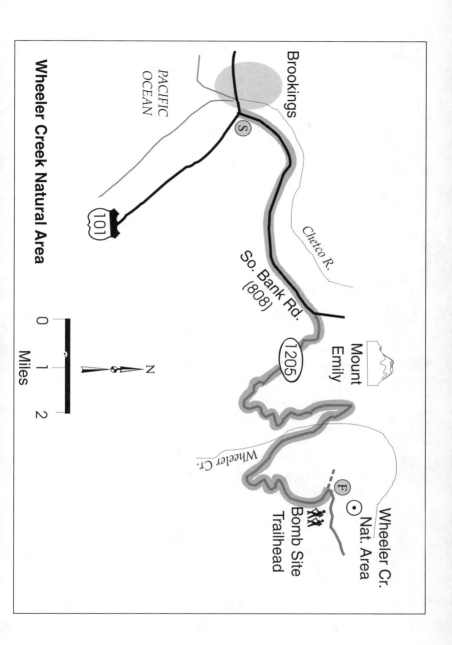

Wheeler Creek Natural Area

Metolius Bench

LOCATION. Central Oregon, between Redmond and Madras, on the east side of the Cascades.

HIGHLIGHTS. Spectacular rimrock above a secluded portion of the Metolius River. The access road crosses all three arms of Lake Billy Chinook reservoir (Deschutes, Crooked, and Metolius rivers). Amazing desert and foothills canyon country.

DIFFICULTY. Easy paved and gravel roads. The last 5 miles are mostly dirt, very dusty, and a little twisty.

DISTANCE. 32 miles from Highway 97 to Monty Campground.

HIGH ELEVATION. 2,300 feet.

MAPS. Round Butte Dam; Fly Creek.

ADMINISTRATION. Deschutes National Forest.

GETTING THERE. From Highway 97, between Redmond and Madras, near Culver, follow signs to Cove Palisade State Park. The route is slightly different but well-marked depending on whether you're coming from the north or south. Either direction takes you through the town of Culver and out to a series of paved back roads. After crossing the Crooked and Deschutes River arms of Lake Billy Chinook, continue on the same road, following signs to Perry South Camp. The road loses the pavement at mile 14 and picks it up again at mile 21, where it drops down to the Metolius River arm of Lake Billy Chinook. At Perry South Camp (mile 27), the pavement ends again and it's a final 5 dirt miles to Monty Campground.

REST STOPS. Cove Palisade State Park; Perry South Camp; Monty Campground.

THE DRIVE. Nearly every state map of Oregon shows it: the Metolius Bench, along the northern bank of the Metolius River. The river, in turn, forms the southern boundary of the Warm Springs Indian Reservation. Metolius Bench is definitely worth seeing, though I found myself wondering why, since this is an area with many spectacular benches (volcanic rimrock), this bench and no other appears on all the maps. But it is a very impressive bench in a very remote, beautiful, and hard-to-reach spot.

Cove Palisade State Park, through which you must go to reach the Metolius Bench, is among Oregon's most spectacular rim-rock-lined river gorges. After driving across the flat desert ranch-land east of the Cascades, with the Three Sisters looming just a few miles west, suddenly the bottom seems to drop out of the universe when you come to Crooked River Canyon, which has near-ly perpendicular 600-foot lava walls on either side. Lake Billy Chinook floods the canyon bottom.

The road then makes its way down to the water's edge, where there is a campground, a store, and a boat ramp. Then it heads up the canyon, crosses a low bridge, and heads back down the

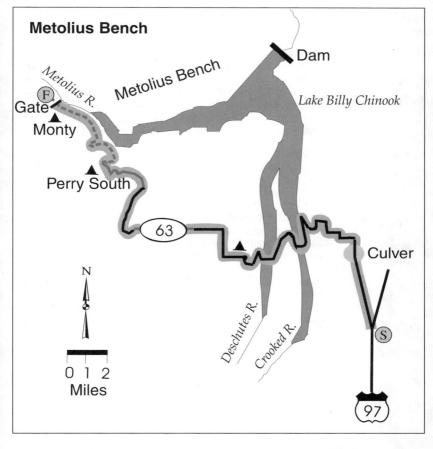

Metolius Bench

Dam

Metolius R.

Metolius Bench

Lake Billy Chinook

Gate

F

Monty

Perry South

63

Culver

S

N

0 1 2

Miles

Deschutes R.

Crooked R.

97

canyon on the opposite side to a gap between Crooked River Canyon and the parallel and nearly identical Deschutes River Canyon. The two canyons meet 0.5 mile down river from the gap, at an immense monolith called the "island." Another campground and store, and some Native American petroglyphs, can be found at the gap.

Beyond the gap, the road makes another drop, almost identical to the Crooked River crossing, into the Deschutes River gorge. It then crosses a second low bridge, makes its way out of the canyon, and heads back into the flat ranch country via a series of steep switchbacks.

After a few more miles on pavement and gravel across the sagebrush desert, the road drops into the canyon of the Metolius River and picks up pavement for a couple of miles as it approaches Perry South Camp and a boat launch. Beyond Perry South, the now narrow dirt road makes its way westward, several hundred feet above the river. That's where the Bench finally comes into view, a wall of lava rimrock between 500 and 1,000 feet high. The Bench is not as steep as the canyon walls of the Deschutes or Crooked river, and of course it's only on one side of the river, but it's quite beautiful. The north side of the river, the side with the

Bench, is the edge of the Warm Springs Indian Reservation. The road runs along the south side of the river.

At Monty Campground, one of the prettiest campgrounds you will find anywhere, you arrive at the free-flowing river above the reservoir, in a stand of pines and cottonwoods, with the Bench towering above the opposite bank. The road continues for several more miles, with much poorer quality. There is a gate just past Monty Campground which was locked when I visited in June, 2001, so I had to cut this trip short. There is a gate just before Monty Campground, too, which was not locked when I visited.

SIDE TRIPS. The Metolius is most famous for its source, a gigantic spring that gushes out of a seemingly random spot in the woods, making it a full-blown river (albeit only 60 miles long) from the very start. Follow signs north from U.S. 20, halfway between Sisters and Santiam Pass, for the Springs of the Metolius. According to the Deschutes National Forest map, if you stay on the road to the spring, heading north past Camp Sherman, and follow a maze of low-quality back roads, you theoretically enter the Warm Springs Reservation and briefly brush the top of the bench.

For the best overview of the confluence of the Crooked and Deschutes canyons, the vista point atop Round Butte is reached via a 5-mile side road north, just before the Crooked River crossing. The dam that impounds Lake Billy Chinook is called Round Butte Dam.

Metolius Arm of Lake Billy Chinook, Metolius Beach on left

Newberry Caldera, Paulina Peak

LOCATION. Newberry National Volcanic Monument, south of Bend in central Oregon.

HIGHLIGHTS. This trip visits Newberry Caldera, a collapsed volcano similar to Crater Lake. Newberry Caldera features the largest obsidian glass flow in the United States, two magnificent lakes, and a spectacular drive to the top of a 7,985 foot peak.

DIFFICULTY. Easy paved road to Newberry Caldera. The wide gravel road to Paulina Peak summit is somewhat steep, and very twisty toward the end.

DISTANCE. 15.5 miles from Highway 97 to the summit of Paulina Peak.

HIGH ELEVATION. 7,985 feet.

MAPS. East Lake; Paulina Peak.

ADMINISTRATION. Deschutes National Forest.

GETTING THERE. Take Highway 97 south for 24 miles from Bend to MP 161, 6 miles north of LaPine. Go east (left) on the paved road where the sign says NEWBERRY CALDERA–PAULINA LAKE–EAST LAKE. It's 12 miles to the Newberry Caldera, Paulina Lake, and the Paulina Peak turnoff (Spur 500). Turn right (south) on Spur 500 at Paulina Lake for Paulina Peak, 3.5 miles away.

REST STOPS. Paulina Lake Resort; Paulina Peak; Giant Obsidian Flow; East Lake.

SPECIAL INFORMATION. This is a National Volcanic Monument and there is a fee station on the entrance road. In 2001, the fee was $5.00 per car, unless you had a Northwest Forest Pass (which is a Forest Service trailhead parking permit), or a Golden Age or Golden Eagle pass.

THE DRIVE. This trip through Newberry National Volcanic Monument (50,000 acres, created in 1990) is a central Oregon highlight. The road from Highway 97 up the side of the volcano and into the caldera basin is paved and easy. Newberry Caldera, unlike Crater Lake and despite a nearly identical geologic history, contains two large lakes, both of which have outlet creeks that carry water out of the caldera. A spectacular cinder cone separates the two lakes, which are both quite deep, over 200 feet, but not nearly as deep as Crater Lake. Paulina Lake covers 1,520 acres while East Lake covers 1,028 acres (by comparison, Crater Lake covers 17,000 acres).

A "caldera" is a large depression formed in a volcano whose top has caved in because the molten magma inside of it either retreated or was expelled. There are several calderas in this volcanic region. Crater Lake is inside a caldera. The Mountain Lakes complex near Lake of the Woods is a caldera, as is the Medicine Lake Highland, just east of Mt. Shasta.

CENTRAL AND SOUTH CASCADES

Soon after the road enters the caldera, the Paulina Peak Road takes off to the right (south). This winding, 3-mile gravel route is steep in spots, with long drop-offs, but wide and not dangerous. The summit is broad with jutting rock outcrops. A short trail from the parking area leads to the top of a promontory that has views of the two lakes, the cinder cone between them, and the obsidian flow. In the distance, on a clear day, you can see from Mt. Hood to Mt. McLoughlin, with the Three Sisters, west of Bend, all over 10,000 feet high, being the most prominent.

SIDE TRIPS. Back on the main Paulina–East Lake Road and continuing eastward, you pass the obsidian flow, then East Lake. The obsidian flow offers a short but extremely impressive hike. This volcanic glass, formed from soupy froth and lava, emerged during the mountain's last eruption, 1,400 years ago.

Nearby volcanic landmarks include Lava River Cave, a mile-long lava tube, just off Highway 97 to the east, 9 miles north of the Paulina–East Lake turnoff (the Forest Service will rent you a lantern); Lava Butte, a huge cinder cone with a lookout and interpretive display on top, located just off Highway 97 to the west, 13 miles north of the Paulina–East Lake turnoff; and the Oregon High Desert Museum, one of the nation's best natural history museums, on Highway 97, 15 miles north of the Paulina–East Lake turnoff. For Surveyors Ice Cave, take Forest Road 21 (gravel) right (east) from East Lake, over the rim and down the mountain through the pine forest. It's 2 miles to the junction with FR 2125 (where you turn right), and 7 more miles on FR 2125 to the ice cave. FR 2125 eventually meets up with FR 22 (here you go right again) and returns to Highway 97. This is an outstanding side trip.

Approaching Paulina Peak

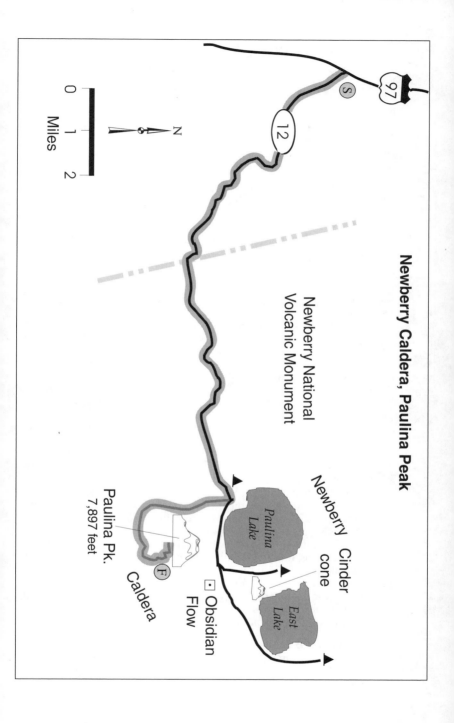

Newberry Caldera, Paulina Peak

Lemolo Lake to Summit Lake

LOCATION. The divide between the Umpqua and Willamette rivers, in the Cascades just north of Diamond Lake.

HIGHLIGHTS. A complicated route featuring Lemolo Lake, spectacular Warm Springs Pass (high above the Middle Fork Willamette River), Timpanogas Lake, Summit Lake, the Middle Fork Willamette River, and Hills Creek Reservoir.

DIFFICULTY. Mostly easy gravel and paved roads, a little washboarded in spots. The road to Summit Lake is low quality.

DISTANCE. 61.8 miles from Highway 138 to Highway 58 (including a 2-mile round trip side trip to Summit Lake).

HIGH ELEVATION. 5,600 feet.

MAPS. Lemolo Lake; Emigrant Butte.

ADMINISTRATION. Umpqua, Willamette National Forests.

GETTING THERE. Seventy-four miles east of Roseburg (near MP 74) on Highway 138, turn left (north) onto paved Forest Road 2610, toward Lemolo Lake. Go 3 miles to paved FR 2614 and turn right (northeast). Go 3 more miles to paved FR 2612 and turn right again (east). Go 0.8 mile to Spur 700 (gravel), where the sign says KELSAY–CALMUT LOOP, and turn left (north). After 6 miles, turn left (north) on Spur 770, where the sign says WARM SPRINGS BUTTE ROAD.

Three miles later, at Warms Springs Pass (unmarked), following signs that say DIAMOND DRIVE, turn right (east) on FR 2154 (the road sign was on the ground when I visited in spring, 2001). After 4.5 more miles, signs at a turnoff right (east) say, TIMPANOGAS ROAD, FR 2154, and DIAMOND DRIVE. This is the turnoff to Timpanogas Lake, 0.25 miles away. Do not take Spur 270 here or you will miss Summit Lake. Immediately after the right turn near Spur 270, go left (north) to remain on FR 2154 (and right for the Timpanogas Lake Campground).

The Summit Lake turnoff is on the right (east), 3 miles past Timpanogas Lake. A 1-mile, low-quality dirt side road leads to the lake. FR 2154 turns to blacktop 4 miles beyond the Summit Lake turnoff. After 2.5 more miles, the route becomes two-lane paved FR 21, paralleling the Middle Fork Willamette River and Hills Creek Reservoir. Thirty miles after the two-lane pavement begins, FR 21 ends at the junction with Highway 58 at Oakridge.

REST STOPS. Diamond and Lemolo Lakes; Timpanogas Lake; Opal Lake; Summit Lake; Indigo Springs; Sacandaga; Campers Flat; Secret, Sand Prairie and Packard Creek campgrounds; Cline-Clark and Ferrin Picnic Sites; Oakridge.

SPECIAL INFORMATION. Going from Diamond Lake to Oakridge dramatically unveils the Middle Fork canyon from Warm Springs Pass, but the route can be just as easily done in the opposite direction.

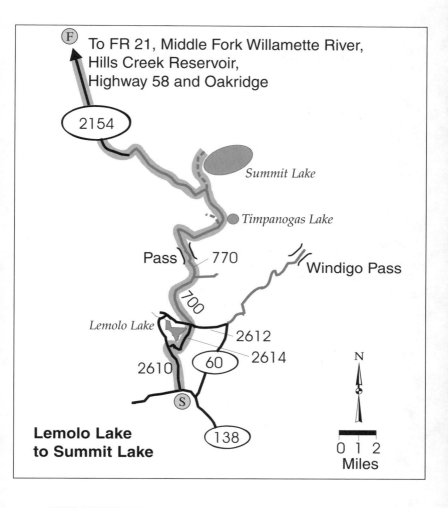

To FR 21, Middle Fork Willamette River, Hills Creek Reservoir, Highway 58 and Oakridge

2154

Summit Lake

Timpanogas Lake

Pass 770

Windigo Pass

700

Lemolo Lake

2612

2610 60 2614

138

N

Lemolo Lake to Summit Lake

0 1 2 Miles

THE DRIVE. When I explored this route in June of 2001, the Diamond Lake Resort, after two weeks of temperatures in the 80s and 90s, was preparing for a busy summer weekend of fishing and swimming. But, much to the surprise of the National Weather Service, it snowed.

I arrived at Diamond Lake (4,900 feet) in a blizzard and figured there was little chance that I'd make it over gravel Warm Springs Pass Road to Summit Lake (I was in a two-wheel-drive car). But I waited a couple of hours until the weather cleared slightly, then headed out. The 5,600-foot pass was spectacular, with snow in the trees and on the ground but amazingly, not on the road. Patches of blue sky and some of the best vistas anywhere in Oregon completed the idyllic scene. I can't promise you'll run into a freak summer snowstorm if you take this beautiful but complicated route, but you will enjoy spectacular scenery and many points of interest.

The first point of interest (see Side Trips below for descriptions of Diamond and Lemolo lakes) is Warm Spring Pass, which affords an amazing view of the Middle Fork Willamette River valley stretching out below, and of the rocky summit of Hills Peak (6,048 feet) to the west. The Middle Fork canyon was carved by an immense valley glacier that originated at Timpanogas Lake.

Timpanogas Lake covers 43 acres in the deep woods. It is the largest of a cluster of glacial lakes and tarns that includes Indigo Lake (3 acres) and Amos (8 acres) and Andy (5 acres) lakes. Opal Lake (12 acres) lies alongside FR 2154 a half-mile past Timpanogas Lake and is home to a small campground. This is not the same Opal Lake as in Drive 12.

Down the road, the 1-mile side trip to Summit Lake is extremely rough, but the immense, tree-lined, 470-acre lake is this trip's highlight. The bouncy Summit Lake road eventually leads to a campground on the lake's north shore. If you keep going, after 4 miles you'll end up at Crescent Lake (3,600 acres), still on an extremely rough road. Crescent Lake (and Summit Lake) are part of the Cascade Lakes group out of Bend. Crescent Lake can also be reached via a paved road from U.S. 97.

FR 2154 picks up pavement a couple of miles past the Summit Lake turnoff, then eventually meets the Middle Fork Willamette River. The final 10 miles of this trip parallel the shore of Hills Creek Reservoir. The river and reservoir here are very nice but not as nice as Warm Springs Pass and Summit Lake. Not in the snow, anyhow.

SIDE TRIPS. Diamond Lake (3,000 acres), at MP 80, 6 miles past the Lemolo Lake turnoff on Highway 138, is one of Oregon's premiere mountain resorts. It offers numerous activities, including Crater Lake National Park (north entrance). There is an excellent restaurant as well as a filling station.

Lemolo Lake, at 175 acres, is much smaller than Diamond Lake, with fewer and lower quality facilities. Two highlights here are Lemolo Falls and Warm Springs Falls. To reach them, continue on FR 2610 past the lake and over the dam. Look for a trailhead for the North Umpqua Trail on the left, 0.5 mile past the dam. It's a 2-mile hike to the 110-foot Lemolo falls, passing many smaller falls on the way. For Warm Springs Falls, stay on 2610 for 3 more miles, to where it cuts away from the North Umpqua River. Turn left onto Spur 680 and proceed for 2 miles. Be careful, since the trailhead is in the middle of a large flat, on the left, and is easy to miss. If you cross Warm Springs Creek, you've gone too far. It's a 0.5-mile hike to a stunning, 70-foot waterfall that tumbles over an outcrop of columnar basalt. (If there are warm springs in the vicinity of Warm Springs Creek, Falls, Pass, or Butte, they aren't on the map.) No signs anywhere direct you to Warm Springs Pass. However, there are signs to Windigo Pass (5,817 feet), 8 miles east of Warm Springs Pass and reached from the Lemolo Lake area via FR 60. There's nothing to see at Windigo Pass, which is surrounded by forest. But it's a major trailhead for the Pacific Crest Trail. The route beyond Windigo Pass eventually emerges at Crescent Lake, but it's a long, slow journey over terrible roads.

Summit Lake (Drive 26)

Miller Lake (Drive 27)

Miller Lake

LOCATION. West of Chemult and northeast of Mt. Thielsen in the southern Cascades.

HIGHLIGHTS. A large beautiful glacial cirque lake with close-up views of the east side of Mt. Thielsen (9,182 feet) as well as the High Cascades. Eastern terminus of the 79-mile North Umpqua Trail.

DIFFICULTY. Easy, mostly level gravel road. Very dusty.

DISTANCE. 12.5 miles from Highway 97 to the road end at Miller Lake.

HIGH ELEVATION. 5,800 feet.

MAP. Miller Lake.

ADMINISTRATION. Winema National Forest.

GETTING THERE. From Highway 97, at MP 202 just north of Chemult, simply head west on Forest Road 9772 where the sign says MILLER LAKE—12.

REST STOPS. Chemult; Miller Lake.

THE DRIVE. The drive to Miller Lake is fairly uniform, traversing a gently upward-trending slope mostly covered with lodgepole pine, an indication that the area has poor volcanic soils (lots of ash) and frequent forest fires. Views of the south-east side of Mt. Thielsen, from the road, are impressive, especially considering that views like this are hard to come by from main highways. The large volcano south of Thielsen, visible from the Miller Lake Road, is Mt. Scott (8,925 feet), highest point in Crater Lake National Park.

It is 12 miles from Highway 97 to the large Miller Lake Campground, on a point of land that juts into the 565-acre, 165-foot deep lake. Half a mile beyond the campground the road ends at a swimming area and picnic site. The trailhead at the east end of the picnic site, by the restroom, is the western terminus of the 79-mile North Umpqua Trail, which opened in 1997 and has its start near the town of Glide, 18 miles east of Roseburg. The trailhead sign says MAIDU LAKE—3½ MILES. At 20 acres and 12 feet deep, Maidu Lake is the largest in the Mt. Thielsen Wilderness (which doesn't have very many lakes), but is much smaller than Miller Lake. It's 3 miles to Maidu Lake: 0.75 miles along the Miller Lake shore, then 2.25 miles through the woods on the North Umpqua Trail.

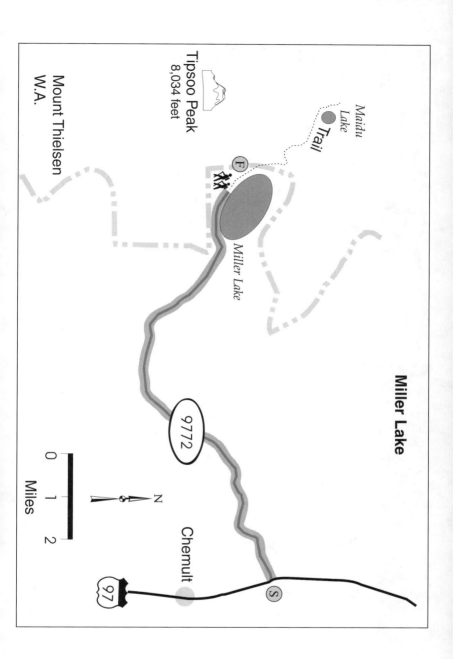

Miller Lake

Maidu Lake

Trail

Tipsoo Peak
8,034 feet

F

Miller Lake

Mount Thielsen
W.A.

9772

N

0   1   2

Miles

Chemult

S

97

Lamb Butte, Olallie Ridge

LOCATION. East of Eugene and Springfield off the McKenzie River Highway, near Cougar Reservoir.

HIGHLIGHTS. Awesome views of the west side of the Three Sisters and Mt. Bachelor, featuring Cougar Reservoir, many trailheads, dense, old-growth Douglas-fir forests, and beautiful subalpine areas.

DIFFICULTY. Easy to moderate, mostly wide gravel road. Some steep drop-offs. May be muddy in spots.

DISTANCE. 27.5 miles from Highway 126 to Horsepasture Trailhead.

HIGH ELEVATION. 5,100 feet.

MAPS. French Mountain; Cougar Reservoir.

ADMINISTRATION. Willamette National Forest.

GETTING THERE. Take Highway 126 east from Springfield for 45 miles to just past the town of Blue River, near MP 45. Turn right (south) onto Forest Road 19, where the sign says COUGAR RESERVOIR. Stay on FR 19 (which makes a hard right after 0.25 miles) for 3 miles to the top of the dam. At the intersection atop the dam, turn left onto FR 1993. At East Fork Campground, 2.5 miles beyond the dam, the paved road crosses a bridge and becomes FR 1994. FR 1993 continues east on the gravel road up the hill on the left. It's 10.5 miles on FR 1993 from the East Fork Campground to the beginning of the fantastic scenery at the Pat Saddle Trailhead. The road becomes one-lane blacktop at mile 20.5, 7 miles before the Horsepasture Trailhead.

REST STOPS. There are campgrounds every couple of miles on Highway 126, two at Cougar Reservoir, and some primitive campsites at the Pat Saddle Trailhead.

SPECIAL INFORMATION. The Olallie Ridge Research Natural Area is not in the same area as Drive 8, which has an Olallie Lake and an Olallie Butte. The highest point in *this* Olallie area is O'Leary Mountain, which seems like a misspelling of Olallie (or vice-versa).

THE DRIVE. This rainy western slope of the central Cascades is the heart of Douglas-fir country. If growing big timber fast is what you're about, this is the place to do it. The drive begins auspiciously, with excellent views of the Cougar Reservoir, which is nestled in a huge canyon walled in by densely forested west-side mountains. The road to the Lamb Butte Scenic Area from Cougar Reservoir is definitely "western slope," with miles and miles of dense, closed-canopy forest that is broken only by occasional logging sites (that's why the road was built). At mile 12, at the Pat Saddle Trailhead, the road finally stops climbing, having gotten to about 5,000 feet. Hike 2.5 miles north on the trail for the summit

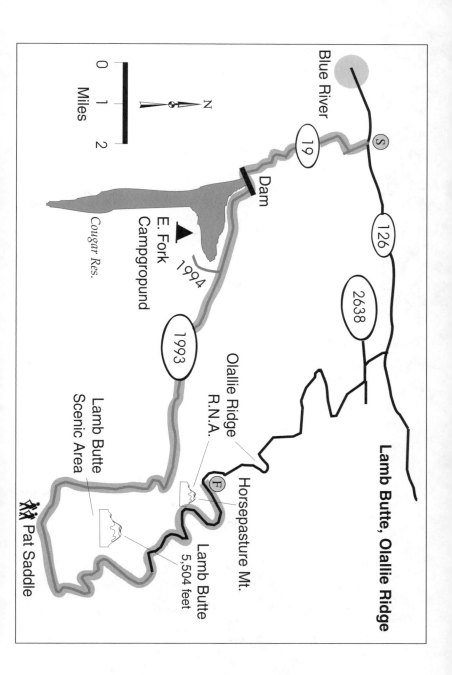

Lamb Butte, Olallie Ridge

Blue River

19

Dam

Cougar Res.

E. Fork
Campgropund

1994

1993

Olallie Ridge
R.N.A.

Lamb Butte
Scenic Area

Horsepasture Mt.

Lamb Butte
5,504 feet

Pat Saddle

S

126

2638

N

0
Miles
1
2

95

of Lamb Butte (5,504 feet), and south for a real long walk through a remote corner of the Three Sisters Wilderness.

Shortly beyond the Pat Saddle Trailhead, the road rounds a bend, emerges from the forest, and treats you to one of the most breathtaking vistas you will ever see, a panorama of the west face of three snow-clad, glaciated volcanoes, all over 10,000 feet and the highlight of the central Oregon Cascades, the Three Sisters. The conical peak to the southeast is Bachelor Butte. Look for evidence of past glaciation in the vast sea of forest and canyons here. Canyons with a "V" cross-section were not glaciated. Canyons with a "U" cross-section were glaciated.

Four miles past Pat Saddle (at MP 16), the road crosses some steep rock slopes and a side road down to Horse Creek. The Lamb Butte Scenic Area is directly above but can't be seen from the road. One mile past the side road, the gravel ends and one-lane blacktop pavement begins. It's 7 more miles through the beautiful sub-alpine scenery of the Olallie Ridge Research Natural Area (green meadows, clumps of noble fir and mountain hemlock, steep rocky slopes) to the Horsepasture Trailhead. Look for a view of Horsepasture Mountain which tells you it's 2 miles to the trailhead. It's less than 1 mile to the summit via the trail, with a terrific vista.

SIDE TRIPS. Beyond the Horsepasture Trailhead, FR 1993 continues through the Olallie Ridge Research Natural Area and 9 miles beyond to FR 2638, Horse Creek Road. If you go left on FR 2638 and continue for 2 miles, you will hit Highway 126 at a point 5 miles past the Cougar Reservoir turnoff. The loop on FR 19, FR 1994, and FR 1993, around Cougar Reservoir, is also very nice.

Mt.Bachelor from Lamb Butte Road

Bohemia Mountain

LOCATION. In the Cascade Mountains east of Cottage Grove, above the Row River.

HIGHLIGHTS. A beautiful drive along the Row River, Brice Creek, Noonday Ridge, and Sharps Creek. A stupendous panorama of the high peaks of the Central Cascades seen from Fairview Lookout, Bohemia Mountain, and the Bohemia Mine complex.

DIFFICULTY. Moderate. Roads range from wide gravel to narrow steep dirt with a few bumps and chuckholes. Worst are the last 0.25 miles of the Fairview Lookout spur. See Side Trips for an alternate route to Bohemia Saddle that is a little more challenging.

DISTANCE. 59 miles from Cottage Grove and back (the route is a loop).

HIGH ELEVATION. 5,933 feet.

MAPS. Rose Hill; Culp Creek; Fairview Peak; Silica Peak.

ADMINISTRATION. Umpqua National Forest.

GETTING THERE. From the main Cottage Grove exit on I-5, head east, away from town, on Row River Road. After 3 miles, you'll come to Shoreview Drive. Shoreview Drive and Row River Road visit opposite sides of Dorena Lake and are of about the same length and quality. They rejoin after 7 miles. At mile 14, you pass Sharps Creek Road, where you'll end up on completion of the Bohemia loop. Soon after, you have the option of going left on Lower Brice Creek Road or crossing a bridge and staying on Row River Road. Go left for Wildwood Falls. Lower Brice Creek and Row River Roads rejoin after 4 miles. If you take Lower Brice Creek, turn right (south) onto Laying Road, stay on it briefly, and then cross the bridge to return to Row River Road.

At mile 18, you'll arrive at the junction with Forest Road 2470 (Brice Creek Road), where the sign says BOHEMIA SADDLE—22. Turn left (east) and follow signs to Bohemia Saddle. The road becomes FR 22 at Champion Creek (see Side Trips below). Twelve miles from the initial "Bohemia Saddle" sign, turn right (west), onto FR 2212. Here you lose the pavement (it's now wide gravel), climb onto Noonday Ridge, and then pass Noonday Saddle and Champion Saddle as you come to Bohemia Saddle. (At every junction, the road becomes a little narrower and bumpier, but it is never terrible.)

At Bohemia Saddle, a 1-mile spur right (west) leads over a steep, narrow, somewhat precarious dirt road to Fairview lookout. Go straight (north) at Bohemia Saddle to return to Row River Road via Sharps Creek. It's 32 miles from here back to I-5.

Three miles down the very steep, curvy road from Bohemia Saddle is a large unmarked junction. Go right (north). It's 6 miles to Mineral Campground, 2 more to paved Sharps Creek Road, 10 miles on Sharps Creek Road to Row River Road, and a final 14 miles on Row River Road back to Cottage Grove.

REST STOPS. There are campgrounds and picnic sites all along Row River and Brice Creek Roads. There is a restroom at Fairview Lookout and a picnic site at Bohemia Saddle. Again, Mineral Campground is located 6 miles down Sharps Creek from Bohemia Saddle. There's a BLM picnic site near the end of Sharps Creek Road.

SPECIAL INFORMATION. Taking the Brice Creek to Sharps Creek (clockwise) direction is much more scenic than going in the opposite direction. Going toward Sharps Creek, the amazing vistas of Bohemia Mountain and Fairview Peak from Noonday Ridge lie in front of you, not behind. In addition, the clockwise route hits the very steep, curvy road from Bohemia Saddle to Sharps Creek in the downhill direction.

THE DRIVE. The Bohemia Mining District originated in the 1860s as one of the few gold-mining areas in the Cascade Mountains. Even though the district is located in the much older Western Cascades, not the High Cascades (which have no gold deposits), and abuts the gold-rich Siskiyou mountains, it was never particularly productive. The district is still active, however, with operating hard-rock gold mines. It also operates a picnic site at Bohemia Saddle, sponsors community events, and patrols the district.

Even without this historic overlay, the loop tour from Cottage Grove to Fairview and Bohemia Mountains is one of Oregon's more spectacular. Beginning in Cottage Grove, the route follows the pastoral Row River past covered bridges and Dorena Reservoir (the name is a combining of "Dora" and "Lena." I'd say Dora got the better of the deal). On Brice Creek Road, the route becomes narrow and shaded, with huge old Douglas-firs, as it passes many recreation sites, trailheads, and smaller waterfalls.

The tour gets truly spectacular upon reaching Noonday Ridge, where you can see Bohemia Mountain (5,990 feet) on the left (south) and Fairview Peak (5,930 feet), with its lookout, on the right (north) 8 miles away. Below Fairview Peak, mine buildings can be seen. And below that, a huge rock expanse has a creek and waterfall running down the middle. In the opposite direction from Bohemia Mountain, from Noonday Ridge as seen from Noonday and Champion Saddles, the high peaks of the Central Cascades line up to the east and south, including the Three Sisters, Bachelor Butte, Diamond Peak, Mt. Thielsen, and Mt. Bailey. But the rhododendrons alone make Noonday Ridge worth visiting in June and early July.

From Champion Saddle, you can drive down the bumpy, zigzagging dirt road to the mines or you can take a short side road left (south) to the old Musick Guard Station, a rustic building which can be rented for overnight accommodations. But the highlight of this area is Bohemia Saddle, with Fairview Peak to the right and Bohemia Mountain on the left. Bohemia Mountain is a handsome peak with jutting rock faces and a flat summit. A trailhead at Bohemia Saddle leads to the summit in 1 mile. A short, low-quality road goes from the saddle to a picnic site, run by the mining district, at the base of a cliff. A 1-mile road takes you from the saddle to Fairview Peak. The summit here offers an impressive view of Noonday Ridge and the High Cascades. There is an

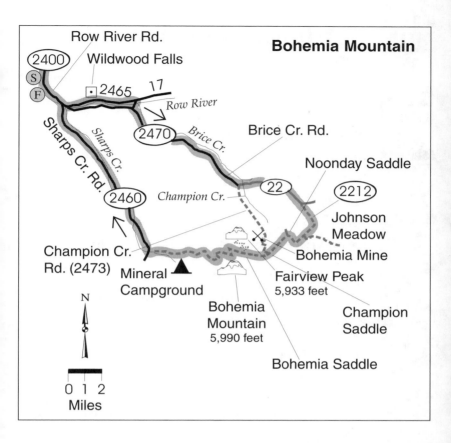

Bohemia Mountain

outhouse, and a lookout tower that visitors are free to climb (at their own risk and only if they don't interfere with the person who is on fire watch). When you've exhausted all possibilities at Bohemia Saddle, you can head quickly down the hill on a narrow, twisty road that plummets back into the dense forest and eventually picks up Sharps Creek Road, returning to pavement and emerging on Row River Road where the tour began.

SIDE TRIPS. There are many side roads and alternate routes for this trip, but none are as scenic as the described tour. If you continue on Brice Creek instead of turning off onto FR 2212, you'll end up at Johnson Meadow and Grass Mountain. Keep going past Grass Mountain and you'll emerge at Oakridge on Highway 58. If you go left (south) instead of right at the unmarked junction 3 miles down Sharps Creek Road from Bohemia Saddle, the road reclimbs the ridge and passes Twin Rocks and Jacks Saddle before dropping back down to Martin Creek and Sharps Creek. Champion Creek Road (FR 2473), up Champion Creek from Brice Creek to Champion Saddle, is extremely rough and a bit challenging, especially toward the upper end. It passes the main Bohemia Mining complex. Road signs on either end of this route advise against taking it.

Umpqua Hot Springs

LOCATION. East of Roseburg, off the North Umpqua Highway.

HIGHLIGHTS. Views of the North Umpqua. A beautiful hot springs and many trailheads.

DIFFICULTY. Easy, mostly level gravel road.

DISTANCE. 4.7 miles from Highway 138 to Umpqua Hot Springs.

HIGH ELEVATION. 3,000 feet.

MAP. Potter Mountain.

ADMINISTRATION. Umpqua National Forest.

GETTING THERE. From I-5 at Roseburg, take Highway 138, North Umpqua Highway, 59 miles east to the Toketee Lake turnoff (Forest Road 34). Proceed 2.5 miles up paved FR 34, then turn right (east) onto to gravel FR 3401. After 2.2 miles on FR 3401, you'll come to the Umpqua Hot Springs parking area.

REST STOPS. Toketee Falls; Toketee Lake; Umpqua Hot Springs.

SPECIAL INFORMATION. Visit Umpqua Hot Springs only if you don't mind seeing naked strangers (including single men), as well as occasional gawkers.

THE DRIVE. The North Umpqua Highway is always a treat, with lots to see and do in the 85-mile drive. Toward the end you pass Diamond Lake (under consideration for designation as a national monument) and Mt. Thielsen, and you wind up near the north entrance of Crater Lake.

One of the nicer things to do en route is stop by Umpqua Hot Springs. From the parking area, a charming footbridge takes you over the North Umpqua River to a couple of rustic campsites and the horrendously steep, 0.25-mile trail to the hot springs. At the hot springs, atop a huge limestone deposit covered with drip marks, the main hot spring is protected by a wooden lean-to and accommodates eight people. Two smaller pools seat three to four each.

Back at the parking area, it's a couple of hundred feet down the road (east) to the Dread and Terror Trailhead of the North Umpqua Trail. The next mile of this trail is the most scenic on the entire 79-mile route. The perfectly level, easy path passes, in short order, an immense gushing spring, a gorgeous campsite, a wall of columnar basalt with water oozing down it, dozens of smaller springs, a huge waterfall, and a pool with water of the most amazing blue color I've ever seen.

SIDE TRIPS. The Toketee Falls Trailhead lies on the left on FR 34, near the Highway 138 junction. It's a 0.5-mile hike to the gorgeous, double-tiered, 90-foot waterfall, which tumbles over a wall of columnar basalt. The trail and observation deck are engineering masterpieces.

CENTRAL AND SOUTH CASCADES

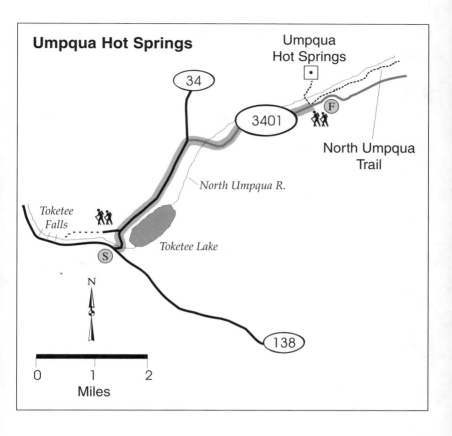

Umpqua Hot Springs

Umpqua Hot Springs

34

3401

North Umpqua Trail

North Umpqua R.

Toketee Falls

Toketee Lake

S

138

N

0   1   2
Miles

To reach Lemolo Falls, continue east on FR 3401, beyond Umpqua Hot Springs, then bear left onto the wide gravel of Spur 800, which you should follow to Spur 840, a narrow, 2-mile dirt road. It's a steep 2-mile hike through a logging clearcut to the thundering, 108-foot falls.

Nearby Lemolo Lake is also worth a visit. When you've seen Lemolo Falls, continue on Spur 800 to the far end of FR 3401. Go left and you'll shortly come out on FR 2610, a couple of miles from Lemolo Lake. Turn left for Lemolo Lake and right for Highway 138. If you decided to take FR 3401 all the way from the hot springs to Lemolo Lake, its much more narrow, steep, and winding than the Spur 800 loop.

Watson Falls, at mile 63 on Highway 138, is the second high-est waterfall in Oregon, at 272 feet, tied with Salt Creek Falls near Willamette Pass, also 272 feet high; Multnomah Falls, east of Portland, is 580 feet high. The eerie, 0.5-mile hike to the base of Watson Falls may be the scenic highlight of southern Oregon, after Crater Lake.

Little River, Quartz Mountain

LOCATION. East of Roseburg, west of the Cascade crest.

HIGHLIGHTS. Rivers, lakes, trails, endless forests, and a challenging drive to an unusual 5,200-foot summit that features quarry tailings, steep cliffs, and views of the High Cascades.

DIFFICULTY. The 2-mile Quartz Mountain Road is steep, filled with tight switchbacks, has at least one area that is badly rutted, and borders on difficult. Forest Road 27 is wide, gravel, and easy.

DISTANCE. 54 miles from Highway 138 to Forest Road 28, including a 4-mile side trip to the top of Quartz Mountain.

HIGH ELEVATION. 5,200 feet.

MAPS. Quartz Mountain; Taft Mountain.

ADMINISTRATION. Umpqua National Forest.

GETTING THERE. From Exit 23 off I-5 at Roseburg, follow Highway 138 east toward Diamond Lake. At mile 15, just before the town of Glide, turn right (south) onto Little River Road, which quickly becomes County Road 17. After 21 miles, the road becomes Forest Road 27, and the pavement is replaced by gravel 2 miles later. From the beginning of FR 27, follow signs for 15 miles to Hemlock Lake. Four miles beyond the Hemlock Lake turnoff, FR 660 (Quartz Mountain Road) takes off left (east). It's 2 miles up FR 660 to the summit of Quartz Mountain. FR 27 ends 10 miles beyond the Quartz Mountain turnoff, on paved South Umpqua Road (FR 28), 21 miles before the town of Tiller.

REST STOPS. Colliding Rivers View Point (in Glide); Wolf Creek Campground; Cool Water Campground; Lake in the Woods Campground; Hemlock Lake Campground; South Umpqua Falls Campground.

SPECIAL INFORMATION. The mileposts on County Road 17 do not correspond to the actual miles driven.

THE DRIVE. This is one of those "hidden gems" you are unlikely to hear about from anybody and of which only local residents are aware. The twisty and fascinating drive to the top of Quartz Mountain is only the icing on the cake, with many other delicious scenic treats preceding it.

The trip begins with a peaceful drive up paved Little River Road, past a stream, farmland, two campgrounds (Wolf Creek and Cool Water), and the trailhead to Wolf Creek Falls (a 2-mile hike). Beyond the Wolf Creek Job Corps Center, the road enters the forest, eventually leaving the river, climbing a bit, and then leveling off at Lake in the Woods (10 miles past the beginning of Forest Road 27). Lake in the Woods is nice but not nearly as pretty as Hemlock Lake, 5 miles down the road.

At mile 15 (from the beginning of FR 27), an unmarked gravel road takes off through the woods to the right (west). This will take you to the West Hemlock Lake Campground and the trail-

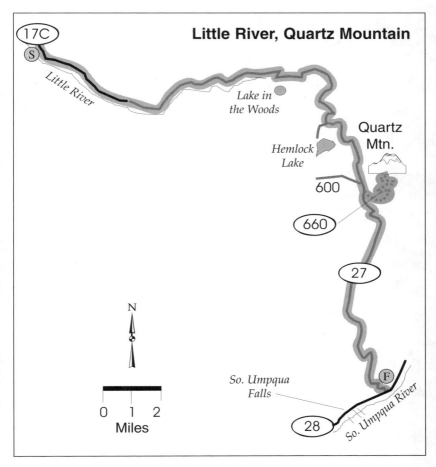

Little River, Quartz Mountain

17C
S
Little River
Lake in
the Woods
Hemlock
Lake
Quartz
Mtn.
600
660
27
N
So. Umpqua
Falls
F
So. Umpqua River
28

0 1 2
Miles

head for the 4-mile Yellowjacket Loop Trail, one of the prettiest trails in the Umpqua National Forest, with wildflower meadows, a side trip to the top of Flat Rock Mountain (5,310 feet), and vistas of the lake, Quartz Mountain, and the High Cascades. If you continue on FR 27 past this turnoff, you will arrive at the main Hemlock Lake boat launch and picnic area in 0.5 mile on the right (west). Hemlock Lake Reservoir is gorgeous, with sparkling blue water surrounded by vast green wildflower meadows and forest stands. Craggy peaks, including the flat side of Flat Rock Mountain, rise up on two sides.

The trip's climax is FR 660, the 2-mile route to the summit of Quartz Mountain. Despite the steepness, multiple tight switchbacks, and the fact that the road is unmaintained (and not shown on the Umpqua National Forest map), there is only one bad spot, which has deep ruts that you can stay out of by straddling them. The summit is an old quarry surrounded by steep cliffs, with views to the east of Mt. Bailey, Mt. Thielsen, and Diamond Peak, which are all in the 8,000- to 9,000-foot range. (Peaks to the west, though also pretty, are in the 5,500- to 6,000-foot range.) The summit of Quartz Mountain has enough level ground to accommodate 100 cars. Climb up the natural rock outcrops along the edge for the best views. The rock tailings, and the natural outcrops looked to me like andesite rock, a type of gray-white lava extremely common in the High Cascades. I was told that they formerly excavated quartz at the site, for use in the Hannah Nickel Mine in Riddle, 65 miles away. The Hannah mine, now closed, was for many years the only operating nickel mine in the United States.

Returning to FR 27, it's 10 fairly uninteresting miles to FR 28, the South Umpqua Road.

SIDE TRIPS. At Colliding Rivers, in Glide, the North Umpqua makes a 90-degree turn directly opposite its confluence with the Little River, so that the two rivers literally collide. There's a vista spot nearby.

Two miles past Hemlock Lake, on the left (east), FR 2781 leads to the Twin Lakes Trailhead, atop Twin Lakes Mountain (5,879 feet), 8 miles away. It's a beautiful drive with views of Quartz Mountain and the High Cascades. To reach the trailhead, follow FR 2781 for 1 mile to Spur 100, on the left. Take Spur 100 (which has many waterbars) for 1.5 miles to FR 2715. Go right on FR 2715 for 0.5 miles to Spur 530, then turn left and proceed 5 miles to the trailhead. Follow the trail for 1 mile to a spectacular rock outcrop overlooking two beautiful glacial cirque lakes. This is a much shorter route than the posted turnoff to the Twin Lakes Trail from FR 27, located 3 miles before Hemlock Lake.

Three miles past Hemlock Lake, Spur 610, to the right (west), brushes after 3 miles the high end of the Yellowjacket Loop Trail. Follow the trail to the left (west) for 0.5 miles to the trail's high spot and vista point, and for another 1 mile to Yellowjacket Meadow.

South Umpqua Falls, on FR 28 near where FR 27 ends, is an enchanting little rest stop where the South Umpqua River fans out over a broad rock face.

Quartz Mountain tailings

Fish Creek Valley

LOCATION. On the crest between the Rogue and Umpqua drainages, just west of Diamond Lake in the southern Cascades.

HIGHLIGHTS. Magnificent meadowed valley, with the two highest peaks in the Rogue-Umpqua Divide Wilderness on either side. Many trailheads. Arguably the most exciting back road in southern Oregon.

DIFFICULTY. Moderate. Can be treacherous early in the season, with mud and snow banks. It's in remarkably good shape for an unmaintained road.

DISTANCE. 13.5 miles from Highway 230 to Happy Campsite in Fish Creek Valley.

HIGH ELEVATION. 5,200 feet.

MAP. Fish Mountain.

ADMINISTRATION. Umpqua National Forest.

GETTING THERE. Take Highway 62 north from Medford past Union Creek. Past mile 57, where Highway 62 swings right (east) toward Crater Lake, continue straight (north) on Highway 230, toward Diamond Lake. Past mile 12 on Highway 230, opposite the Hamaker Campground turnoff, turn left (north) onto gravel FR 6560, where the sign says BUCK CAMP. After 5.5 miles up FR 6560, atop the divide, the route becomes FR 37. Turn left (west), 0.5 miles beyond the divide, onto Spur 800, then continue for 3.5 miles past Lonesome Meadow and turn left again (still west) onto Spur 870, the Fish Creek Valley Road. It's 4 miles up Spur 870 to the road end, just past Happy Campsite.

REST STOPS. Hamaker Campgrounds; Happy Campsite; Watson Falls Trailhead.

SPECIAL INFORMATION. Spur 800 is shown on the Forest Service map as a loop and signs at the turnoff say INCENSE-CEDAR LOOP. But this is not a loop. There is a colossal washout just before the road rejoins FR 37.

There is no reason why this trip cannot be done from the Umpqua side of the divide (though it's a little longer), taking Highway 138 to FR 37, at the Watson Falls turnoff at mile 63. Proceed south to Spur 800.

THE DRIVE. Although the final 4 miles of this exquisite, seldom visited route offers world-class vistas of breathtaking beauty, this route is scenic from beginning to end. A highlight of the early portion of this steep, winding drive on Forest Road 6560 is the view of Buck Canyon, just north of Fish Mountain, the highest point, at 6,789 feet, in the Rogue-Umpqua Divide Wilderness. Look for the canyon on the left, just past the Spur 400 turnoff. Continuing on FR 6560 the route crests at a pretty, beargrass-filled clearcut. Soon after, Spur 800 is a little narrow but very pretty as it rises to a high elevation in a woods of white fir, noble fir, mountain hemlock, and lodgepole pine. After 2 miles, you come to the junction with Spur 870, the Fish Creek Valley Road.

Fish Creek Valley Road, a 4-mile beauty of a route, is unusual because the Wilderness boundary runs along either side of the road edge. The road essentially plunges into the heart of the 33,200-acre Wilderness. Toward the road's far end, the valley widens out to a meadowed expanse, with the blocky outcrop of Rattlesnake Mountain rising across the valley to 6,556 feet. You'll catch glimpses of Fish Mountain from the Fish Creek Valley Road but it's hard to see unless you hike across the valley to Rattlesnake Mountain and look back.

A slew of trails take off near Happy Campsite, at mile 4. One of them climbs 6 miles up Rattlesnake Mountain, another drops over into Buck Canyon, and yet another follows the crest of the Rogue-Umpqua divide to Hershberger Lookout (see Drive 33). Castle Rock, visible from the road end, is a huge rocky spire jutting up from the middle of the valley.

SIDE TRIPS. For a real challenge, the road to the far end of the Rattlesnake Mountain Trail is long but lots of fun. Continue north on FR 37, beyond the Fish Creek Valley and Spur 800 turnoff, until you pick up the pavement. About 1.2 miles later, look for Spur 200 on the right and a paved (for 200 feet) but unmarked turnoff on the left immediately after. If you pass Spur 100 and cross Rogue Creek, you've gone too far. FR 37 ends at the Watson Falls parking area (see Drive 30). Watson Falls is Oregon's second highest waterfall.

The unmarked road to the left, just past Spur 100, is FR 3702, whose number was somehow omitted from the most recent Umpqua National Forest map. Nevertheless, follow FR 3702 for 3.5 miles to Spur 500, then follow Spur 500 to the end, 5 miles later. This moderate-to-difficult road is slow, with a few rough spots, wet spots, bouldery spots, and narrow spots, and dozens of waterbars. The trailhead sign is located at a little switchback, 0.3 miles from the road end. You may or may not make it up the very steep, final pitch to the actual trailhead. It's a challenge. The view of Mt. Bailey as you approach the road end is outstanding.

Rattlesnake Mountain, Fish Creek Valley

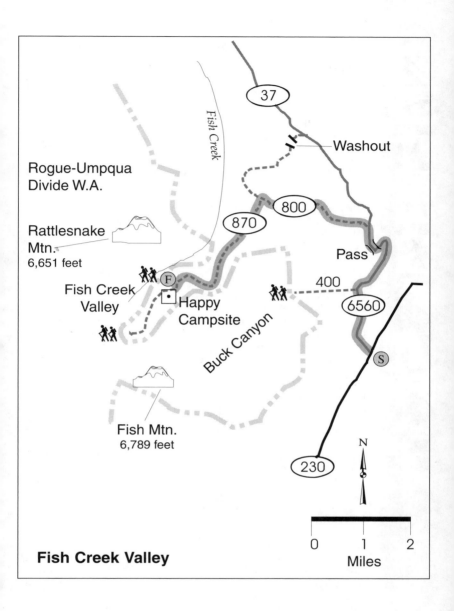

Rogue-Umpqua
Divide W.A.

Fish Creek

37

Washout

800

870

Pass

400

6560

Rattlesnake
Mtn.
6,651 feet

F

Fish Creek
Valley

Happy
Campsite

Buck Canyon

S

Fish Mtn.
6,789 feet

230

N

0   1   2

Miles

Fish Creek Valley

Hershberger Lookout

LOCATION. Between Medford and Crater Lake near the southeast edge of the Rogue-Umpqua Divide Wilderness.

HIGHLIGHTS. A magnificent old fire lookout, with views of Crater Lake, the Rogue-Umpqua Divide range, the upper Rogue Valley, and Rabbit Ears. Spectacular wildflower display.

DIFFICULTY. Moderate. Wide, curvy gravel and dirt road for 18 miles. Mile 19 is steep, narrow, and rough.

DISTANCE. 19 miles from Highway 230 to lookout.

HIGH ELEVATION. 6,285 feet.

MAP. Buckeye Lake.

ADMINISTRATION. Rogue River National Forest.

GETTING THERE. Take Highway 62 north from Medford to Union Creek. Where 62 swings right (east) toward Crater Lake, past MP 57, continue straight on Highway 230 toward Diamond Lake. One mile later, turn left (west) across the Rogue and onto gravel Forest Road 6510. Follow it for 8 miles (with a left turn at mile 2), to the junction with FR 6515. Turn right (north) and follow FR 6515 for 8.5 miles to Horse Camp, where it becomes Spur 530 (FR 6515 veers right here). There are signs to Hershberger Lookout at each of these junctions. You'll pass a trailhead at the switchback at mile 18.5 and arrive at the lookout at mile 19.

REST STOPS. Horse Camp; Hershberger Lookout.

THE DRIVE. The drive on FR 6510 and FR 6515 winds somewhat boringly for 16 miles through old logging areas. But it picks up markedly as it approaches Horse Camp, a grassy flat with a little spring and campsite. Immediately past Horse Camp, you get your first glimpse of the canyon-laden Umpqua side of the Rogue-Umpqua Divide.

Especially note the wildflowers that begin just before Horse Camp and continue to the lookout. The display is breathtaking. You will see Indian paintbrush, columbine, sweet pea, lupine, saxifrage, bleeding heart, and many others. Two trails takes off at the switchback 2 miles past Horse Camp. For a short, beautiful hike, try the Acker Divide Trail on the left (west), which crosses a creek and a wet floral meadow after 1 mile. There is a stand of Alaska yellow cedar, which is rare in southern Oregon, by the creek. From the road end, at the abandoned lookout perched on a craggy outcrop directly above Horse Camp, you can see the Crater Lake rim, Mt. Thielsen, Mt. Bailey, Fish Mountain, and the valley of the Rogue. Look for the section of the Rogue where the old riverbed filled up with ash from the Crater Lake (Mt. Mazama) eruption, which happened some 7,000 years ago, and after which the river recut a channel though the ash.

SIDE TRIPS. At Horse Camp, a road takes off right (the continuation of FR 6515) and leads after 1.5 miles to the base of Rabbit

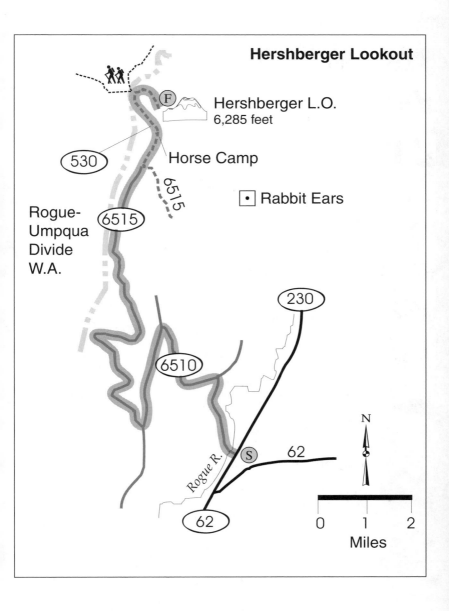

Hershberger Lookout

Hershberger L.O.
6,285 feet

530

Horse Camp

6515

Rabbit Ears

Rogue-
Umpqua
Divide
W.A.

6515

230

6510

Rogue R.

62

62

N

0   1   2
Miles

Ears, which is the innermost lava conduit of an ancient volcano that long ago eroded away. The reason there are such formations in the Rogue-Umpqua Divide is that the mountain chain is part of the Western Cascades, a volcanic system much older than the towering peaks of the High Cascades, such as Mt. Loughlin, the Crater Lake rim, and Mt. Shasta.

Blue Canyon, Smith Rock

LOCATION. East of Medford, south of Crater Lake, at the western edge of the Sky Lakes Wilderness.

HIGHLIGHTS. Close-up views of Devil's Peak and Mt. McLoughlin, the Sky Lakes' two highest peaks. Smith Rock and Blue Rock aren't bad either.

DIFFICULTY. Easy gravel road, except for the last mile which is narrow and a little bumpy as it climbs a rocky hill.

DISTANCE. 25.2 miles from Butte Falls to Blue Rock.

HIGH ELEVATION. 6,500 feet.

MAPS. Rustler Peak; Mt. McLoughlin.

ADMINISTRATION. Rogue River National Forest.

GETTING THERE. Take Highway 62 north from Medford to the Butte Falls Road turnoff. Turn right (south) and drive 17 miles on the highway to the town of Butte Falls. Then continue past Butte Falls 1 mile to the Prospect turnoff. Turn left (east) across the bridge and proceed 2 miles to gravel Rancheria Road. Turn right (south) and stay on Rancheria, which becomes Forest Road 32, for 15 miles. FR 32 eventually merges with FR 37. After 0.8 mile on FR 37, a red gravel road, FR 3770, takes off right (south). Follow FR 3770 for 5.6 miles to the Blue Canyon Trailhead and for 0.8 more mile to the Blue Rock vista point at the road end.

REST STOPS. Parker Meadows Campground (0.5 miles past the FR 3770 turnoff on FR 37); Blue Canyon Trailhead; Blue Rock.

THE DRIVE. This trip offers the best Sky Lakes Wilderness views to be had without actually entering the Wilderness. While the drive through Butte Falls and up FR 32 and FR 37 is very nice, the scenery really starts to cook on FR 3770. Look for a turnout 1 mile up FR 3770, with a view of Devil's Peak, second highest peak in the Sky Lakes Wilderness at 7,582 feet. This is the closest you can get to Devil's Peak by car, although the summit is visible from I-5, north of Medford.

Farther up the road, Devil's Peak is replaced by a magnificent close-up vista of Mt. McLoughlin. At 9,495 feet, McLoughlin's imposing volcanic cone is the highest peak in the Sky Lakes and southern Oregon. Then, amid emerald meadows and towering Shasta red firs, you arrive at the fancy Blue Canyon Trailhead. If you follow the trail on foot, you'll hit Round Lake after a 1-mile downhill walk. Another mile takes you to the beautiful but unstocked Blue Lake, with its massive, tortured lava-rock headwall.

Past the trailhead, the road quality deteriorates for the final mile as it crosses a thinly soiled, rocky meadow and dead-ends atop a little outcrop called Blue Rock. Smith Rock, an ice-cream cone spire, rises out of Blue Canyon, not far away. (Blue Rock is not the least bit blue. It is a light buff tan. Blue Lake is blue, though.)

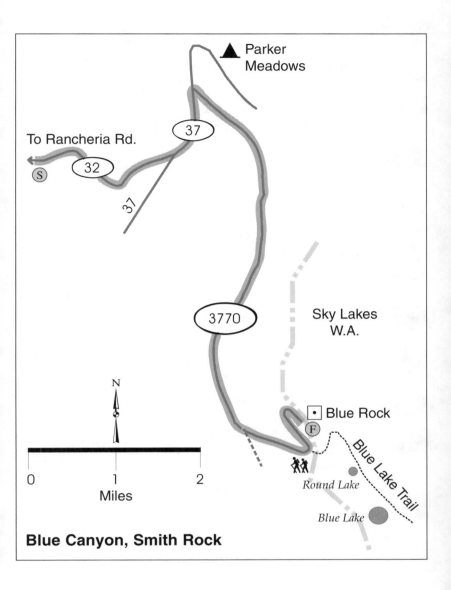

Blue Canyon, Smith Rock

SIDE TRIPS. The west side of the Sky Lakes Wilderness is riddled with excellent dirt and gravel roads, most of which access trails that tend to be much more scenic than the roads. You might drop by Willow Lake on your way up from Butte Falls, which has a campground, a resort and marina and a fine swimming area. To get there, keep going on the Butte Falls Road for 10 miles past Butte Falls, instead of turning onto the Prospect Road.

Pelican Butte

LOCATION. West of Klamath Falls, near Lake of the Woods.

HIGHLIGHTS. A fantastic drive to an 8,036-foot summit that has views of the Sky Lakes and Mountain Lakes Wildernesses, Mt. McLoughlin, Upper Klamath Lake, and the Klamath Basin.

DIFFICULTY. Moderate to difficult. Narrow, switchbacked, occasionally muddy, and rutted dirt road. Waterbars.

DISTANCE. 14.5 miles from Highway 140 to the summit.

HIGH ELEVATION. 8,036 feet

MAPS. Lake of the Woods North; Pelican Butte.

ADMINISTRATION. Winema National Forest.

GETTING THERE. From Highway 62 in White City, near Medford, take Highway 140 east toward Lake of the Woods and Klamath Falls. At mile 41, past Lake of the Woods, Forest Road 3651 takes off left (north), toward Cold Springs. Drive 9.5 miles up FR 3651 to the Pelican Butte turnoff, Spur 980, on the right (east), and then 5 miles up Spur 980 to the summit.

REST STOPS. Cold Springs Trailhead and Campground are located 1 mile past the Pelican Butte turnoff on FR 3651.

THE DRIVE. The gravel road from Highway 140 to the Pelican Butte turnoff is not a very interesting drive. However, the view from atop Pelican Butte reveals that the route follows the densely-forested canyon between Mt. McLoughlin, southern Oregon's highest peak (9,495 feet), and Pelican Butte, southern Oregon's third highest peak (8,036 feet). Aspen Butte, in the Mountain Lakes Wilderness, ranks second.

The fun dirt road to the Pelican Butte summit begins in a dense, brushy woods at the turnoff from FR 3651 onto Spur 980. The first 2 miles are bumpy, occasionally rutted, and sometimes muddy, with jutting branches scraping the sides of your car. You eventually emerge onto a series of short, tight switchbacks that feature an unfolding panorama of the eastern Sky Lakes Wilderness below. The road is a little wider and less bumpy on the switchbacks than in the woods.

The summit is a level flat that is capped by a lookout tower and a microwave repeater. A metal ladder climbs to the bottom of the walkway around the little house on top of the lookout. But you can't reach the walkway or house, because of a locked gate. Pelican Butte has been under study as a proposed ski area. There is presently snow-cat skiing but no lifts.

The summit vantage point offers an amazing panorama of the Sky Lakes Wilderness. It's so good that I thought I could see where the glaciers that shaped the region began and ended. That is not as clear from Devil's Peak or Mt. McLoughlin. But looking out from Pelican Butte, it's as though the long-departed ice sheets left behind a road-map, especially the Cherry Creek Glacier,

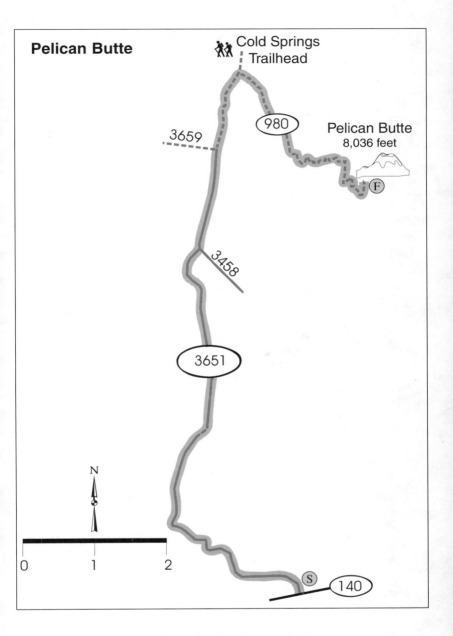

Pelican Butte

Cold Springs Trailhead

Pelican Butte
8,036 feet

980

3659

3458

3651

N

0   1   2

S   140

which carved the Sky Lakes Basin and which once wrapped around Pelican Butte's north flank.

From the summit, also look for Mt. McLoughlin to the southwest, the Sky Lakes and Blue Lake Basins directly west, Devil's Peak to the northwest, Klamath Basin to the east, and the Mountain Lakes caldera to the south. On Pelican Butte's northeast flank, a cute little glacial cirque contains two tiny lakes, Francis and Gladys.

Sand Creek Pinnacles

LOCATION. Southeast corner of Crater Lake National Park, north of Klamath Falls.

HIGHLIGHTS. An unusual perspective on the Crater Lake National Park Pinnacles area beyond what is seen from inside the park. The route passes an abandoned entrance station of historical interest. Easy, 0.75-mile trail.

DIFFICULTY. Easy, wide, level, straight, gravel roads.

DISTANCE. 14 miles from Highway 62 to Sand Creek Trailhead via Sun Mountain Road.

HIGH ELEVATION. 5,400 feet.

MAP. Sun Pass.

ADMINISTRATION. Winema National Forest; Crater Lake Forest Cooperative.

GETTING THERE. From Highway 62 southeast of Crater Lake National Park, proceed until you are either 1 one mile north of Fort Klamath (Dixon Road [624], go east) or 2 miles south of Fort Klamath (Sun Mountain Road [2300], go north). At both junctions, signs point up paved roads to Jackson Kimball State Park. Dixon Road gets there in 1 mile, Sun Mountain Road gets there in 3. Beyond the state park entrance, Forest Road 2300, now gravel, continues north for 4 miles to Sun Pass and 3 more miles to FR 2304. Turn left (west) on FR 2304 and proceed 4 miles to the trailhead parking area at the road end.

REST STOPS. Jackson Kimball State Park.

THE DRIVE. This lovely and interesting little trip begins at Jackson Kimball State Park, a pretty campground on the Wood River. The river meanders across an emerald meadow, much of which is ranch land, with the high, often snow-covered volcanic peaks of the Crater Lake rim rising directly west. Beyond the state park, the gravel road climbs through pine forests toward Sun Pass. What could be excellent views westward, of the Wood River valley and the Crater Lake rim, are obscured by a narrow strip of trees alongside the road. You get the idea that it's a very pretty vista but there's no place to stop to take a photo.

At Sun Pass, a nondescript hilltop with a pine plantation, the road starts gently downhill toward the junction with FR 2304. At the junction, a sign says PINNACLES TRAILHEAD—4. On FR 2304, after 1.5 miles, you will pass a pullout and vista area where there are no signs. But stop anyway, because the spot overlooks a segment of Sand Creek that has spire-like pinnacles rising on both sides of the narrow, steep-walled, 100-foot-deep canyon.

Sand Creek, and the adjacent Lost Creek, were both inundated with Mt. Mazama ash some 6,000 to 7,000 years ago, during the major eruption that ended with the mountain collapsing into itself and the formation of Crater Lake. Subsequently, escaping gasses hardened some of the deposits so that when flowing water

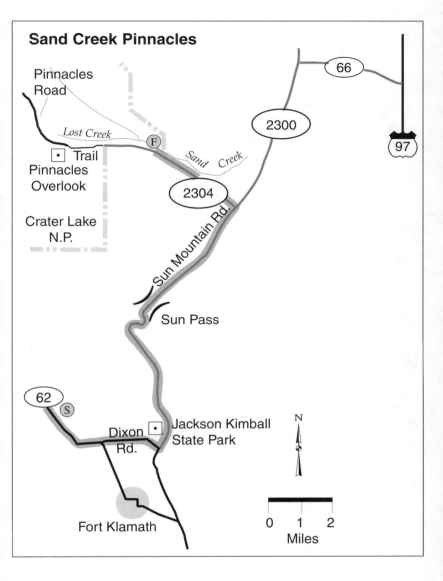

Sand Creek Pinnacles

began cutting a channel through the ash, the harder spots eroded more slowly than the surrounding material.

Over the next 3 miles on FR 2304 the view to the right (north) reveals ever more impressive pinnacle formations along Sand Creek, with Mt. Scott (8,929 feet), highest point in Crater Lake National Park, rising immediately beyond, to the north. The trip's highlight is the short (0.75-mile) trail connecting the end of FR 2304 with the paved Pinnacles Road inside the park. The Pinnacles Road dead-ends at a parking area and observation deck.

According to a sign at the FR 2304 trailhead, FR 2300 used to be Highway 97, the main thoroughfare from Klamath Falls to Bend. FR 2304 also used to be the paved east entrance to the national park. When they rerouted Highway 97, in the 1950s, use of the east entrance dropped to almost zero and it was abandoned in 1959. The pavement was later ripped out and the last 0.75 miles were turned into a trail. The huge old stone entrance sign, however, exactly like the impressive signs on Highway 62 and elsewhere as you enter the park, is still there alongside the trail, about 0.25 mile up.

A quarter-mile beyond the trail entrance sign, Sand Creek merges with Lost Creek, and you will see that both creeks are lined with pinnacle formations. (Mt. Scott still forms an impressive backdrop.) Soon after, the Pinnacles Overlook, with its cars, tourists, and observation deck, comes into view on Lost Creek. Having hiked in on the trail, you have a much better perspective than the tourists, who see only this one spot and are probably unaware that the level ridgetop on the opposite side of the creek drops immediately down to Sand Creek and more pinnacles on the other side. (You, on the other hand, have just seen the confluence of the two creeks.)

But the pinnacles around the observation deck are the most impressive. There are more of them, they are higher, and a band of pink runs through them. Lost Creek forms a meander immediately below that undercuts the canyon's south face, creating greater and steeper erosion with more exposed pinnacles.

Some of the pinnacles look very fragile, being 200 to 300 feet high and less than five feet in diameter near the top. I pondered this as I stood on the observation deck. There was a housewife standing next to me taking photos.

"It wouldn't take much to knock that thing over," I commented to her, pointing at the tallest, slenderest projection. "All you'd have to do would be to climb down into the canyon and kick a few rocks out from the base." The woman looked at me aghast, didn't say anything, backed slowly away, then turned and ran.

I would not do such a thing, of course. Besides, the spires are much stronger than they look, otherwise there would be fallen spires amid the intact ones. And they probably would have disappeared centuries ago.

SIDE TRIPS. To reach FR 2304 from Highway 97 southbound, look for the Klamath Marsh and Silver Lake turnoff 15 miles south of the junction with Diamond Lake Highway and Highway 138. Head west, away from Silver Lake on gravel FR 66 on the opposite side of the highway. It's 3 miles on FR 66 to FR 2300. Go left (south) on FR 2300 and continue for 6 miles to the FR 2304 junction, where you will turn right.

Klamath Canyon

LOCATION. The Oregon–California line, between Klamath Falls and Ashland.

HIGHLIGHTS. In an area not normally thought of as desert or canyon country, a spectacular semidesert canyon, featuring a road that follows both the canyon rim and the water's edge.

DIFFICULTY. Moderate to difficult. Patches of snow in winter. Steep segments with extremely muddy patches in fall, winter, and spring due to all-terrain-vehicle (ATV) activity.

DISTANCE. 21 miles from Highway 66 at the Topsy Campground turnoff to Copco Bridge.

HIGH ELEVATION. 3,900 feet.

MAP. Chicken Hills.

ADMINISTRATION. BLM Lakeview District.

GETTING THERE. Leave I-5 at Exit 14 (Ashland) and take Highway 66, which is Emigrant Lake Road then Greensprings Road, east toward Keno. The trip begins at MP 44, just over the Klamath River bridge, where you turn right and go south toward Topsy Campground. Stay on the main gravel road past the campground and follow along the rim, then the river, to Copco Bridge.

REST STOPS. Topsy Picnic site (just west of the Klamath bridge on Highway 66); Copco Lake; several fishing access points.

SPECIAL INFORMATION. This trip runs north to south, although it can be done in the opposite direction with the downhill portions becoming steep, muddy upgrades. Watch out for ATV riders.

THE DRIVE. Southern Oregon and far northern California are neither canyon country nor desert. Many longtime residents are therefore surprised when I tell them of an immense semidesert canyon right in their backyard. Very few are aware of this spectacular and challenging drive, one that underscores the diversity and the infinite surprises the region has to offer. The Klamath is the only river besides the Columbia to breech the Cascade Range, and it does so right here! The river originates in Upper Klamath Lake, just east of the High Cascades, near Klamath Falls.

From the pretty little reservoir where Highway 66 crosses the Klamath, a dirt road takes off through the forest, heading south. There are no road signs, but if you head south along the rim and don't take any side roads which veer sharply right or left, you should remain on course. (It's 1.5 miles from Highway 66 to Topsy Campground.)

This road's initial 10 miles follow the canyon rim and feature frequent outstanding vista points. This fire-prone area is occupied by a youngish forest of Douglas-fir and ponderosa pine. Just below the rim, the immense and steep canyon appears more typical of the central Oregon desert, with its lava plateaus and barren rimrock, than of the High Cascades. But this is definitely the High Cascades, despite the moderate elevations (3,900 feet at Highway 66; 2,500 feet at Copco Lake).

At mile 8, look for a wide gravel side road on the left (east), which takes you to the California town of Dorris (15 miles). After 10 miles, the road descends into the canyon with many steep, very rough downgrades, even though it loses only 1,000 feet in 3 miles. Note the change in vegetation from montane forest (Douglas-fir, ponderosa pine) to a semidesert of grass, valley oak, widely spaced ponderosa pine, lots of brush, and even a little sagebrush and juniper. The increased aridity occurs partly because of the loss of elevation and partly because you are entering the Shasta Valley, a high-desert pocket in the rainshadow directly east of Mt. Shasta and the Marble Mountains.

The road, now following the river's edge, crosses the state line 5 times between miles 12 and 14. This is mostly private property owned by the power company that runs the dams. Several designated recreation spots, with pit toilets, are available for fishing, picnicking, and admiring the wide, beautiful river and steep-sided canyon. The dirt road ends at the bridge and turnoff to the Copco Lake store. If you head west on the pavement, away from the store, you'll come to the Mallard Cove recreation site after 2 miles. The site offers picnicking and an outstanding view of the lake.

Beyond Copco Lake, the Klamath flows into Iron Gate Lake, then past the town of Hornbrook before entering the lower Klamath Canyon, one of northern California's many outstanding scenic wonders. The river meets the Pacific at the fog-shrouded town of Orick.

SIDE TRIPS. At MP 42 on Highway 66, turn right (south), where the sign says JOHN C. BOYLE POWER PLANT. It's 4.2 miles to a power plant at the bottom of the canyon, below the dam, with fantastic views of the canyon and spillway. At mile 0.4, go straight, not left (left will take you to the dam). At mile 4.5, a narrow, paved side road heads steeply downhill to a boat launch amid white oaks, ponderosa pines and much rock and grass. Parking is limited at the boat launch and river rafters leave their vehicles in a parking area up on the main road. The 15-mile river run to Copco Lake is supposed to be outstanding. Beyond the boat launch turnoff, the west-side road becomes extremely narrow and rocky. It follows the river for 8 more miles, then cuts away.

To do the route south to north, leave I-5 at the Henley-Hornbrook Exit, 6 miles into California. Proceed east, toward Hornbrook, following signs to Copco Lake. It's 3 miles to Agar Road (go right, over the Klamath), 4 more miles to Agar-Beswick Road (go left) and 13 more miles to Copco Lake (20 miles from I-5). This is all paved and signed. At Copco Lake, just before the bridge over the Klamath to the store, a gravel road takes off right. That is the far end of the road from Highway 66.

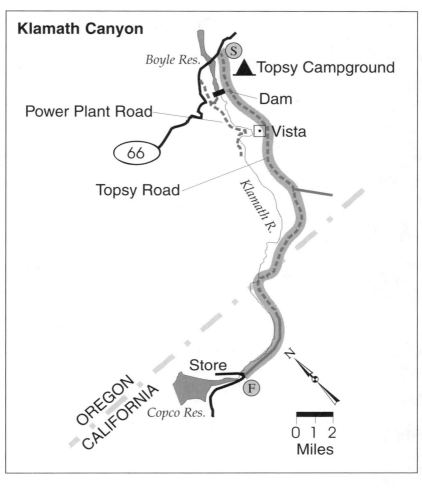

Klamath Canyon

Boyle Res.

Ⓢ ▲ Topsy Campground

━ Dam

Power Plant Road

☐ Vista

⑥⑥

Topsy Road

Klamath R.

OREGON
CALIFORNIA

Store

Ⓕ

Copco Res.

N

0 1 2
Miles

Spillway, Klamath Canyon

Marial Road

LOCATION. North of the Rogue River, between Grants Pass and Gold Beach, at the eastern tip of the Wild Rogue Wilderness.

HIGHLIGHTS. A dizzying, curvy road to one of Oregon's most remote communities, with an old ranch and museum, and a spectacular trail.

DIFFICULTY. Moderate. Despite the steepness, occasional washboarding, curves, and dirt surface, Marial Road is well maintained. Mt. Reuben Road, up from Grave Creek, contains a very steep 3-mile segment.

DISTANCE. 35.6 miles from Grave Creek Bridge to the road end just past Marial.

HIGH ELEVATION. 3,500 feet.

MAPS. Dutchman Butte; Mt. Bolivar; Galice; Mt. Reuben; Bunker Creek; Kelsey Creek; Marial.

ADMINISTRATION. Siskiyou National Forest.

GETTING THERE. A few miles north of Grants Pass, leave I-5 at the Merlin exit and proceed 23 miles west on Merlin-Galice Road, past Galice to the Grave Creek Bridge and the boat landing. Once over the bridge, turn left and head up the mountain on 34-8-1, gravel Mt. Reuben Road, for 15 miles. (The road is very narrow, winding, and steep for the 3 miles between Whiskey Creek Road and Sawmill Gap.) At mile 15.1, the road merges with the upper end of Whisky Creek Road and becomes 32-7-19.3. At mile 15.6, you pick up 32-8-31, a one-lane blacktop from Glendale. Turn left, toward Powers, and go another 5 miles to the Marial Road (32-9-14.2). Gravel Marial Road is 15 miles long, very steep, and very curvy. The last mile, to the trailhead, is a little rough and muddy.

REST STOPS. Tucker Flat Campground.

THE DRIVE. Marial is a tiny community smack in the middle of the 47-mile Wild and Scenic section of the lower Rogue canyon. It's the only spot on the river between the Grave Creek landing, near Grants Pass, and Foster Bar, near Agness, that is accessible by car. And it's a heck of a ride. Just reaching the Marial turnoff from the Glendale-Powers Road is quite a trip. Once onto the Marial road, you're in for a thrilling, 15-mile downward spiral. The only level spot comes at Big Meadows, at mile 10, a large grassy opening with a house.

Eventually, the river comes into view. Soon after, you pass Tucker Flat Campground (on the right), and the Rogue River Ranch (on the left) with its little museum. The ranch is historic because the Rogue Valley's very first settlers, in the 1820s, lived nearby. Marial is also the location of Oregon's oldest known Native American archaeological site. There is no store and there are no services in Marial, but there is a Forest Service guard station and a few houses. If you continue through town to the road

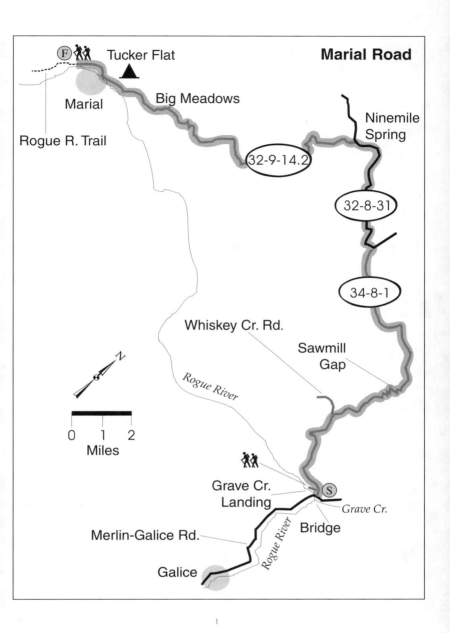

end, you'll end up at a trailhead. Hiking west, the initial 2 trail miles traverse the river's most scenic section, passing Mule Creek Canyon, the Coffee Pot, Stair Creek Falls, and Blossom Bar Rapids. The latter is considered the river's most challenging rafting run.

SIDE TRIPS. For the Mt. Bolivar and Hanging Rock trails, continue west toward Powers on 32-8-31, which becomes FR 3348. See Drive 17.

Illinois River Canyon

LOCATION. Off Highway 199, southwest of Grants Pass.

HIGHLIGHTS. A long, sometimes rough dirt road along one of Oregon's most magnificent and unusual federally protected Wild and Scenic rivers.

DIFFICULTY. Easy. Moderate toward the end. The most difficult segment, approaching Store Gulch, was recently regraded and widened.

DISTANCE. 18 miles from Highway 199 to Briggs Creek.

HIGH ELEVATION. 1,500 feet.

MAPS. Cave Junction; Eight Dollar Mountain; Pearsoll Peak.

ADMINISTRATION. Siskiyou National Forest.

GETTING THERE. Twenty miles southwest of Grants Pass, turn right (west) at Selma off Highway 199 onto Illinois River Road (County Road 5070, becoming Forest Road 4103). The road is paved for 6 miles then becomes narrow, winding, dirt, and bumpy for 12 miles to the terminus at the Briggs Creek Picnic Site and Trailhead. The last mile can be a little muddy.

REST STOPS. Store Gulch Campground; Briggs Creek Picnic Site; dozens of beautiful aqua swimming holes along the road.

THE DRIVE. Arguably southern Oregon's most scenic byway (see Author's Favorites), this road runs for 18 miles through the Wild and Scenic section of the Rogue's principal tributary. To rafters, this is a more challenging run than the lower Rogue, and the canyon is even more spectacular. But the best parts lie beyond the road end. You do get to see an outstanding canyon from your car, though, with the orange cone of Pearsoll Peak rising up from the water's edge halfway between Highway 199 and Briggs Creek. At 5,098 feet, Pearsoll is the highest summit in the Kalmiopsis Wilderness. To climb it, see Drive 40. The orange rock is weathered serpentinite, a nutrition-poor substance which is host to dozens of endangered species. You can identify serpentinite not only by the orange color but by the stunted, sparse vegetation. And, by the way, what looks like ponderosa pines on serpentinite are actually Jeffrey pines, which in Oregon grow only on serpentinite.

The best part of this trip is the many beautiful aqua-colored swimming holes. The myrtlewood groves and side creeks aren't bad, either.

The road ends at Briggs Creek, the beginning of the 21-mile Illinois River Trail. After crossing a footbridge into the Wilderness, then traversing an old orchard, the trail goes high above the river. If you hike 2 miles, to the east fork of York Creek, you'll find a patch of kalmiopsis plants, an exceedingly rare, dwarf azalea after which the Wilderness is named.

SIDE TRIPS. For McCaleb Ranch, Illinois River Falls, Chetco Pass, and Pearsoll Peak, see Drive 40.

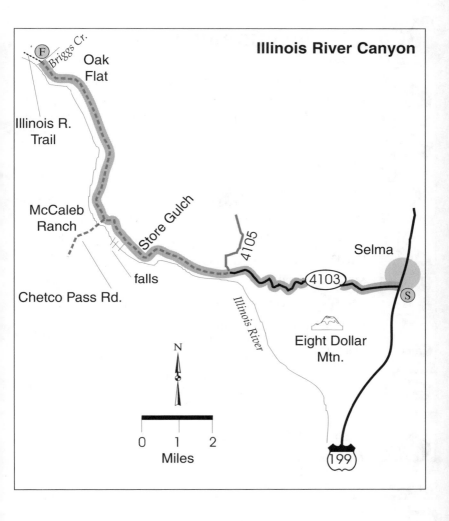

Illinois River Canyon

Briggs Cr.

Oak Flat

Illinois R. Trail

McCaleb Ranch

Store Gulch

falls

Chetco Pass Rd.

4105

Selma

4103

Illinois River

Eight Dollar Mtn.

N

0   1   2
Miles

199

2002 FIRE. Forest road 4103 is open and unchanged although it passes through heavily burned areas. Many side roads are closed. Recent salvage logging on private land damaged the last half-mile and the route is confusing as it has many unmarked spurs. Where the road ends at the Illinois River Trailhead, the footbridge was badly damaged and may have been removed. The picnic table may also have been removed due to the hazard of falling tree limbs.

Chetco Pass

LOCATION. Off Highway 199, southwest of Grants Pass.

HIGHLIGHTS. A challenging drive down to the Illinois River, then over a low-water bridge and back up to a high pass at the edge of the Kalmiopsis Wilderness. Trailhead to Pearsoll Peak. Side trip to Illinois River Falls.

DIFFICULTY. Difficult. The road down to McCaleb Ranch from the Illinois River Road is extremely steep and rough. They fix it occasionally but the repairs don't seem to last long. Across the river, the road up to Chetco Pass is steep, deeply rutted, with four-wheel drive definitely recommended.

DISTANCE. 5 miles from Illinois River Road to Chetco Pass.

HIGH ELEVATION. 3,500 feet.

MAP. Pearsoll Peak.

ADMINISTRATION. Siskiyou National Forest.

GETTING THERE. Twenty miles southwest of Grants Pass, turn right (west) at Selma off Highway 199 onto the Illinois River Road (County Road 5070, becoming Forest Road 4103). At the little hilltop (at mile 10), turn left onto Spur 87, the road to McCaleb Ranch. It's 1 mile to the river, then 4 more miles to Chetco Pass. The road is sometimes gated just beyond McCaleb Ranch, in which case you will need to forget about the journey. It happens.

REST STOPS. McCaleb Ranch; Chetco Pass.

THE DRIVE. The road from FR 4103 down to McCaleb Ranch can be an adventure in itself. There's a turnoff (left) to a parking area at mile 0.7, with a trail from there to a pedestrian suspension bridge across the river. Or you can keep driving, around a rocky switchback and down to the water's edge, then across a low-water wooden bridge that is inundated when the water is high. McCaleb Ranch, a pioneer settlement now owned by the local Boy Scout Council, occupies the large flat on the far side of the river. If you camp in the vicinity, respect the peace and solitude of the caretakers. There's a parking area just over the bridge.

The road to Chetco Pass, straight ahead and uphill, is sometimes gated, though usually not. It is exceptionally steep, with long, precarious drop-offs, and ruts that will swallow your vehicle if you fall into them rather than straddle them. But Chetco Pass is fantastic, with woods, meadows, and serpentinite outcrops. The gated road beyond the pass leads to some chromite mines inside the Kalmiopsis Wilderness. The road right, up the hill, will take you halfway to the summit of 5,098-foot Pearsoll Peak, highest point in the Kalmiopsis. Most people hike to the summit from Chetco Pass because the road up from the pass is even worse than the road up from the river.

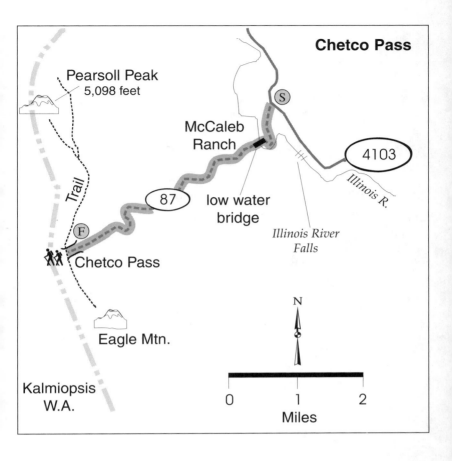

SIDE TRIPS. Illinois River Falls is a must-see. Either hike down via the pedestrian suspension bridge and turn left, along the river, or cross the low-water bridge and head, on foot, in the same direction. It's 0.5 mile to the aptly named Fall Creek, with the falls appearing soon after. The falls aren't very big—they're more of a steep rapid—but the rocky chasm through which they flow is impressive.

2002 FIRE. From FR 4103 the area was heavily burned and several large Port Orford cedar stands were destroyed. The caretaker's house at McCaleb Boy Scout Ranch burned to the ground, although the low-water bridge and the swinging footbridge are unharmed. The first part of the road remains unstable. The road from the ranch to Chetco Pass has a new Port Orford cedar gate,* closed November 1 to June 1 (you're unlikely to make it over the bridge then anyhow). While this road has been improved in recent years, it is still primitive. The sign at the turnoff from Illinois River Road may be down.

---

* See note at Drive 20.

Onion Mountain

LOCATION. In the hills directly west of Grants Pass.

HIGHLIGHTS. Beautiful Shan Creek Canyon, and a panorama of Grants Pass and the Rogue Valley followed by Onion Mountain Lookout and an even better panorama.

DIFFICULTY. Easy to moderate, on wide, somewhat steep gravel roads. If you venture beyond Onion Mountain, there are some moderate-to-difficult spots. See Side Trips.

DISTANCE. 16.1 miles from Highway 199 to the lookout.

HIGH ELEVATION. 4,200 feet.

MAPS. Wilderville; Onion Mountain.

ADMINISTRATION. Siskiyou National Forest.

GETTING THERE. From Grants Pass, take Highway 199 southwest to the Applegate River bridge. Just over the bridge, turn right onto Riverbanks Road (260). Follow the pavement 6 miles to Shan Creek (Forest Road 2706), then turn left (west). The pavement yields to gravel after 1.5 miles. It's 8 miles to the Shan Creek View Point and 8.5 miles to FR 2509 (gravel). Go right on FR 2509 and proceed for 0.8 mile to a three-way junction. The last mile is gated because the lookout is for rent. The new outhouse at the Shan Creek picnic site was vandalized and will be replaced. If you see anybody messing with it, get a license number and call the police.

REST STOPS. Shan Creek View Point; Onion Mountain Lookout.

THE DRIVE. FR 2706 is a favorite backcountry drive among Grants Pass residents. The dramatic, rocky, serpentinite canyon of Shan Creek (look for an old mine on a particularly precarious hillside across the creek) culminates at a charming little viewpoint with a restroom and picnic table. The canyon perfectly frames the confluence of the Applegate and Rogue Rivers, the city of Grants Pass, and Mt. McLoughlin on the horizon.

Beyond the viewpoint, turning onto FR 2509, the way levels off and becomes much easier (for a mile, anyhow) as the steep, brushy flank of Onion Mountain comes into view. If the lookout road is closed, you'll have to walk the steep, shaded 0.8 miles. But it's well worth it, as this is one of Oregon's few remaining active fire lookouts. From the lookout, the view west of the Illinois Canyon, Pearsoll Peak, and York Butte is almost as dramatic as the view east, of Grants Pass and the Rogue Valley.

SIDE TRIPS. For a real adventure, return to Grants Pass by continuing ahead on FR 2509. The road soon becomes extremely narrow and goes steeply downhill, with a few rough spots that a low-clearance car might not negotiate, especially in spring and fall. FR 2509 eventually emerges onto FR 25 at Lone Tree Pass. From there, turn right for a beautiful, paved drive down Taylor Creek to the Rogue River Canyon in the Galice area. See Drive 44.

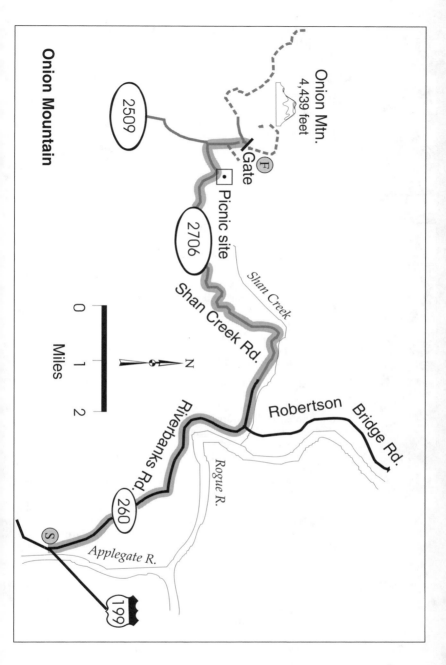

An easier, albeit not quite as scenic alternate return route is to backtrack on FR 2509 past the upper end of Shan Creek Road, to the junction with FR 25, which is paved. Follow it out to Highway 199 at Hays Hill, 8 miles beyond the Riverbanks turnoff.

2002 FIRE. Forest roads 2706, 2509, and 056 were all unaffected. The last mile is gated because the old lookout is for rent.

Josephine Creek, Onion Camp

LOCATION. Southwest of Grants Pass, near the town of Selma.

HIGHLIGHTS. A long, winding road, stupendous vistas, and multiple trailheads.

DIFFICULTY. Easy to moderate. Paved for 1 mile, then one-lane blacktop to just past the Illinois River bridge. Then mostly wide, gravel road.

DISTANCE. 18.5 miles from Highway 199 to Onion Camp.

HIGH ELEVATION. 4,400 feet.

MAPS. Cave Junction; Josephine Mountain.

ADMINISTRATION. Siskiyou National Forest.

GETTING THERE. Go 23 miles southwest from Grants Pass on Highway 199. Three and a half miles beyond Selma, a sign pointing left reads KALMIOPSIS WILDERNESS—17 MILES. Follow this road, Forest Road 4201, across the Illinois River bridge and proceed 17 miles up the steep but wide gravel route to the Babyfoot Lake turnoff, on the left. The Onion Camp turnoff is also on the left, 1.5 miles past the Babyfoot Lake turnoff. The short Onion Camp spur road is gated of late, making it a 0.25-mile walk in.

REST STOPS. Onion Camp; Whetstone Butte Trailhead.

THE DRIVE. Only one highway sign in the universe directs traffic to the immense Kalmiopsis Wilderness, and that is the turnoff from Highway 199 to Forest Road 4201. Luckily, you don't need to hike into the wilderness to appreciate the area's splendor. The beginning of the road, with Eight Dollar Mountain on the right and the Illinois River on the left, is quite scenic in its own right. (Eight Dollar Mountain has been often tested for nickel mining potential, but in 30 years nothing has materialized.) This is a serpentinite area of stunted vegetation and endangered plants. Just before the National Forest boundary, look to the left for a large darlingtonia bog, a marsh populated with fly-eating darlingtonia (cobra) plants, along with tiger lilies and azaleas.

After crossing the Illinois at a beautiful bridge and swimming hole, the road follows Josephine Creek for a bit, then heads up the mountain. (Josephine Creek was one of southern Oregon's original gold-mining areas. The county is named after it.) The road up the hill to Onion Camp is predictably long and curvy, but wide and pleasant, with excellent vistas of the Illinois River Valley. (See Side Trips for a couple of dandy excursions.)

Onion Camp is a three-slot campground with a meadow, a creek, and a bunch of trailheads. One mile beyond the Onion Camp turnoff (which is on the left), on FR 4201 just past the Fall Creek turnoff (on the right), there is an excellent view of the barren, brown rock summit of Whetstone Butte sloping down into the Illinois River Canyon. A 1.5-mile trail (beginning on the left side of the road), will take you to Whetstone Butte, which features views of the entire Kalmiopsis Wilderness, from the upper Chetco

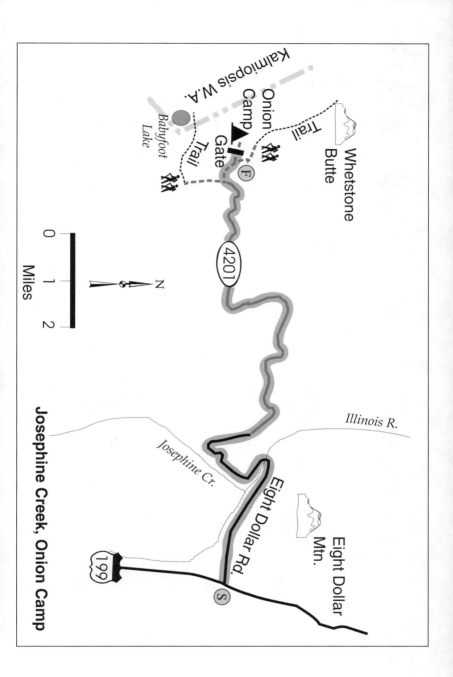

Josephine Creek, Onion Camp

drainage to the Big Craggies. They recently put up a pit toilet at the Whetstone Butte Trailhead.

SIDE TRIPS. Shortly beyond the Illinois River bridge, where the main road (FR 4210) swings right and starts uphill, a dirt road takes off left. If you follow it for 1 mile, you'll come to a rare hanging bog, on the side of a hill instead of in a depression. Look for fly-eating darlingtonia plants, butterworts (another insect eater), and the endangered and gorgeous Waldo gentian.

The Babyfoot Lake Road, FR 861, a 1-mile side trip left at mile 17, leads to the Babyfoot Lake Trailhead. The road itself isn't very interesting, but the 1.5-mile trail beyond it is quite popular. There are lots of rare Brewer spruces at the tiny glacial cirque lake.

2002 FIRE. Forest roads 5240, 4201, and 142 were unaffected. There is a new sign at the Babyfoot Lake Trailhead, and at other Kalmiopsis trailheads, asserting that the Kalmiopsis Wilderness area trails have not been assessed since the Biscuit Fire and may contain numerous fallen snags and unstable holes from burned-out tree roots. Although the roads traverse many burned areas, their condition otherwise remains the same.

Illinois River bridge, Eight Dollar Road to Onion Camp

Tennessee Lookout

LOCATION. Illinois River Valley southwest of Grants Pass, near Kerby.

HIGHLIGHTS. A rough road to a lookout site in a highly scenic region that is underlain by vast areas of serpentinite rock. One of southern Oregon's original and most productive gold-producing areas beginning in the 1850s, this is still a busy gold-mining region.

DIFFICULTY. Difficult. The road to Tennessee Pass is steep and narrow, with very deep waterbars. The final 0.8 miles to Tennessee Lookout is even steeper, narrower, and bumpier than the rest of the route, with jutting rocks, overhanging tree limbs, and bottomless drop-offs. The roads from Tennessee Pass down to Josephine Creek are a little better, but still difficult.

DISTANCE. 5 miles from Highway 199 to the top of Tennessee Mountain.

HIGH ELEVATION. 3,227 feet.

MAP. Cave Junction.

ADMINISTRATION. Siskiyou National Forest.

GETTING THERE. From Highway 199 at Kerby, head northeast on Finch Road where the sign says TENNESSEE L.O.—5 MILES. Proceed along Finch Road for 1 mile, over the west fork of the Illinois River, to West Side Road. Turn right and continue for 0.5 miles to a gate and a cyclone fence. The unmarked Tennessee Pass Road takes off left there (for the record, it's Spur 011). Follow the road 2 slow miles to Tennessee Pass. At the pass, take Spur 921, right and uphill for 1.5 miles, to the top of Tennessee Mountain. Do not take Spur 915.

REST STOPS. Tennessee Pass; Tennessee Lookout.

SPECIAL INFORMATION. The miners who maintain these roads and drive them frequently are reasonably friendly but might try to discourage you from spending too much time in the area. They would apparently rather not have tourists looking at their diggings. My advice is to avoid the mining sites along Josephine Creek, although the creek itself is incredibly scenic.

THE DRIVE. Fortunately, the most scenic part of this trip is the journey to Tennessee Pass and Tennessee Lookout, not Josephine Creek, where the miners hang out. The road to Tennessee Pass is narrow and curvy, with deep waterbars every few feet.

Tennessee Pass affords an outstanding view of the precipitous road gouged into Tennessee Mountain, plus panoramic views into the canyons of Free and Easy Creek and Josephine Creek. At the pass, follow Spur 011 left for 0.5 miles to a little rocky knob for a fabulous overview of the roads descending to the creek and climbing the mountain. Then go back to the pass. Spur 921, from the pass to the summit, is much like the road you came in on except narrower and steeper, with long, steep drop-offs. The waterbars aren't as deep here. But the last 0.8 miles to the summit will bounce you around, pinstripe your paint job, and demolish your radio antenna (from overhanging tree branches).

The view from the rocky, barren summit is spectacular. You can see the entire Josephine Creek drainage and most of the central Illinois River area, including Eight Dollar Mountain and the Hungry Hill and Onion Camp ridge (Drive 42). In the other direction, you can see the main Illinois River Valley and Highway 199. A fire lookout at the summit was torn down years ago but the structure's base remains. When I visited in December 2000, it was brilliantly sunny but the valley around Kerby was filled with fog and the surrounding ridge tops all had a sparkling dusting of snow.

SIDE TRIPS. From Tennessee Pass, it's 3 miles on Spur 011 down to Josephine Creek. The road crosses the creek, doubles back on the opposite bank, and then heads up Canyon Creek, dead-ending at a very remote trailhead near the Kalmiopsis Wilderness.

To reach Free and Easy Pass, on the other side of Tennessee Mountain from Tennessee Pass, take the dirt road right, off of FR 921, just past an opened road gate and just before a gravel borrow site. It's 1 mile to Free and Easy Pass on a road that is similar to the Tennessee Pass Road, except a little muddier and lower in elevation.

The story I heard years ago from a retired miner is that prostitutes used to wait at Tennessee Pass to meet the returning gold miners. Miners on the way in sometimes were able to procure the women's services with the promise to pay on the way out. But the miners would come out via Free and Easy Pass. Hence the name. I suspect the prostitutes caught on quickly.

2002 FIRE. This mostly private and Bureau of Land Management area was largely unaffected. It gets very muddy in wet weather.

Top of Tennessee Mountain

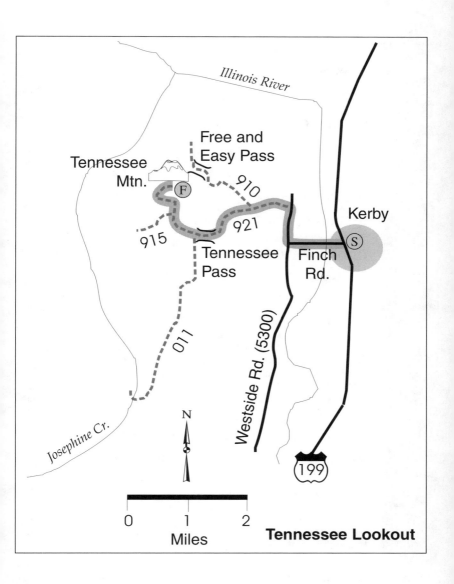

Tennessee Lookout

Taylor Creek, Flat Top

LOCATION. West of Grant Pass and southwest of the Rogue River Canyon.

HIGHLIGHTS. Vistas of the rugged summits and canyons of the Rogue–Illinois River region, ending with a hair-raising ride to the most beautiful creek on Earth.

DIFFICULTY. Mostly easy gravel road. The road from Flat Top to Silver Creek is moderate. If you make it beyond the gate, it's difficult and then some.

DISTANCE. 29 miles from Merlin-Galice Road to Old Glory Mine.

HIGH ELEVATION. 4,400 feet.

MAPS. Galice; Chrome Ridge; York Butte.

ADMINISTRATION. Siskiyou National Forest.

GETTING THERE. Leave I-5 at Exit 63, Merlin, and proceed west on Merlin-Galice Road through Merlin, past the Hellgate overlook and over the bridge to Briggs Valley Road (Forest Road 25), where the sign says BIG PINE CG—13 MILES. Turn left onto the one-lane blacktop and proceed 14 miles to the FR 2512 junction. Turn right onto FR 2512. Immediately after, pass the two entrances to Sam Brown Campground. The pavement ends just past the campground. It's 9.8 miles from the FR 2512 junction to a large three-way junction near Flat Top Mountain. Go right, uphill, for Spur 090 and the 5.2-mile drive to Old Glory Mine at Silver Creek.

REST STOPS. Tin Can; Big Pine and Sam Brown Campgrounds; Old Glory Mine.

SPECIAL INFORMATION. The last 1.5 miles to Silver Creek are gated in winter to prevent the spread of Port Orford cedar root rot. The area beyond the gate is officially a "nonmotorized use only area," although the road is legally accessible to miners and in fairly good condition. The gate is closed but unlocked in summer.

THE DRIVE. The paved drive up Taylor Creek to Big Pine Campground is deservedly popular. Look for a tremendous water-fall across a huge rock canyon at mile 1, a built-up, improved vista point at mile 2, another waterfall at mile 4, and many lovely creek-side spots. At Big Pine, a short, 0.125-mile trail leads to one of the world's largest ponderosa pines.

Beyond Sam Brown Campground, on FR 2512, it's 5 gravel-topped miles to Chrome Ridge Road (FR 2402), on the right. (See Side Trips for more on FR 2402.) Continuing on FR 2512, the route winds through a serpentinite area with long vistas, sparse, stunted forests, and many orange rock outcrops. Spur 048, left from FR 2512 at the FR 2402 junction, offers an easy 1-mile side trip with fantastic views from atop an orange cliff. It's a little narrow and rough, though. Don't go too far down the road because trees gradually encroach on the road and you'd have to back out.

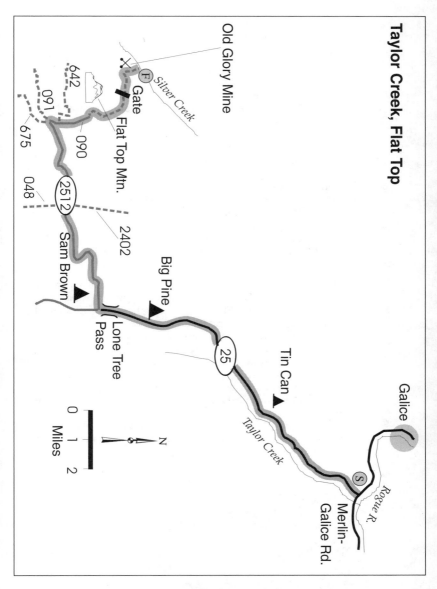

For the 5 miles beyond the FR 2402 junction, FR 2512 alternates between the north and south sides of Chrome Ridge. Turn right onto Spur 090 at the three-way junction. Spur 090 heads up hill briefly, follows the ridge top to a large rock outcrop (Flat Top Mountain), then careens into the canyon in a series of tight switchbacks. The road here is fairly well maintained but very steep and narrow. It is gated 1.5 miles from Silver Creek. See Special Information above.

Where the road hits Silver Creek at Old Glory Mine, walk down the steep bank to one of the most beautiful streams on Earth. The clearest water you'll ever see courses through a channel of perpendicular rock walls, narrow corridors and fern grottos on its way to the Illinois River.

SIDE TRIPS. Chrome Ridge Road (FR 2402) is a long, slow 13-mile route ending on the Bear Camp Road near Hansen Saddle. It's not as scenic as FR 2512 but it's a fun cut across. (See Drive 45.)

Continuing up FR 2402 (becoming Spur 675) from the Spur 090 turnoff, you'll come to the York Butte Trailhead after 1 mile. It's a beautiful, reasonably easy 1.5-mile walk to the York Butte summit, which features a view straight down into the Illinois River Canyon and across to Pearsoll Peak (see Drive 40).

The middle road at the Flat Top junction, Spur 091, is the notorious Bald Mountain Road, which was very controversial when built as a logging spur in 1980 because of the proximity to the north Kalmiopsis roadless area. It ties into the Illinois River Trail on Bald Mountain and offers excellent views of Chinaman Hat, Silver Creek Canyon, and the Illinois River Canyon. The Forest Service is considering gating Spur 091. If it is gated, Spur 642, taking off left from Spur 090 just beyond the Spur 091 turnoff, also offers an excellent view of Chinaman Hat.

2002 FIRE. Forest roads 25 to 2512 to 190 were heavily impacted by the Biscuit Fire from Sam Brown Campground west. Where Chrome Ridge road and FR 2512 west were main fire lines, the brush and trees have been removed along the edges. In general, the fire line was effective: the burn was almost entirely confined to the west and north of the two roads. Beyond the Chrome Ridge road junction, views northward are into Little Todd Creek, which was completely burned. Spur 090 into Little Todd Creek had not been inspected as of winter 2003 beyond the Port Orford cedar gate* at 1.5 miles from Silver Creek. Road signs were unaffected and FR 25 and 2512 remain an amazingly scenic drive. In the vicinity of Spur 091, there may be some kalmiopsis plants; I also saw a burned Port Orford cedar and Brewer spruce here.

_____
* See note at Drive 20.

Jeffrey Pines, Flat Top Road

Burnt Ridge, Brandy Peak

LOCATION. The coastal mountains between Grants Pass and Gold Beach.

HIGHLIGHTS. An extremely popular route with high peaks and long vistas. Begins on the lower Rogue at Galice and emerges on the even-lower Rogue at Agness. Much botanical interest.

DIFFICULTY. Easy. Bear Camp Road is one-lane blacktop. Burnt Ridge Road is wide and gravel.

DISTANCE. 36 miles from Merlin-Galice Road to Forest Road 33.

HIGH ELEVATION. 4,975 feet.

MAPS. Agness; Galice; Mt. Peavine; Hobson Horn; Brandy Peak.

ADMINISTRATION. Siskiyou National Forest.

GETTING THERE. From Exit 63 on I-5, north of Grants Pass, take Merlin-Galice Road west through Merlin to the turnoff left (Forest Road 23), just before Galice, where the sign says GOLD BEACH—67 MILES. Burnt Ridge Road (FR 2308) takes off at Bear Camp Summit on FR 23 at mile 19. Burnt Ridge Road ends at mile 36 where it meets FR 33, or 30 miles from Gold Beach. At the end of Burnt Ridge Road, turn left (west) for Gold Beach.

REST STOPS. Galice; Bear Camp; Cougar Lane.

SPECIAL INFORMATION. The river outfitters usually plow Bear Camp Road in mid-May. This road can be driven in the opposite direction.

THE DRIVE. The only problem with this beautiful and popular drive is the frequent river outfitters on their way from Galice to pick up rafters in Agness. Other than that, it's a fantastic drive.

FR 23 follows Galice Creek for 5 miles, then begins climbing. You lose the centerline at mile 10. Further up, you are treated to many long vistas and some beautiful marble outcrops. Just past Bear Camp summit, a picnic site offers a commanding view of the Rogue River Canyon, although you can't see the river. A short trail from Bear Camp summit, on the south side of FR 23 where it is intersected by Burnt Ridge Road, leads to a grassy opening with many endangered wildflowers and an extremely rare, for the southern Coastal Ranges, occurrence of Pacific silver fir. The trail system in the Burnt Ridge and Brandy Peak area is under construction.

Beyond Bear Camp on Bear Camp Road, 5,316-foot Brandy Peak's blocky crag dominates the horizon to the south. Sixteen more miles of downhill twists and turns takes you to FR 33 at Cougar Lane, which is a little store directly across the Rogue River from Agness. Go right for Agness (6 miles), and left for Gold Beach.

SISKIYOUS

For Burnt Ridge Road, FR 2308, turn left at Bear Camp summit. This route treats you to much more rugged terrain than Bear Camp Road, and even better vistas. The route skirts the base of Brandy Peak. In the opposite direction, travelers are treated to tier after tier of mountain ridges, ending with the snow-capped cone of Mt. McLoughlin on the eastern horizon. Holding a contour high above Indigo Creek, the route eventually makes its way through coastal old-growth forests, emerging on FR 33 one mile south of where FR 23 comes out.

SIDE TRIPS. Hobson Horn is noteworthy because of a fire lookout and an abundance of Brewer spruce, one of North America's rarest and most beautiful trees. A trail there leads to Silver Peak and the Illinois River. To reach Hobson Horn, turn left (south) from FR 23 at mile 12, then right (west) onto FR 34-9-35, which becomes FR 2411. It's 4 easy miles to the Hobson Horn Trailhead.

Bear Camp Pasture is located (on the left) 0.5 miles before Bear Camp summit. A short, steep road leads to a picnic table at the meadow's edge. There's also a beautiful little spring, a creek, and several endangered wildflowers.

Spur 016, the first right (north) off of Burnt Ridge Road, leads steeply downhill to a small meadow in a tiny glacial cirque on Brandy Peak's north face. The meadow contains a small stand of Alaska yellow cedar, an extremely rare tree for the southern coastal ranges.

A badly burned knobcone pine (right) and Douglas-fir off Bear Camp Road, September 2002 after the Biscuit Fire.

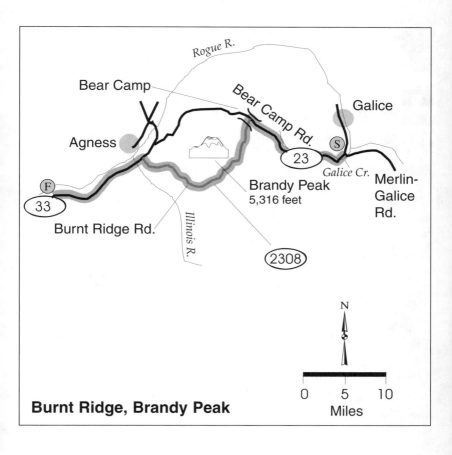

Burnt Ridge, Brandy Peak

0   5   10
Miles
N

2002 FIRE. Both FR 23 (Bear Camp Road) and FR 2308 (Burnt Ridge Road) were main fire lines. On FR 23, the burned areas are mostly in the south, although the fire jumped the road in a few places. On FR 2308, the burn zone is confined to the east and north. The routes offer wide panoramas into the upper Silver and Indigo creek drainages where the fire burned irregularly. Along FR 2308, Brandy Peak, and the beautiful little glacial cirque visited by Spur 016, did not burn. The cirque contained a small stand of Alaska cedar, common in the Central and North Cascades but extremely rare in the Siskiyou Mountains. Indigo Prairie (turnoff at mile 12)—caused by fire originally and slowly filled in over the past 100 years with Douglas-fir—has now been substantially enlarged. Road conditions and signs were unaffected.

Silver Creek Falls

LOCATION. West of Grants Pass, off Bear Camp Road on the way to Gold Beach.

HIGHLIGHTS. A spectacular waterfall near a remote creek.

DIFFICULTY. Easy to moderate except for the last couple of miles, which can be treacherous in wet weather.

DISTANCE. 9.4 miles from Forest Road 23 to the falls.

HIGH ELEVATION. 3,600 feet.

MAPS. Hobson Horn; York Butte.

ADMINISTRATION. Siskiyou National Forest.

GETTING THERE. From I-5, take Merlin-Galice Road (at Exit 63) through Merlin to Forest Road 23 and then turn left (west), toward Gold Beach. At mile 9.7, the second Chrome Ridge exit (there are two side roads on the left here, and one on the right), turn left onto FR 35-9-1. Take the road that goes downhill and to the right, go along the creek and continue following the creek. After 1.8 miles, turn left onto Road 35-9-14, where the sign says HAWK'S CREEK. After 2.1 miles on FR 35-9-14, at a small saddle, turn left, downhill, on a very narrow road. It's 5.5 rough, curvy miles to the road end at the falls.

REST STOPS. Galice; Silver Creek Falls.

THE DRIVE. The drive along upper Silver Creek, at the beginning of the route, showcases the extensive stands of western hemlock, a fairly uncommon tree in the Siskiyous and one that is extremely beautiful. Lower Silver Creek (below the falls), is my nominee for the prettiest mountain stream on Earth (see Drive 44).

Turning off of Silver Creek Road, the spur road winds through logging areas before emerging at a remote dirt road amid old-growth forest. After 3 steep curvy miles, the road hits bottom at an old cabin and follows the creek for 2.5 level miles. It then ends at a little parking area next to Silver Creek, just above the water-fall. Take the main trail (right, then left) for the best view of the 80-foot falls. The path winds steeply downhill for 1.5 miles to the falls' base.

(By the way, this is one of three falls with variations of the name "Silver Falls" in Oregon of which I'm aware. There is one at Silver Falls State Park, near Salem. It is spectacular but extremely well visited. There is one at Golden and Silver Falls near Coos Bay [see Drive 16]. And of course there is this one, off Bear Camp Road, which is the most remote and difficult to reach. It's also mighty beautiful.)

2002 FIRE. The fire badly impacted the route that includes FR 35-9-1, 35-9-4, and 2600/050. The road signs—poor to begin with—may have been further damaged or destroyed. In this case, the route description above may be your best guide. All BLM roads off Bear Camp Road were closed until spring 2003 and I am

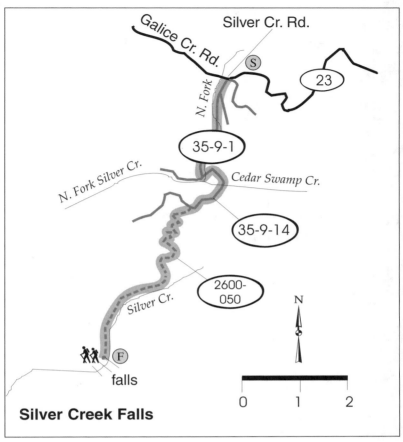

Silver Creek Falls

Patchy burned areas and clearcuts (higher up) as seen from upper Silver Creek Road.

told that there are numerous snags across this route. Forest road 2600/050, the steep, winding, narrow, often muddy road down to the falls, is scheduled for maintenance (finally!).

Black Butte

LOCATION. Southwest of Cave Junction in Oregon's extreme southwest corner, crossing over into California.

HIGHLIGHTS. Starting in the fascinating Takilma community, this is a beautiful drive that culminates at a craggy summit and an overlook of the East Fork Illinois River canyon. You will see some unusual botany, impressive glacial geology, and the Siskiyous' most impressive peak cluster.

DIFFICULTY. Easy. A wide gravel road (except near the end, where it's a wide dirt road).

DISTANCE. 15.8 miles from the Takilma Road/Happy Camp Road junction to Black Butte Trailhead.

HIGH ELEVATION. 4,800 feet.

MAPS. Takilma; Polar Bear Mountain.

SPECIAL INFORMATION. The Takilma community, a cluster of odd-looking houses along the East Fork Illinois River, dates to the 1960s counterculture movement. Residents are friendly but don't like to be gawked at, so be low key and respectful.

ADMINISTRATION. Siskiyou National Forest.

GETTING THERE. Take Highway 199 to Cave Junction and go east on Caves Highway (OR 46). Turn right onto Holland Loop after 2 miles and then right again onto Bridgeview-Takilma, Forest Road 5820, after 2 more miles. Go 4 miles on Takilma Road, to the Happy Camp Road turnoff. It's 1 more mile to Takilma village on the same road, which becomes FR 4904. Bear left 4 miles beyond Four Corners, where the centerline ends. Turn right 1.8 miles later and go over Dunn Creek onto FR 4906 (there's a sign for this road only if you are coming from the opposite direction), which becomes Spur 053 near its end. It's 10 miles up FR 4906 and Spur 053, to the trailhead at Black Butte.

REST STOPS. Dunn Creek bridge; trailhead at Black Butte.

THE DRIVE. The drive from Four Corners to Black Butte crosses the Oregon state line just before the Dunn Creek bridge. Much of the route was severely impacted by the massive Longwood Gulch fire in 1987. The burn was heavy in spots, but watch for places the fire mysteriously bypassed.

After winding for several miles through logging areas, the road comes out on Spur 53 high above the East Fork Illinois River, with glacially smoothed rock lining the canyon and Black Butte's looming summit dead ahead. This is a serpentinite area of stunted Jeffrey pine, western white pine, and lots of grass, rock, and manzanita. A long trail into the Siskiyou Wilderness leads to Polar Bear Mountain, El Capitan and Young's Peak, a high peak cluster that can be seen in the distance as you enter the Illinois River Valley heading south on Highway 199. The path connects with the upper end of the East Fork Trail (of the Illinois River)

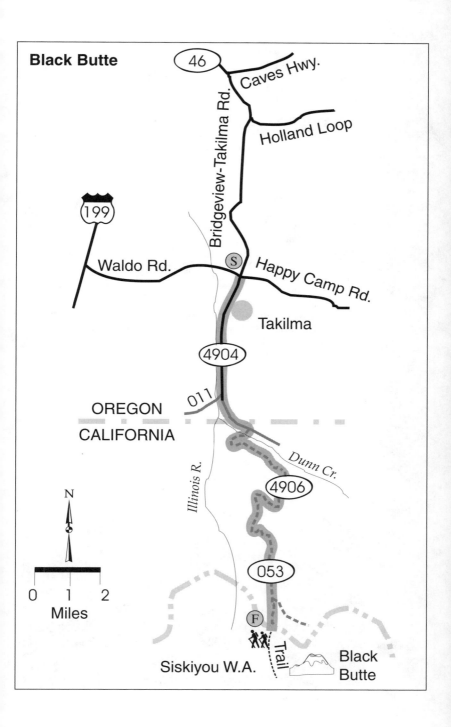

after 4 miles. If you keep going for 1 mile on Spur 053 past the trailhead, you'll come to a tiny glacial cirque that contains a pretty corn lily meadow. There's no trail but it's fun to stop and explore. The road here is lined with Brewer spruce, once thought to be one of North America's rarest trees.

SIDE TRIPS. To reach the lower end of the East Fork Trail, where the centerline ends on FR 4904, bear right on Spur 011 and proceed for 0.5 mile to the bridge where the blacktop ends. Across the bridge, turn left and go 0.3 miles to a boulder-lined turnout which may be marked as a trailhead. There's an excellent swimming hole just before the turnout.

The drive into California to the Young's Valley Trailhead at the far end of the Black Butte Trail is absolutely spectacular, with close-up views of Young's Valley, El Capitan, and Preston Peak. The latter may be the two most imposing summits in the Siskiyous. To reach the Young's Valley Trailhead, continue past Cave Junction southwest on Highway 199. Seven miles into California, turn left up Knopke Creek Road (18N07). Follow it 14.5 curvy miles to the "T" junction with FR 18N02, just before Sanger Lake. Turn right onto 18N02 and proceed 1.5 miles up the narrow, gravel road to the boundary of the Siskyou Wilderness. The last 1.5 miles used to be one of the more adventurous 4WD roads, but it has since been improved. 18N07 may be gated due to Port Orford cedar root rot control.

North Fork Smith River, on the way to Sourdough

Sourdough Camp

LOCATION. Between Cave Junction and Brookings, at the southern tip of the Kalmiopsis Wilderness.

HIGHLIGHTS. At the end of a long, bone-jarring, amazingly scenic road, a spectacular river confluence in one of Oregon's most remote locations.

DIFFICULTY. Difficult. The road is steep only in a few spots, but it's rocky, rutted, and can get muddy. To prevent erosion, the last 4 miles have deep waterbars.

DISTANCE. 27 miles from Highway 199 to Sourdough Camp.

HIGH ELEVATION. 3,140 feet.

MAPS. O'Brien; Buckskin Peak; Biscuit Hill.

ADMINISTRATION. Siskiyou National Forest.

GETTING THERE. Take Highway 199 to O'Brien and turn right onto Lone Mountain Road (County Road 5550, becoming Forest Road 4402). The pavement ends after 2 miles, where a sign says WIMER WAGON ROAD. (Although you will make several turns, remain on FR 4402 for the entire 27 miles to Sourdough.) Where a sign says SOURDOUGH—14 MILES and you turn left (west), the road becomes extremely low-quality, with many jutting rocks and deep ruts. Over the next 10 miles, you'll run into three ambiguous junctions with no road signs. Turn right at each of these junctions. The first junction has SOURDOUGH spray-painted on an old metal signpost. The second has SD and an arrow carved in a tree. And the third has SOURDOUGH written in marker on a plastic milk jug! (If the milk jug is gone, don't worry. The next sentence will steer you in the proper direction.) Where a sign facing in the other direction says END COUNTY ROAD MAINTE-NANCE (you'll see the rather prominent back side of the sign, which is the only road sign for miles), you've entered California. The road, now FR 305, gets much better for 2 miles. At a hilltop junction with three side roads, take FR 206 right (north; FR 206 becomes FR 4402 again on reentering Oregon). From there, it's 4 miles to Sourdough. Do *not* take Spur 450.

REST STOPS. O'Brien; North Fork Smith Bridge; Sourdough Camp.

THE DRIVE. Looking at a map, Sourdough Camp, apparently in the middle of nowhere, always seemed to me like a wonderful place. I tried to get there 25 years ago, but I turned back for fear of wrecking my low-clearance car, just 1 mile onto the jeep road. But it was worth the 25-year wait.

The route begins with a drive along the West Fork Illinois River. Look for patches of insect-eating darlingtonia plants along the creek in this serpentinite ecosystem. Just over the Whiskey Creek bridge, you'll see a turnout and a parking area on the left. Park and explore on foot the streamside meadow with its many endangered wildflowers, including the reclusive California lady slipper orchid.

The 4WD road begins beyond an enchanted forest with a rhododendron understory. After a couple of creek fordings (you'll make it), there will be a wooden bridge over the north fork of Diamond Creek. Meandering through wooded side creeks, the road contours around immense, sparsely vegetated mountainsides. Everything looks huge here, with rounded summits, deep canyons and a tiny thread of road gouged into the rock. This is a serpentinite area with stunted forests (except along the creeks) of incense-cedar, Jeffrey pine, and western white pine. When you finally hit Spur 206, you enter an area of lush coastal forest, mostly Douglas-fir, red alder, and tanoak. Fall Creek, where a little bridge goes over the top of a 25-foot waterfall, means you're almost there.

Sourdough Camp is a grassy flat on the North Fork Smith River. The highlight is the river's confluence with Baldface Creek, which at that point is as wide as the river. The river emerges from a narrow canyon just above Sourdough Camp. The creek is fast, wide, and bouldery. The river is the western boundary of the Kalmiopsis while Baldface Creek forms the eastern boundary. The confluence is the southern tip of the immense Wilderness.

SIDE TRIPS. Turn left where the sign says SOURDOUGH—18, U.S. 199—11 and you'll end up at the Patrick Creek Resort. The road crosses over from Shelly Creek to Patrick Creek at an impressive rocky saddle. The gravel road (right) where the sign says SOURDOUGH—14 used to lead to Rough and Ready Lakes via one of the best 4WD roads around. But it is now closed after 4 miles. You can hike the last 6 miles, along Baldface Ridge, to two extremely beautiful, shallow, gem-like pools with many botanical oddities and spectacular vistas everywhere.

At the junction of FR 305 and FR 206, stay on FR 305 for 2.5 miles to reach an overlook of the North Fork Smith River canyon and bridge. Just beyond the bridge are a boat ramp and a brand new outhouse.

2002 FIRE. The Biscuit Fire took its toll on the route that includes FR 5550, 4402, 305, and 208 which was a main fire line in some places. The road to the "Sourdough-14" sign was widened and re-graveled. Beyond, the low-quality road now has waterbars. Because of steep grades and deep mud, avoid driving this section in winter. The bridges at Diamond and Fall creeks were "compromised" by the fire but are driveable (the Diamond Creek bridge never did look safe). Three incidental road markers described under "Directions," 1 mile before, 1 mile after Diamond Creek, and at the turnoff from FR 305 to Spur 206, are presumed gone (including the sign written with a marker on a plastic milk jug). These are all right turns. The last 4 miles on FR 206 have been much improved. Now, the road ends just past Fall Creek, 1/2-mile before Sourdough Camp. Amazingly, Sourdough Camp was not burned.

If you continue straight on the gravel at the "Sourdough-14" sign instead of turning left, you will arrive at a trailhead on the left after 4 miles; the 3-mile path leads to the summit of Biscuit Hill.

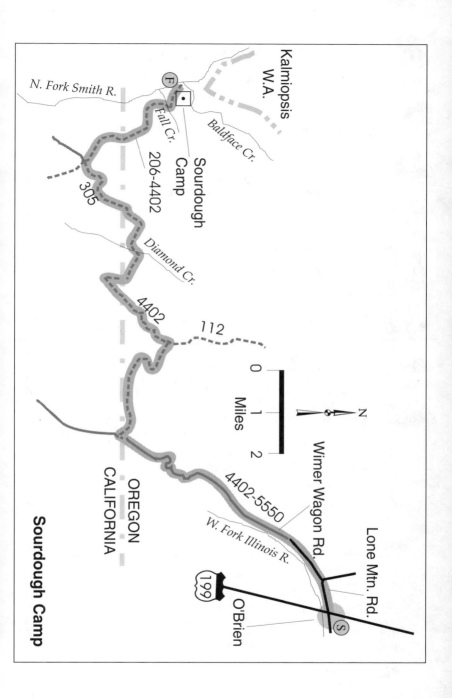

Sourdough Camp

Bolan and Tannen Lakes

LOCATION. South of Cave Junction off Highway 199, near the California line.

HIGHLIGHTS. Rocky crags, vistas of the Illinois River Valley and Klamath River Canyon, and some beautiful alpine glacial cirque lakes.

DIFFICULTY. Easy gravel and dirt roads, unless you take the short side trip to Bolan Lookout, which is of moderate difficulty.

DISTANCE. 21.6 miles from Happy Camp–Takilma Junction to Tannen Lake Trailhead.

HIGH ELEVATION. 5,100 feet.

MAPS. Takilma; Oregon Caves.

ADMINISTRATION. Siskiyou National Forest.

GETTING THERE. Take Highway 199 south from Grants Pass to Cave Junction. Go east on Caves Highway (OR 46) toward Oregon Caves National Monument. Two miles up, turn right on Holland Loop and go 1.5 miles, then go right again on Bridgeview–Takilma Road for 4 miles, where the road to Happy Camp takes off left. Go left on Happy Camp Road (Forest Road 5828, becoming FR 48). At the summit of Happy Camp Road (mile 13 from Four Corners), turn left onto FR 4812. At mile 3.8, go left for Bolan Lake (on Spur 040) or right for Tannen Lake (on Spur 041). It's 2.5 miles from this junction to Bolan Lake and 4.8 miles from the junction to the Tannen Lake Trailhead.

REST STOPS. Bolan Lake; Tannen Lake Trailhead.

THE DRIVE. The Takilma–Happy Camp Road is one of Josephine County's most dramatic. From the junction near Takilma, the narrow paved highway winds high into the mountains with increasingly spectacular views of the Illinois River Valley and the Siskiyou crest. At the road's summit, as you weave along the state line, you start to glimpse vistas of California's Klamath Canyon, with the Marble Mountains rising on the other side.

Bolan Lake sits in a pleasant little glacial cirque accessible only by unpaved road. It's fairly popular, with a busy campground. Just before Bolan Lake, the 0.75-mile road (right) to Bolan Mountain Lookout (elevation 6,263) is very steep, with loose rock. But the payoff, the view from the lookout, is magnificent.

From the FR 4812 and Spur 041 junction, the 4 miles to the Tannen Lake Trailhead may be Josephine County's prettiest mountain drive, with the narrow dirt road skirting the rocky cliffs and crags of Althouse Mountain (elevation 6,326). It's an easy, 0.5-mile hike from the trailhead to Tannen Lake, nestled in a small glacial cirque with a steep headwall on the flank of Tannen Mountain (elevation 6,298). The lake has a brushy shore and a silty bottom, but the setting is lovely.

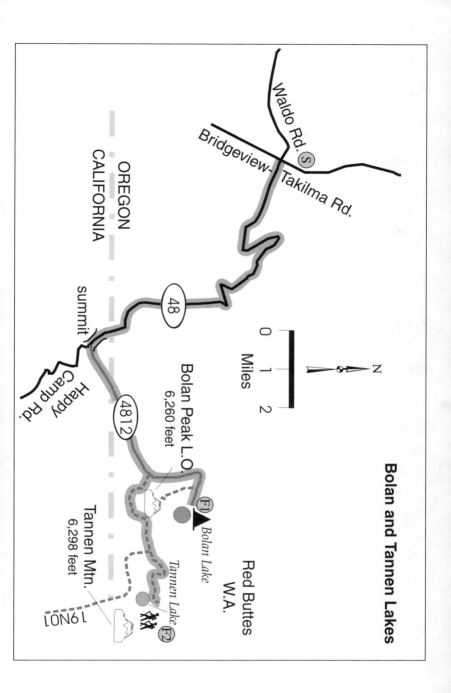

Bolan and Tannen Lakes

Waldo Rd.

Bridgeview–Takilma Rd.

S

48

OREGON
CALIFORNIA

summit

Happy Camp Rd.

4812

Bolan Peak L.O.
6,260 feet

Tannen Mtn.
6,298 feet

19N01

F1

Bolan Lake

Tannen Lake

F2

Red Buttes
W.A.

N

0   1   2
Miles

SIDE TRIPS. Thompson Ridge Road (19N01), to the right (south) from King's Saddle, 1 mile before the Tannen Lake Trailhead, is worth a look. The dirt road features a spectacular view from high above Tannen Lake, and a 0.75-mile trail (the Boundary Trail) that leads to the Tannen Mountain summit. Back on paved Takilma–Happy Camp Road, if you continue over the summit toward Happy Camp for about a mile, you'll come to a vista point near a Brewer spruce grove, the only Brewer spruce I know of that is accessible via paved road. And as long as you're on the Caves Highway (see Getting There), you should have a look at the popular Oregon Caves National Monument.

Whiskey Peak

LOCATION. Upper Applegate area, between Grants Pass and Jacksonville, near the California line.

HIGHLIGHTS. Spectacular drive to an abandoned fire lookout. Tremendous views of the Middle Fork Applegate River and the Red Buttes.

DIFFICULTY. Moderate. Slow, occasionally steep gravel road. Devil's Climbout, just past Whiskey Peak, is a terrific drive that looks scarier than it actually is.

DISTANCE. 27 miles from Highway 238 to Whiskey Peak.

HIGH ELEVATION. 6,450 feet.

MAPS. Grayback Mountain; Carberry Creek.

ADMINISTRATION. Rogue River National Forest.

GETTING THERE. From south of Grants Pass or Jacksonville on Highway 238, the Applegate River Road, turn south on Forest Road 10, Thompson Creek Road, at the town of Applegate. Proceed 10 miles to the hilltop where the pavement ends, then bear left and continue 3.5 more miles on FR 1030 to gravel FR 1035, on the right. Follow FR 1035 for 10.5 miles to Spur 350, also gravel. Turn right and go 3 more miles around a long switchback to the road crest and the trailhead for the half-mile summit trail.

REST STOPS. Applegate; Whiskey Peak; Applegate Lake.

SPECIAL INFORMATION. A sign at the turnoff onto FR 1035 claims that the road is impassable 8 miles ahead, due to a washout. This, however, is incorrect. The washout occurred during the devastating floods of New Years Day, 1997, but has long since been repaired.

THE DRIVE. The drive on Highway 238 up the Applegate Valley to the village of Applegate, and the drive up Thompson and Carberry creeks from the village of Applegate to Applegate Lake are beautiful. The side trip from Carberry Creek to Whiskey Peak is especially beautiful. From FR 1030, FR 1035 and Spur 350 climb and climb, reaching an elevation of well over 6,000 feet. The view improves with every mile, especially after the long, tight switchback on Spur 350. You finally arrive at the trailhead for the rocky mile-long path over barren scree to the lookout. The trailhead is the gated road on the right, just before the road crest.

The view from the summit (6,489 feet) reveals the full rugged splendor of the high Siskiyous. Looking north, you can see down into the Steve Fork Canyon. The vistas west and southwest overlook the dramatic Middle Fork Applegate River canyon. Low Gap, 1,000 feet directly below and to the west, can be driven to from Whiskey Peak via Devil's Climbout, a very steep, primitive, but fun road with tight switchbacks. The Azalea Lake Trail, highlight of the Red Buttes Wilderness, begins just south of Low Gap (off FR 1040), at the Fir Glade Trailhead, and passes Pyramid Peak and Buck Peak, both of which are visible from Whiskey Peak.

The rocky north face of Whiskey Peak is home to Brewer spruce, Baker cypress, and Alaska cedar, all exceedingly rare in the Siskiyous.

SIDE TRIPS. The Devil's Climbout turnoff (Spur 700), is on the right at the gap just past the Whiskey Peak road summit. It's a little over a mile from there to FR 1040. If you continue on Spur 350, the road dead-ends after a mile, with some breathtaking vistas similar to those from Whiskey Peak. If you continue on FR 1035 past the Spur 350 turnoff, you'll end up at a vista overlooking the Middle Fork Canyon, with the precipitous Red Buttes rising immediately south. Keep going on FR 1035 and you'll drop down and cross the Middle Fork, eventually emerging at the upper end of Applegate Lake. If you continue south on FR 1030, you'll come out at the upper end of Applegate Lake after 4 more miles. Turn left from there for a paved loop back to Highway 238.

Observation Peak, Silver Fork Meadow, Siskiyou Crest

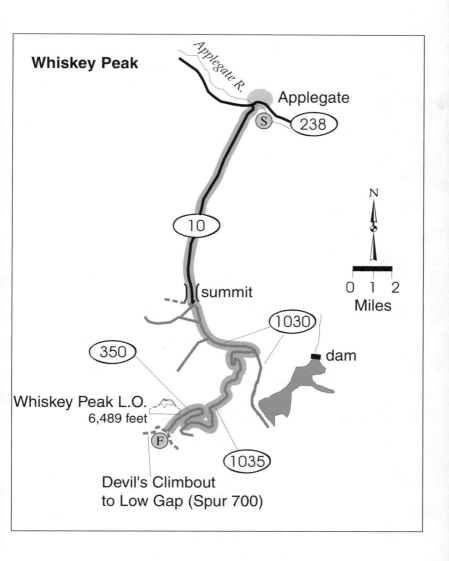

Whiskey Peak

Applegate R.

Applegate

S

238

10

)(summit

N

0 1 2
Miles

1030

350

dam

Whiskey Peak L.O.
6,489 feet

F

1035

Devil's Climbout
to Low Gap (Spur 700)

Siskiyou Crest, Mt. Ashland

LOCATION. The Oregon–California line between the Applegate River Valley and Ashland.

HIGHLIGHTS. A magnificent drive among the high peaks of the Siskiyou Mountains, paralleling the state line and crossing a 7,061-foot pass. Side trips include the summit of Mt. Ashland, highest peak in the Siskiyous at 7,533 feet, and Dutchman Peak, the Siskyous' second highest peak, at 7,418 feet.

DIFFICULTY. Moderate. Long gravel and dirt road, occasionally steep and washboarded. Areas of sharp switchbacks.

DISTANCE. 37 miles from Applegate Road to I-5.

HIGH ELEVATION. 7,061 feet.

MAPS. Squaw Lakes; Dutchman Peak; Siskiyou Peak; Mt. Ashland.

ADMINISTRATION. Rogue River National Forest.

GETTING THERE. From Highway 238 between Jacksonville and south Grants Pass, at the town of Ruch, head south on the Applegate River Road. At mile 9, turn left (east) onto Forest Road 20 (Beaver Creek Road), where the sign says DUTCHMAN PEAK— 17 MILES, and MT. ASHLAND. Continue on FR 20 past Mt. Ashland to I-5.

REST STOPS. Stores at Ruch and McKee Bridge; Beaver Sulphur Campground; Dutchman Peak Lookout; Wrangle Campground; Mt. Ashland Ski Area.

SPECIAL INFORMATION. This trip may be driven in either direction. I chose west to east mainly because it starts closest to my home. Note: The road crosses the Pacific Crest Trail at Jackson Gap, then crosses or touches it six more times between there and I-5.

THE DRIVE. This slow, sometimes steep, and always spectacular route may be the ultimate drive through the Siskiyou Mountains. The Siskiyous are part of the Klamath Mountains, an ancient, very rugged range jammed between the much more extensive Cascades and the Coast Range. Other Klamath ranges include the Trinity Alps, Trinity Divide, and Marble Mountains, all in northern California.

Beginning at the Applegate River Road, Beaver Creek Road (FR 20), paved for the first 5.5 miles, follows Beaver Creek and passes Beaver Sulphur Campground at mile 3. At mile 5.5, the route become gravel. At mile 8, it starts inscribing switchbacks steeply uphill, and you'll see views of the Grayback Peak area of the Siskiyous to the west. Grayback Peak (7,055 feet), is the highest summit in Josephine County.

At mile 10.5, the route arrives at a summit, with a close-up view of Deadman Point (5,890 feet) to the northeast. Soon after, the road narrows and becomes mostly dirt as a terrific view of the

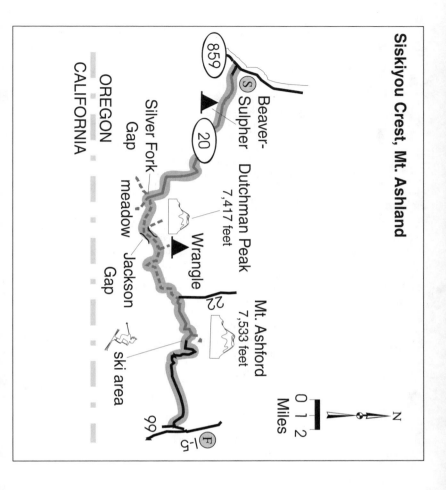

high Siskiyous unfolds to the south and west. Most prominent are Red Butte (6,733 feet) and Preston Peak (7,309 feet), both of which from here appear higher than Dutchman Peak, though they are not.

Things become even more spectacular at Silver Fork Gap, at mile 14, as you approach the 7,000-foot level. Silver Fork Meadow, far below, sweeps dramatically up to Jackson Gap (7,061 feet) and Observation Peak (7,340 feet). Dutchman Peak is just out of view here, to the north. This panorama is prettiest when there is still a little snow around (before July 4, most years), though this area is also located where snow is most likely to block your way. To visit Silver Fork Meadow, follow the road sign at Silver Fork Gap that says DONOMORE MEADOWS (FR 2025), but go only 1 mile. An unmarked trail by the creek (left) leads to the meadow. See Side Trips.

Back on the main road, at Jackson Gap and mile 16.5, the highest point of this route, a 1.5-mile side road leads to Dutchman Peak Lookout. Just before Jackson Gap, there's a shortcut (left, north) to the lookout, where you see not only the main ridge of the Siskiyous to the south and west, but, for the first time on this trip, Mt. Shasta to the south and the Marble Mountains and Trinity Alps to the southwest, all in California. That is the view you will see to the south from here to the end of the trip.

From Jackson Gap, it's 2 miles to the short, 0.25-mile turnoff (left, north) to Wrangle Campground at the base of Red Mountain. Wrangle Gap lies a mile east of the Wrangle Campground turnoff, on the other side of Red Mountain, which is a large serpentinite outcrop. The meadows at Wrangle Campground and Wrangle Gap contain many rare and endangered wildflower species.

The next landmarks are Siskiyou Gap, at mile 22, and the junction with FR 22 at mile 23 (see Side Trips). As you round Siskiyou Peak at mile 24, the basin to the west of Mt. Ashland comes into view, with Mt. Ashland dominating. This is an area of forested pockets of mountain hemlock and Shasta red fir, and of broad meadows that contain clumps of brushy-looking quaking aspen. There's a small picnic site and an even smaller campground on the stretch between here and the Mt. Ashland Ski Area.

The turnoff to the Mt. Ashland summit comes at mile 28, on the left (northeast). It's a 1-mile drive to the top (see Side Trips). Back on the main road, you pick up the pavement just before the Ski Area, at mile 29. From the ski area, it's 7 miles through forest, brush, and steep southern drop-offs, to the frontage road that parallels I-5. A final mile on the frontage road takes you to the I-5 Mt. Ashland interchange.

SIDE TRIPS. To do this trip east to west, leave I-5 at Exit 6, the Mt. Ashland exit. Follow the frontage road (Highway 99) south for 1 mile, then turn right (west), onto Mt. Ashland Road (FR 20), following signs to the Ski Area.

For a real adventure, the Donomore Meadow Road (FR 2025) from Silver Fork Gap not only leads to Silver Fork Meadow and Donomore Meadow, it follows the crest of the Siskiyous to Alex Hole and Condrey Mountain (7,112 feet), both extremely scenic. The road crosses into California at mile 6. Dry Lake Lookout is also worth a visit.

FR 22 is paved, wonderfully scenic, and leads to the Wagner Butte Trail after 5 miles. Wagner Butte is 7,140 feet high and overlooks Medford and Ashland. The Wagner Butte Trail gives you an idea of what the experience of Mt. Ashland might be if there weren't a road to the top. FR 22 leads down Wagner Creek to the town of Talent.

The Mt. Ashland summit road is steep, very narrow, and a little precarious (especially if you drive a school bus full of college students up it, which I once did). There are several buildings at the top, plus a small, lakeless glacial cirque and lots of stunted, windswept (a condition called "krummholz") mountain hemlock.

Lower Deschutes River

LOCATION. North-central Oregon. North of Madras, southeast of The Dalles.

HIGHLIGHTS. Oregon's most wild and scenic river at its wildest and most scenic.

DIFFICULTY. Easy. Paved for the first 8 miles. Wide, gravel road for the last 17 miles.

DISTANCE. 25 miles from Maupin to the road end.

HIGH ELEVATION. 900 feet.

MAPS. Maupin; Sherars Bridge; Sinamox.

ADMINISTRATION. BLM Prineville District.

GETTING THERE. From Madras, go north on Highway 97 for 27 miles to Highway 197, then go left, northwest. In Maupin, the Lower Deschutes Scenic Byway takes off north, from the east side of the bridge over the Deschutes River. The sign says DESCHUTES RIVER RECREATION AREA. It's 1 block from the main highway to the beginning of the byway (which has a bunch of signs at the turnoff, none of which say anything about the Lower Deschutes River Road). At mile 8, go right (east) briefly on Highway 216 (toward Grass Valley), then hang a left (north) shortly after on gravel Deschutes River Access Road. Continue 17 more miles to the road end.

REST STOPS. There are campgrounds, picnic sites, outhouses, and boat launches every couple of miles.

SPECIAL INFORMATION. As this is the route to Oregon's most popular river rafting run, not too far from Portland, traffic can be heavy. Maupin, which since the creation of the National Wild and Scenic River has transformed from a sleepy little ranching town to a major recreation jumping-off point, can be a madhouse. The canyon can get hot in mid-summer.

THE DRIVE. The Deschutes experience begins 10 miles south of Maupin on Highway 197 (heading north), when the surface of the earth suddenly drops away and the vast, barren Deschutes River Valley is revealed from a hilltop aerie. The highway soon begins a long descent and, just when you think it can descend no further, it makes a number of final switchbacks before arriving at Maupin and the Deschutes River Bridge. Beyond the bridge, the road climbs and climbs and climbs.

This is a mighty popular place. When I visited, on the weekend before July 4, a never-ending parade of rafts made their way downriver, with a proportionate number of shuttle vehicles plying the paralleling road. I'm told the river run is fairly placid, with only a couple of Class II rapids (out of six increasingly difficult classes). So it's not like the Lower Illinois or the Rogue.

And there are prettier canyons to be found in Oregon. The Deschutes at Lake Billy Chinook, south of Madras, is one; Kiger

Gorge in the Steens is another; and of course there's Hells Canyon. However, the Lower Deschutes is undeniably beautiful. Both sides are lined with steep, grassy slopes and tan rimrock, with nary a tree anywhere. There is a railroad track on the bank opposite the road. Bring sunscreen.

The highlight of this trip comes when the road's initial 8 paved miles briefly join up with Highway 216 at Sherar's Falls, where the river compresses into an impressive rapid. Wooden scaffolds built alongside enable the local Native Americans to net the leaping salmon. Sherar's Falls divides the river in two river rafting areas. From Maupin to the falls is 10 miles. From the falls to the mouth is about 30 miles.

A couple of miles beyond Highway 216, the gravel road climbs a big hill that affords a fine panorama in both directions, with a railroad bridge below. After that, the route settles down and follows the shore, with turnouts every couple of miles. The route dead-ends at a gate 17 miles from Highway 216. To reach the Columbia, you must walk 13 miles. Or get yourself a raft (and a permit).

SIDE TRIPS. Another unpaved road runs upriver (south) from Maupin for about 8 miles. Heading north on Highway 197, the road takes off left (south) at a switchback 1 mile before the Maupin bridge. The road is not much different than the route described above, except it is a little narrower and not quite as busy.

At the Highway 216 junction, a 3-mile side trip (west) will take you out of the canyon to tiny White River Falls State Park. The waterfall is impressive, about 80 feet high, and it splits into several channels as it tumbles over the lava rimrock.

By all means, visit the mouth of the Deschutes. To get there, continue west on Highway 216 back to Highway 197, then head north 28 miles to I-84. Get on I-84 westbound at Exit 88, then get off again at Exit 97 and follow Highway 206 eastbound for 2 miles past the Deschutes mouth to Deschutes River State Recreation Area. In pioneer days, the Columbia Gorge was a major route of travel, and the wide Deschutes River presented a significant obstacle. According to an interpretive sign, wagons were floated across, livestock swam across, and the Native Americans ferried people in canoes in exchange for "brightly colored objects." A trailhead (Equestrian Trail), located at the recreation area's extreme south end, accesses the closed road paralleling the river.

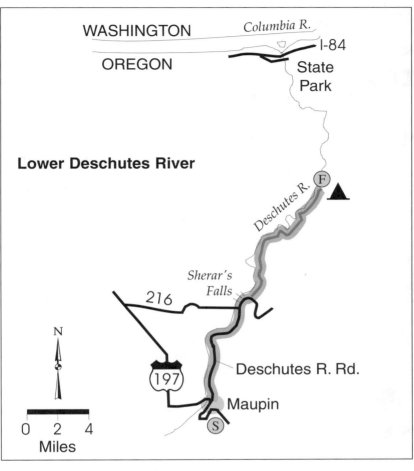

WASHINGTON   *Columbia R.*
                                    I-84
OREGON   State
                          Park

Lower Deschutes River

Deschutes R.   (F) ▲

Sherar's
Falls

216

N

197   Deschutes R. Rd.

0 2 4   Maupin
Miles   (S)

Rafters, Lower Deschutes Canyon

Stein's Pillar, Ochoco Crest

LOCATION. In the Ochoco Mountains east of Prineville, near the Mill Creek Wilderness.

HIGHLIGHTS. A 350-foot-tall rock spire and a beautiful drive along the crest of the Ochoco Mountains.

DIFFICULTY. Moderate. Most of the route is easy gravel or dirt, and portions are paved. Forest Road 3320 can get muddy and a portion of FR 27, near the drive's far end, is very narrow.

DISTANCE. 32.8 miles from Highway 26 back to Highway 26.

HIGH ELEVATION. 6,181 feet.

MAPS. Ochoco Reservoir; Wildcat Mountain; Salt Butte; Stephenson Mountain; Opal Mountain.

ADMINISTRATION. Ochoco National Forest.

GETTING THERE. From Prineville, take Highway 26 east for 8 miles to paved Mill Creek Road (which becomes FR 33), just past Ochoco Reservoir. Turn left (north), and proceed 16 miles, past the Brennan Palisades turnoff (where the pavement ends) and Stein's Pillar, to the hilltop junction with dirt FR 3320. Go right (northeast) on FR 3320. Proceed 4 miles to FR 27, which is one-lane blacktop, then go right (east) again. Three miles later, the pavement veers left while FR 27, mostly dirt, bears right. Take FR 27 (right) back to Highway 26, following the sign that says HIGHWAY 26—9.

REST STOPS. Ochoco Lake; Ochoco Divide.

SPECIAL INFORMATION. Easily done in the opposite direction.

THE DRIVE. Central Oregon's Ochoco Mountains are an ancient uplift with a volcanic overlay. They contain some of the state's oldest rock. The highest Ochoco peak is 6,926-foot Lookout Mountain, located 15 miles southeast of Stein's Pillar. The highest peak on the described loop route around the Mill Creek Wilderness is the 6,181-foot crest known only as View Point.

To reach Stein's Pillar, take Mill Creek Road, a pleasant route that leads to and encircles the 17,400-acre Mill Creek Wilderness, whose main feature is Twin Pillars. Mill Creek Road's lower portion features piney woods with flat pasture in the middle. The pavement ends at mile 5, at the Brennan Palisades turnoff.

To hike to the base of Stein's Pillar, take Spur 500 right, at mile 7, one mile before the pillar. Go 1 mile to the end and then follow the 1.5-mile trail. Stein's Pillar itself, a lava plug that was formerly the central conduit at the core of a now-defunct volcano, is passed at mile 8. Beyond that, the road follows Mill Creek for 3 more miles, to Wildcat Campground and the lower end of the Twin Pillars Trail.

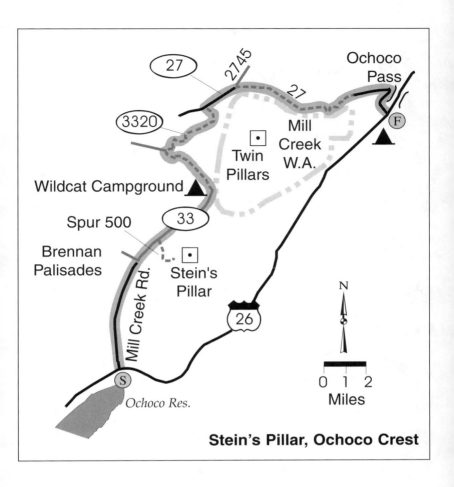

Stein's Pillar, Ochoco Crest

Above Wildcat Campground, the road leaves the creek and begins seriously climbing and twisting, eventually meeting FR 3320 at the hilltop. FR 3320, somewhat poorer in quality, also climbs and curves, through a large burn area with many seedling plantations, before meeting paved FR 27, whose blacktop ends 3 miles later at the junction with FR 2745.

The 9.8-mile dirt road along the Ochoco crest offers many views in both directions. Early on, you will pass the upper trailhead for the Twin Pillars Trail. The road then goes by a series of lovely hilltop meadows that alternate with forests of pine, Douglas-fir, noble fir, and some larch. A short spur road right (south) at the crest (mile 5 of 9), leads to the View Point, which offers a vista south down Mill Creek into the Mill Creek Wilderness, and north into the vast central Oregon rimrock and lava plateau country.

Beyond the crest, the road becomes very narrow for a while but then widens and picks up pavement for the last 3 miles before meeting Highway 26 at the Ochoco Divide (4,720 feet). There's a campground at the pass and a rest area 1 mile south on Highway 26.

SIDE TRIPS. To view the palisades, go left on FR 3370 from Mill Creek Road, then right, then left. It's 1.5 miles to the Brennan Palisades, with no signs other than the one at the turnoff. The palisades are a series of tan lava bluffs. The Painted Hills Unit of John Day Fossil Beds National Monument is located 15 miles north of the Ochoco Divide on Highway 26, or 3 miles before the town of Mitchell. The Painted Hills, a series of multi-hued volcanic ash and mud outcrops, should not be missed. They boast some lovely short trails and a fantastic overlook.

Painted Hills, near Ochoco Mountains

Clarno Palisades, John Day Fossil Beds National Monument (Drive 54)

John Day River, Fossil Beds

LOCATION. North-central Oregon, near Fossil.

HIGHLIGHTS. A short but interesting drive along the Wild and Scenic John Day River. Outstanding side trips.

DIFFICULTY. Moderate. Slow, narrow, bumpy, and muddy, with a few large whoopsies (large depressions). Mostly level, though.

DISTANCE. 4 miles from Highway 218 to the gate.

HIGH ELEVATION. 2,200 feet.

MAP. Clarno.

ADMINISTRATION. State and private.

GETTING THERE. From Highway 97 at Shaniko, north of Madras 50 miles, turn right (east) onto Highway 218, toward Antelope. It's 12 miles to Antelope and 15 miles from Antelope east to the Clarno bridge over the John Day River. Near an abandoned house on the west end of the bridge, take the turnoff to the unpaved road (there is no sign). Follow the dirt road north (left) 4 miles to the gate.

REST STOPS. Clarno State Wayside; Clarno Unit of John Day Fossil Beds National Monument; Fossil.

THE DRIVE. This cute little fellow is only 4 miles long and will probably take no longer than 20 to 30 minutes, but it's a nice diversion when combined with a tour of the John Day Fossil Beds. The sometimes-muddy route, with a grass center strip, winds slowly around hay fields, meets the river, then winds around more hay fields. The canyon is very wide here, with a series of rimrock hills far in the distance on either side.

After 3.5 miles, the road cuts across one of those colorful ash and mud formations like those at Painted Hills (see Drive 53), except this one is mostly white, with a little pink. The road is much fun here, with lots of bounces. Beyond the mud outcrop, the road crosses some sagebrush hills above the river before deadending at a gate. There, you must turn around and go back.

SIDE TRIPS. The Clarno Unit of John Day Fossil Beds is 2 miles east of the Clarno bridge on Highway 218. The unit consists of a row of tan palisades along the road. According to the interpretive sign, the palisades are made of compacted volcanic mud and ash that inundated the forest here 45 million years ago and preserved tree leaves, trunks, and small animals.

Fossil, population 500, located 20 miles east of the Clarno Bridge on Highway 218, is Oregon's second smallest county seat (Gilliam County). The smallest is Moro, population 250, seat of Sherman County, which abuts Wheeler County to the northeast. This is a region of many more cows than humans.

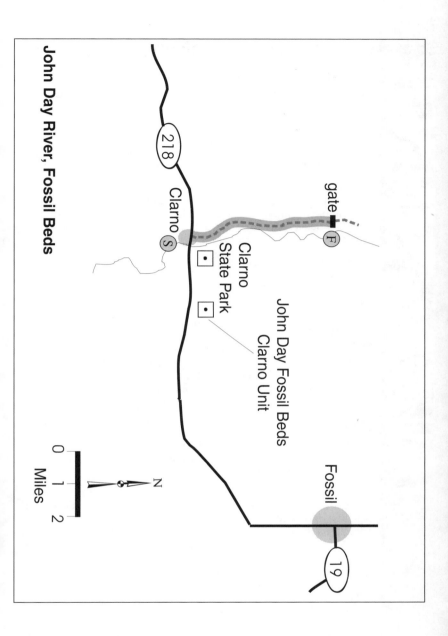

John Day River, Fossil Beds

Lower Imnaha Canyon

LOCATION. Extreme northeast corner of Oregon, on the Snake River near the Idaho line.

HIGHLIGHTS. A remote and spectacular road to the bottom of Hells Canyon, the deepest canyon in North America. Incredible side canyons tower above the Wild and Scenic Imnaha River and adjacent creeks. A true adventure and the best drive in this book.

DIFFICULTY. Moderate to difficult. Narrow, long, extremely curvy dirt road with some very steep and rather rough sections. A sign at the beginning of the drive claims that you need high clearance, which you do not (except in spring when creeks run across the road). The road is paved for 6 miles and dirt for 24 miles.

DISTANCE. 30 miles from Imnaha to Dug Bar.

HIGH ELEVATION. 2,500 feet.

MAPS. Imnaha; Haas Hollow; Cactus Mountain.

ADMINISTRATION. BLM Vale District.

GETTING THERE. From Highway 82 in the middle of Joseph, southeast of the larger town of Enterprise, follow paved Little Sheep Creek Road left (east) toward Imnaha, 30 miles away. The Lower Imnaha Road begins in Imnaha and is well-signed. Go left (north). Follow the road for 30 miles to Dug Bar.

REST STOPS. Imnaha; Imnaha Crossing; Dug Bar.

SPECIAL INFORMATION. Watch out for river outfitter shuttle vehicles, the only traffic you're likely to encounter. There's a boat ramp at Dug Bar.

THE DRIVE. For years, I assumed that the two most noteworthy unpaved drives in Oregon were the Hat Point Road (see Drive 57) and the Steens Mountain Loop (see Drive 67). I was wrong. The winner is the drive down the Lower Imnaha River to the bottom of Hells Canyon. Not only does this road offer the most breathtaking scenery of any trip in this book, but the drive retains a sense of primitive adventure, whereas the Steens and Hat Point roads have been "upgraded" in recent years, so that while still unpaved and incredibly beautiful, they aren't very challenging. That is not the case here.

The journey begins innocently enough, following a regular old canyon with a few houses for 6 miles via a paved road. At a little tree-shaded house just beyond a bridge across the river the pavement ends and the road takes off rudely and bumpily up a steep hill. It climbs to a vista point at the boundary of the national recreation area, with a view back down to the river. When I visited in July of a very dry year, I noted several arid waterfalls that would surely be impressive during the wet season.

After contouring across steep, grassy hillsides for 4 miles, the route drops back down to the water's edge, with its cottonwoods and brush, and remains there for the next 10 miles. At mile 16, the

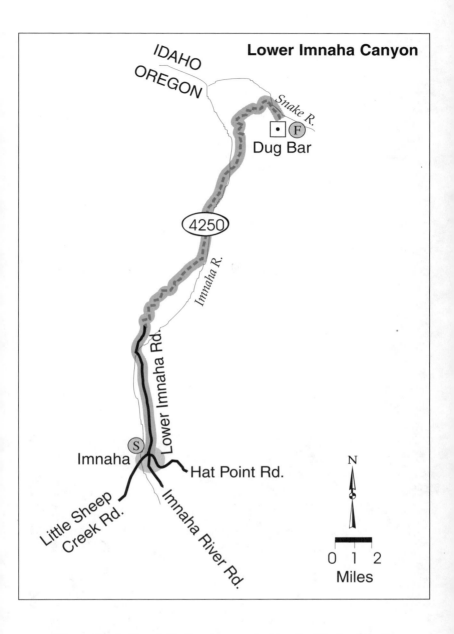

Lower Imnaha Canyon

Thorn Creek Guard Station is passed. At mile 19, the Imnaha River is crossed a second time. There is a pit toilet at this second bridge.

Shortly beyond the bridge, the drive gets very interesting (if it wasn't already). There's not enough room in the canyon for a road to the mouth of the Imnaha River, which squeezes through a very narrow rock cleft. Instead, you climb 1,000 feet, cross a grassy ridge, and drop down the other side. It is the 6-mile climb up, looking back on the Imnaha Canyon and a row of side canyons, that offers what may be the most incredible scenery this writer has ever seen. You see what looks like giant inverted sailboats. There are at least three: barren, eroded rock ridges made of bedded lava flows. The ridges flare out toward the bottom, then narrow to a jutting "keel" as they rise. Except these keels are 2,500 feet high!

At mile 24, you cross the ridge and begin the slow, multi-switchback drop down to the river. And yes, the walls of Hells Canyon are very impressive, with their approximately 3,500-foot rise (they're not that high here). They aren't inverted sailboats but they are impressive. The part of Hells Canyon that is over 7,000 feet deep, immediately below Hat Point, lies 35 miles upstream.

Eventually, Dug Bar appears in the distance. After going through an unlocked gate, then another gate, you will be there, at the little Dug Bar boat launch. The only shelter from the intense dry-season heat is a large cottonwood tree. I'm told the people who live in the two houses are river outfitters. I'm also told that fishing in the river is mostly for warm-water fish, catfish and bass.

Chief Joseph and his Nez Perce followers camped at Dug Bar in 1877 during their attempted flight to Canada with the U.S. Army in pursuit. They crossed the Snake not far away.

SIDE TRIPS. See Drives 57 and 58, which also begin at Imnaha.

Lower Imnaha River Road

Lostine River, Eagle Cap

LOCATION. Extreme northeast Oregon, in the Wallowa Mountains, south of Enterprise.

HIGHLIGHTS. A gorgeous drive along a National Wild and Scenic River, with a view of the dominant peak in the Eagle Cap Wilderness, Eagle Cap.

DIFFICULTY. The road is paved at first, then wide gravel, then narrow gravel, but it is all easy and level. Can be heavily trafficked in summer.

DISTANCE. 18 miles from Highway 82 to the road end.

HIGH ELEVATION. 6,000 feet.

MAPS. Lostine; North Minam Meadows.

ADMINISTRATION. Wallowa-Whitman National Forest.

GETTING THERE. From LaGrande, take Highway 82 northeast into the Wallowa Valley for 55 miles to the town of Lostine, between Wallowa and Enterprise. Turn right (south) onto the Lostine River Road (which becomes Forest Road 8210). It's 18 miles to the road end at the Wilderness boundary.

REST STOPS. There are nine campgrounds on Lostine River Road.

THE DRIVE. The Wallowa Mountains have been called the "Alps of North America." With their jagged, nearly vertical granite ridges, they are the kind of mountains you see in fanciful landscape paintings but rarely in real life. They are also the only Rocky Mountains range in Oregon, which explains why the Wallowa Valley is the state's only area containing Rocky Mountain juniper instead of western juniper. The only auto route that deeply penetrates the Wallowas is the Lostine River Road, with the Wilderness boundary paralleling both sides of the road for the last 7 miles.

Autumn is an excellent time to visit by car, when the crowds are gone and the larch trees are in color. Larches are members of the pine family, and their needles turn orange and drop off in fall. The trees are scattered throughout the northern Rockies and northern Cascades but are usually not noticed except in fall and spring. They seem to be most abundant, and grow the largest, in the mountains of northeast Oregon. They have a distinctive cinnamon-colored bark in northeast Oregon, which is not the case elsewhere. Quaking aspen and bigleaf maple also put on an outstanding autumn show in the Wallowas.

Lostine River Road begins on the wide Wallowa River Plain, with the mountains abruptly rising to the south. Ten thousand years ago, four immense, north-flowing glaciers oozed out onto the plain. The largest glacier formed Wallowa Lake. The longest glacier carved the Lostine River Canyon. Approaching the national forest boundary before entering the canyon on Lostine River Road, look for an outwash plain coming out of the canyon mouth, and an immense lateral moraine (gravel pile) left by the retreating glacier. The moraine, on the east side of the outwash plain, is seen as a long, narrow row of hills parallel to but away from the river.

Throughout most of the canyon, the terrain immediately adjacent to the river is rather gentle, since the valley bottom was widened and flattened by the glacier (although the canyon around Pole Bridge is narrow and dramatic). Not far away from the level valley bottom, huge, glacially-smoothed rock walls shoot skyward. Trails out of the Lostine Canyon are extremely steep, with multiple switchbacks. Once out of the canyon, they level off as they visit high meadows, exquisite alpine lakes, and some of the world's best scenery.

While you can catch a glimpse of Eagle Cap, framed by the Lostine Canyon, as you approach the town of Lostine on Highway 82, the knockout view of Eagle Cap turns up at mile 15 on Lostine River Road (the road ends at mile 18). Eagle Cap, at 9,595 feet, is not the highest peak in the Eagle Cap Wilderness. Three are higher, including Matterhorn Peak at 9,832. But Eagle Cap is the hub from which the major ridges of the Wallowa Mountains all radiate.

The river continues for 5 miles beyond the road end, to Upper Lake at the beginning of the Wallowa's largest cluster of cirque lakes, north and east of Eagle Cap. Hiking trails from the road end will take you there.

SIDE TRIPS. For an abbreviated version, over a somewhat poorer road, of the Lostine River drive, Hurricane Creek is great fun. In Enterprise, take Hurricane Creek Road right (south), which becomes FR 8205. It's 5 miles to the beginning of the canyon and 4 miles up the canyon to the road end.

Wallowa Lake, of course, is the area's automobile highlight and should not be missed. Take Highway 82 through Joseph to Wallowa Lake State Park, at the lake's far end. The Mt. Howard tramway, near the state park, operates in summer and winter but not in spring or fall. There are many other points of interest in the

High Wallowas, Lostine Canyon, Wallowa Valley

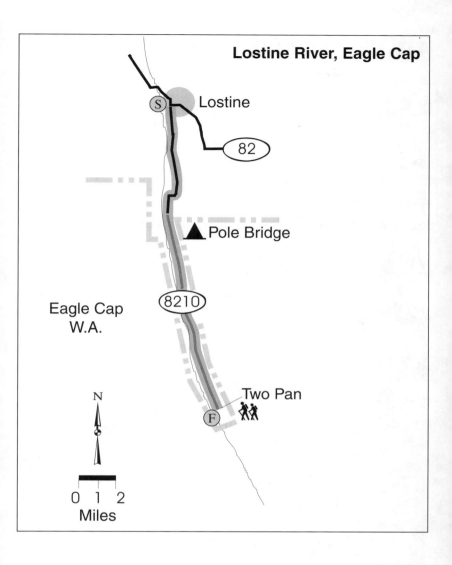

Lostine River, Eagle Cap

Lostine

82

▲ Pole Bridge

8210

Eagle Cap
W.A.

Two Pan

N

0 1 2
Miles

area, including the downtown Joseph historic district and the Chief Joseph Cemetery Historical Monument. Chief Joseph was the gallant and eloquent Nez Perce leader who attempted to lead his people to Canada in 1877 but was thwarted by the U.S. Army. He is buried at Wallowa Lake. (See also Drive 55.)

USELESS TRIVIUM. "Wallowa" and "Walla Walla" are actually the same Native American word, which means "many rivers."

Hat Point, Hells Canyon

LOCATION. Extreme northeast corner of Oregon.

HIGHLIGHTS. The only auto-accessible vista into the deepest part of Hells Canyon, North America's deepest river gorge.

DIFFICULTY. Easy (but see Special Information). Lots of traffic in summer.

HIGH ELEVATION. 6,982 feet.

MAPS. Imnaha; Hat Point.

DISTANCE. 24 miles from Imnaha to Hat Point.

ADMINISTRATION. BLM Vale District.

GETTING THERE. From Highway 82 in the middle of Joseph, southeast of the larger town of Enterprise, follow paved Little Sheep Creek Road left (east), toward Imnaha, 30 miles away. Hat Point Road (Forest Road 4240, also called Grizzly Ridge Road) begins in Imnaha and is well-signed. Drive on FR 4240 for 22.5 miles to the Memaloose Forest Service station and landing strip. Turn right at Memaloose, onto Spur 315, and proceed 1.5 more miles to the Hat Point parking area.

REST STOPS. There are five established vista points on Hat Point Road, including Hat Point, plus two campgrounds near the end.

SPECIAL INFORMATION. For decades, Hat Point Road was reputed to be one of Oregon's most difficult, axle-eating drives. Even before 1994–95, however, when the road was greatly improved, it wasn't nearly as bad as its reputation. When I drove it in 1987, it was relatively tame, except for one short stretch near the beginning. In 1996, it was all easy. Nevertheless, dire warnings about what an awful, terrifying drive it is continue to sully the road's reputation.

THE DRIVE. Every leg of this journey is more mind-boggling than the last, beginning with the Grande Rhonde and Wallowa valleys. The drive from Joseph along Little Sheep Creek, with its towering brown mesas, is outstanding. And the 24-mile Hat Point Road ranks among the most breathtaking anywhere.

For the first 18 miles, travelers on the one-lane gravel Hat Point Road are treated to frequent turnouts with ever-improving views of the Imnaha River Canyon. Look for brown mesas and rimrock in the canyon, with the high Wallowas rising across the canyon to the southwest.

At mile 18, the road reaches the top of a level mesa and begins a gradual 180-degree turn. For the final 6 miles, the route follows a ridgetop that peers into Hells Canyon on the Snake River. It's a 1-mile elevation drop from Hat Point to the Snake River (a 5,582-foot drop, actually, from 6,982 feet at the rim, down to about 1,400 feet—deeper than Arizona's Grand Canyon). On the Idaho side, Hells Canyon plunges to the Snake River from He Devil

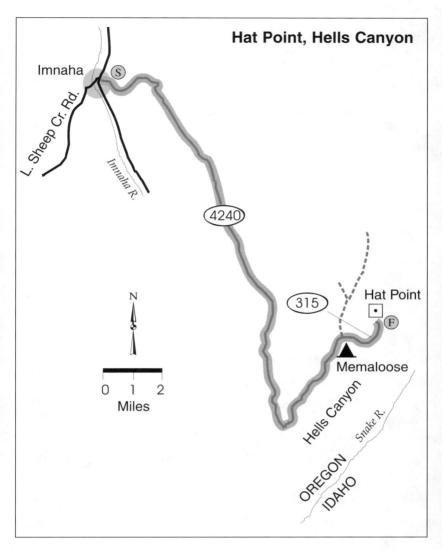

Hat Point, Hells Canyon

Imnaha

L. Sheep Cr. Rd.

Imnaha R.

(S)

4240

315

Hat Point

(F)

Memaloose

Hells Canyon

Snake R.

OREGON

IDAHO

N

0   1   2
Miles

Peak (9,393 feet) in the Seven Devils Mountains, for a drop of nearly 8,000 feet.

The Snake River Canyon is not nearly as extensive as the Grand Canyon, and it lacks the colorful rock formations and grand mesas. Looking down from Hat Point, in fact, it may be difficult to grasp how truly deep the canyon is, although it is definitely a world-class vista. If you have any doubts about its depth, try hiking the trail from Hat Point to the river. And if you still have doubts, try hiking back up.

Most of the forests on the ridgetop were burned in a series of fires between 1987 and 1995. What forests remain consist of small, upper-elevation conifers such as subalpine fir and mountain hemlock. They contrast sharply with the grassland and cottonwoods at Imnaha.

At mile 22, you arrive at the Memaloose Forest Service station. Go straight on FR 4240 to explore the ridgetop for 5 more miles and access a number of trailheads at the edge of the Hells Canyon Wilderness. Turn right at Memaloose for the Hat Point area, which is highly developed, with vista points, interpretive signs, and much parking. The lookout tower is not open to the public. (An oft-repeated story explains that Hat Point was named when an early visitor, on horseback, had his hat blow off into the canyon. That's what happens when you wear wide-brimmed cowboy hats.)

SIDE TRIPS. FR 4240 beyond Memaloose is discussed above. The dirt road is poorer in quality (a little bumpy) than the road leading to Memaloose. If the Hat Point Road is snowed over, the Lower Imnaha River Road makes an awfully scenic alternative. See Drive 55.

Hells Canyon Overlook, Upper Imnaha Road

Imnaha River Road

LOCATION. Extreme northeast corner of Oregon.

HIGHLIGHTS. Wild and Scenic Imnaha River upstream from the town of Imnaha. Hells Canyon overlook.

DIFFICULTY. Easy, level gravel for 30 miles, then paved.

DISTANCE. 65 miles from Imnaha to Halfway.

HIGH ELEVATION. 4,400 feet.

MAPS. Imnaha; Sheep Creek Divide; Jaynes Ridge; Puderbaugh Ridge; Duck Creek; McLain Gulch; Halfway.

ADMINISTRATION. Wallowa-Whitman National Forest.

GETTING THERE. From Highway 82 in the middle of Joseph, southeast of the larger town of Enterprise, follow paved Little Sheep Creek Road left (east) toward Imnaha, 30 miles away. The Imnaha River Road begins in the town of Imnaha. Go right (south), where the sign says HALFWAY—64. Proceed for 30 miles on the gravel to paved Forest Road 39 and turn left, again towards Halfway, now 35 miles away. Twenty-five miles further on, you'll hit Highway 86, where you turn right and continue for a final 10 miles to Halfway. Highway 86 ends up in Baker City on I-84, 50 miles past Halfway.

REST STOPS. Imnaha; a couple of campgrounds on FR 39; Hells Canyon Overlook; Halfway.

SPECIAL INFORMATION. A sign at its beginning warns that the road is rough and unpaved for 26 miles. It is actually unpaved for 30 miles, but the only roughness is occasional washboarding. The first road sign confirming that you're on the Imnaha River Road comes at mile 24. This trip is just as easily driven in the opposite direction.

THE DRIVE. This is the third of three backcountry drives that begin in the town of Imnaha, in the Hells Canyon country in Oregon's extreme northeast corner (see also Drives 55 and 57). It's the longest of the three routes and the only through road. The charming little town of Halfway, 66 miles from Imnaha, is well worth visiting.

The upper Imnaha River canyon isn't nearly as spectacular as the drive from Imnaha to the Snake River, on the Lower Imnaha River Road (but then, nothing is as spectacular as that). And it isn't as impressive as the view of the upper Imnaha canyon from Hat Point Road. It is impressive, though. For the most part, the valley is rather wide, with much adjacent flat land, hay fields, and occasional ranches. The first few miles offer outstanding views of Grizzly Ridge, immediately east. That's the ridge that contains Hat Point, with the deepest part of Hells Canyon, North America's deepest river gorge, on the other side.

Eventually, Grizzly Ridge fades away and you're left with a regular old canyon. At mile 15, the canyon narrows for a couple

NORTHEAST OREGON

of miles and gets quite pretty. There are at least three bridges across the medium-sized river (or large creek) during the 30 miles of unpaved road.

At mile 30, you hit pavement at FR 39 and leave the Imnaha River behind. The river cuts west here, into the high Wallowas, while you continue south. Six miles later, you arrive at the turnoff, on the left, for the Hells Canyon Overlook. (See Side Trips. Do not overlook this attraction.) Past the Overlook turnoff, the roads wind through woods and farmland for 30 more miles.

The town of Halfway (which is considering a legal name change to "Half.com"), is adorable, with lots of quaint little home-grown tourist shops, much like Joseph. The best part is the beautiful green valley with the high Wallowas rising abruptly to the north. The main peak is Red Mountain, which is in fact red, with the more typical white granite peaks behind it and to the right. Halfway is not quite on the 45th parallel, half way between the Equator and the North Pole. It's close, though. It's also almost (but not quite) half way between Baker City and Joseph.

SIDE TRIPS. The Hells Canyon Overlook is a 3-mile side trip on a paved road to a national recreation area interpretive site. The canyon is "only" 4,000 feet deep here, compared to 7,000 feet 30 miles down river, below Hat Point. The overlook is well upriver from Hells Canyon Dam but you can't see the river or the reservoir. However, the contrast between the gentle forests you've been driving through and the world suddenly breaking away to this immense, jumbled, barren landscape is startling and impressive.

Upper Imnaha Canyon

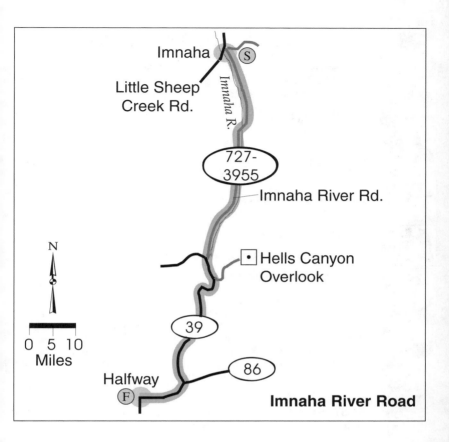

Imnaha

Little Sheep
Creek Rd.

Imnaha R.

727-3955

Imnaha River Rd.

Hells Canyon
Overlook

N

0 5 10
Miles

39

86

Halfway

Imnaha River Road

Snake River Road

LOCATION. Northeast Oregon, on the Snake River along the Idaho line, between Baker City and Ontario.

HIGHLIGHTS. Intimate access to the Snake River above Hells Canyon Dam. Impressive canyon, seen mostly from water level, with an outstanding overlook near the beginning.

DIFFICULTY. Easy, wide gravel. A little curvy. Washboarded in spots. Can be a little trafficky and therefore dusty.

DISTANCE. 48 miles from Richland to the Farewell Bend entrance to I-84.

HIGH ELEVATION. 3,200 feet.

MAPS. Sturgill Creek; Connor Creek; Olds Ferry NW; Olds Ferry.

ADMINISTRATION. BLM Vale District.

GETTING THERE. First get to Richland. The fun way to accomplish this is to come from Halfway, which means you've just been either to Hells Canyon Dam in Idaho or Oregon's Wallowa Valley via a long, circuitous road. From I-84 at Baker City, it's 38 miles to Richland via Highway 86. Once in Richland, turn right (south) where the sign says HUNTINGTON—42. In Huntington, it's 6 more miles to the southbound I-84 entrance, at Farewell Bend.

REST STOPS. Richland; many campsites and boat launches along the river; Huntington; Farewell Bend.

SPECIAL INFORMATION. Richland to Huntington is the preferred direction for this trip because of the dramatic drop into the Snake River Canyon after climbing the hills from the farmland south of Richland.

THE DRIVE. This trip visits the Brownlee Reservoir on the Snake River above Hells Canyon Dam and Brownlee Dam. It does not visit the free-flowing river and definitely does not visit the part of Hells Canyon that is over 7,000 feet deep. But the drive does offer 28 miles of uninterrupted, intimate contact, at water level, along the bottom of an impressive gorge, with the Oregon–Idaho line running up the middle.

From Richland, the road lights out across patchwork farms, past a backwater of Brownlee Reservoir, and up into the grass- and sagebrush-covered hills. The Wallowa Mountains can be seen rising to the north. The pavement ends after 4 miles.

Following many twists and turns, the road crests at an impressive vista, then begins a long descent to water level. The next 28 miles are fairly uniform, with steep canyon walls dropping abruptly down to the river on both sides and the road literally gouged into the rock. There are many lovely vistas up river and down river. The route passes occasional houses and small side canyons. This is a popular fishing area, mostly for catfish and bass.

NORTHEAST OREGON

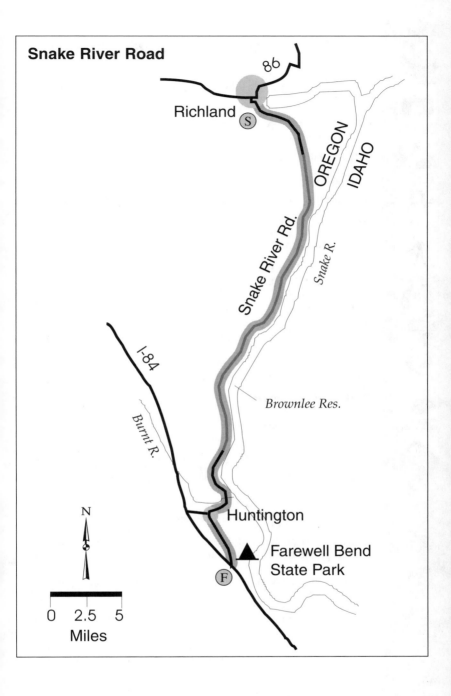

Snake River Road

Richland

86

OREGON

IDAHO

Snake River Rd.

Snake R.

I-84

Brownlee Res.

Burnt R.

N

Huntington

Farewell Bend
State Park

0   2.5   5
Miles

After 36 miles, the pavement begins again. Two miles later, at a railroad bridge, the road cuts inland (west), away from the river and uphill, arriving at Huntington 6 miles later, following a rather dramatic descent.

South Fork John Day River

LOCATION. The absolute dead center of Oregon, east of Prineville.

HIGHLIGHTS. A pleasant backcountry drive along a Wild and Scenic River canyon, truly emerging in the middle of nowhere.

DIFFICULTY. Easy, wide gravel road.

DISTANCE. 31 miles from Dayville to County Road 63.

HIGH ELEVATION. 3,400 feet.

MAPS. Dayville; Aldrich Gulch; Supplee Butte; Izee.

ADMINISTRATION. BLM Prineville District.

GETTING THERE. On Highway 26 from Dayville, between Fossil and John Day, go south on County Road 42 (South Fork Road), following signs to CR 63 (shown on the Ochoco National Forest map as CR 67) toward Izee. Turn right (west) after 31 miles, when you hit the pavement at CR 63 and proceed for 90 miles through Paulina to Prineville.

REST STOPS. Dayville; Paulina.

SPECIAL INFORMATION. Either direction works fine.

THE DRIVE. This is an easy and charming little drive that will get you off the highway and away from traffic after you've toured the John Day Fossil Beds and are seeking an alternate route back to the Prineville and Bend area. It's a Wild and Scenic River but it's a very gentle wildness, if you can picture such a thing. The little canyon is quite pretty, rising above hayfields and a small, kind of brushy river. Go left at the fork at mile 9, toward Izee. You can go right, but the road dead-ends after 1 mile.

At mile 10, the canyon narrows considerably and ponderosa pines begin to show up. The highlight is the main trailhead for the Black Canyon Wilderness Area (13,400 acres) at mile 12. Black Canyon is exquisite, with black rock cliffs on either side and big fat red ponderosa pines shading the trail. The pine scent is heavenly.

The canyon widens out again at mile 18 but remains piney. At mile 25, you pass the junction with FR 58 (on the right or west), which also leads to Paulina. (According to the map, FR 58 is an extreme "longcut" to Paulina and you're better off continuing on South Fork Road to CR 63.) South Fork Falls turn up 1 mile beyond the FR 58 junction. The pretty, braided waterfall, about 30 feet high, spills through a narrow, brushy gorge. There are no good photo spots.

The junction with paved Highway 63 ranks among the loneliest places in Oregon. There are no signs whatsoever, but logic dictates that you go right (west). If you do, you'll end up in Paulina, then Prineville after crossing 90 miles of ranch and range land.

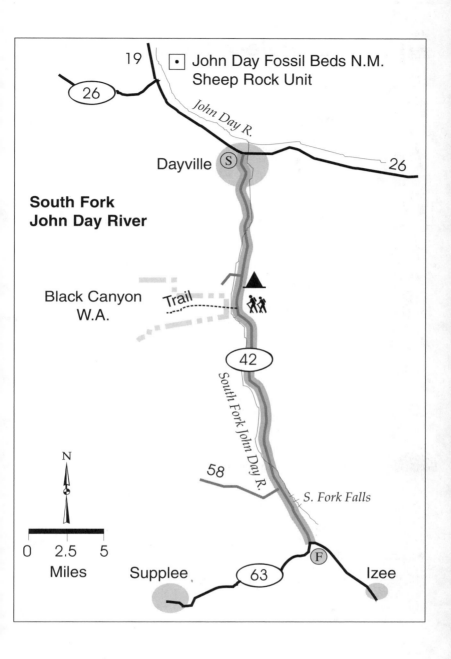

19

□ John Day Fossil Beds N.M.
Sheep Rock Unit

26

John Day R.

Dayville Ⓢ

26

**South Fork
John Day River**

**Black Canyon
W.A.**

Trail

42

South Fork John Day R.

N

0   2.5   5
Miles

58

S. Fork Falls

Ⓕ

Supplee

63

Izee

SIDE TRIPS. The Sheep Rock Unit of John Day Fossil Beds National Monument (the monument's largest unit) is located 7 miles west of Dayville, at the junction of Highway 19 and Highway 26. The canyon of the John Day River on Highway 19 is impressive, with towering Sheep Rock being the most out-standing formation. Turnouts explore some of the ash and mud fossil beds. An old ranch house serves as a fantastic visitor center.

Hole-in-the-Ground

LOCATION. Central Oregon, in the lava country southeast of Bend.

HIGHLIGHTS. A great big volcanic crater. In fact, two of them.

DIFFICULTY. Easy. The road from Highway 31 is wide and gravel, except for the last few hundred feet to the overlook. The road back out to Highway 31 is narrow and incredibly dusty, with one steep spot. See Side Trips for something a little more challenging.

DISTANCE. 4.1 miles from Highway 31 to Hole-in-the-Ground.

HIGH ELEVATION. 4,700 feet.

MAP. Hole-in-the-Ground.

ADMINISTRATION. Deschutes National Forest.

GETTING THERE. From Bend, take Highway 97 south for 30 miles to LaPine. Two miles south of LaPine, turn left (east) onto Highway 31, toward Silver Lake. At mile 22, on Highway 31, turn left (north) onto Forest Road 3125, a wide gravel road with a sign that says HOLE-IN-THE-GROUND. After 3 miles, a gravel side road (FR 3130) takes off south (right). It's one more mile to the short Hole-in-the-Ground access spur on the left (0.1 mile long). FR 3130, now a narrow dusty dirt road, takes you back to Highway 31 in 3 miles (via FR 3145), emerging 1 mile before the Christmas Valley and Fort Rock turnoff.

REST STOP. Hole-in-the-Ground; Fort Rock.

SPECIAL INFORMATION. I included Big Hole as a Side Trip in this chapter rather than giving it its own chapter because it's very close by and because, although it is an interesting little drive, the actual crater is kind of indistinct.

THE DRIVE. Hole-in-the-Ground has a geological history identical to that of nearby Big Hole (see Side Trips). Although smaller than Big Hole (0.5 mile in diameter versus 1 mile), Hole-in-the-Ground is the more impressive because it is deeper and unforested (or much less forested). Both are formerly underwater volcanic craters (actually, collapsed lava domes or "maars"), plopped in the middle of a lodgepole pine area. They are both at a higher elevation than Christmas Valley proper, and both are on the sandy (or ashy) volcanic soil that lodgepole pine simply adores.

As you approach the rise of the Hole-in-the-Ground rim, the pines give way to juniper and sagebrush. You end up at a little overlook spot with a fascinating panorama of the crater, best described as a "big hole." There is a small lake on the bottom at certain times of year.

SIDE TRIPS. *To visit Big Hole:* Coming from LaPine on Highway 31, go to mile 19, which is 1.5 miles before the Hole-in-

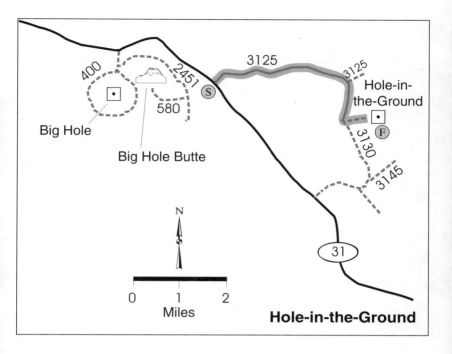

Hole-in-the-Ground

the-Ground turnoff. Look for a stop sign on the right (southwest). There are no signs at the Big Hole turnoff but you can see some of the bluffs just before it from Highway 31. Immediately after turning off the highway, you are faced with a three-way junction. Spur 400 is the 3-mile loop road around the crater, a narrow dirt route through a lodgepole pine forest. It's a fun, bouncy little primitive road but there's no place on it where you can see the entire crater, as you can at Hole-in-the-Ground. The road to the top of Big Hole Butte is FR 2541, on the left (east). The Forest Service map says "241," which is not correct.

The top of Big Hole Butte doesn't offer much more of a perspective on Big Hole than does the loop road. The view from the summit in the Big Hole direction (west) is obscured by trees and you can see only pieces of the crater. It's a terrific drive, though. To get to the summit, go left (east) on wide gravel FR 2451 for 2 miles to Spur 580, on the right (south). Spur 580 is narrow and steep with lots of bumps and dips. However, it's also fairly straight and soft and has a sort of "U"shaped profile, which keeps you on the road. Let's just say I enjoyed Spur 580.

The summit contains the pilings from an old lookout tower. While the view westward of Big Hole crater is disappointing, the view east is incredible. You can see, among other things, Christmas Valley and Fort Rock. And you can see Hole-in-the-Ground. At least I'm pretty sure it's Hole-in-the-Ground. It's a big crater located right where H-I-G is supposed to be, in a line between Big Hole Butte and Fort Rock, except the crater you see is full of trees. As I mentioned earlier, H-I-G is not full of trees (there are a few). I have no explanation for why H-I-G looks like it's full of trees when seen from Big Hole Butte.

While in the neighborhood: A rock shaped like a fort! What could have been better for the 19th century military types who once administered the region? Fort Rock is a collapsed dome of underwater pillow lava not unlike Hole-in-the-Ground and Big Hole, except it's higher and more fortress-like, with steeper sides, due to lakeshore erosion. To reach Fort Rock, turn off Highway 31 (left, or east, if coming from LaPine) onto Christmas Valley Road and proceed 7 miles to Fort Rock village. It's 2 miles left (north) from the village to Fort Rock proper, which can be seen for miles and miles (follow the signs if you must). If you drive up to the rock and walk around, it's even more fort-like, with high rock walls on three sides and a commanding view of the surrounding desert.

Fort Rock, near Hole-in-the-Ground

Crack-in-the-Ground

LOCATION. Southeast of Bend, north of the town of Christmas Valley.

HIGHLIGHTS. A remarkable 2-mile-long fissure in the central Oregon lava plateau. The road leads to a fire lookout.

DIFFICULTY. Easy, wide, mostly level, gravel road. Arrow-straight for the first 4 miles, then a little curvy.

DISTANCE. 14 miles from Christmas Valley Road to Green Mountain Lookout.

HIGH ELEVATION. 5,100 feet.

MAP. Crack-in-the-Ground.

ADMINISTRATION. Deschutes National Forest.

GETTING THERE. From Christmas Valley, head east for 1 mile on the main highway (Christmas Valley Road) to a gravel side road going north (left), with a BLM sign that says CRACK-IN-THE-GROUND—7.5. This is not the same road that heads north 2 miles east of town, which according to the official state highway map connects with Lost Forest Road. The Crack-in-the-Ground road is not shown on the official state highway map. It's 7.5 miles to Crack-in-the-Ground and 6.5 miles farther to Green Mountain Lookout.

REST STOPS. Christmas Valley; Crack-in-the-Ground; Green Mountain Lookout.

SPECIAL INFORMATION. A sign at the turnoff from Christmas Valley Road has a picture of a car (a big sort of low-rider from the 1960s) with a bar across it that says NOT RECOMMENDED. Cars aren't recommended? Maybe they mean two-wheel drive cars, or low-clearance cars. But this is a pretty good road. Maybe it applies to driving on the lower-quality side roads that riddle the area and can get very soft and sandy. If you stay on the main route, however, the only potential problem I see is that the road's lower portion can flood during the rainy season, requiring higher clearance. But the rainy season lasts about eight minutes a year in this arid region.

THE DRIVE. Crack-in-the-Ground is one of Oregon's most unusual geological features. To get there, follow the gravel road from Christmas Valley Road. The first 4 miles are arrow-straight and run alongside Christmas Lake, a big, usually dry alkali flat on the right. The straight part of the road also crosses some sage-brush-covered sand dunes, with much sand on the road.

Eventually, the road veers left and climbs the low lava hills and dunes, amid sagebrush and junipers, arriving at the little Crack-in-the-Ground parking area at mile 7.5. It's a 0.2-mile hike to the actual fissure, which averages 40 feet deep, 5 to 10 feet wide, and is a little over 2 miles long. There are trails along the bottom and along the rim. In summer, in the oppressive desert

SOUTHEAST OREGON

heat, the bottom trail is wonderful, almost magical. Since the entire region is underlain by lava flows, which frequently crack as they cool, and as the land slowly shifts, one wonders why there aren't more big cracks. But there apparently aren't.

Continue down the gravel road for 6 more miles to the Green Mountain Lookout (elevation 5,100 feet). You'll pass a lava field and a big volcanic cinder cone on the way. At Green Mountain, it's a short climb up wooden stairs to the lookout deck, from which you can seemingly see a million miles in every direction. Look for the sand dunes to the east, passed on the way to Lost Forest (Drive 63). They're especially obvious if it's windy and the sand is being whipped up.

SIDE TRIPS. While in the vicinity, the Lost Forest and sand dunes (Drive 63) should not be missed.

Crack-in-the-Ground

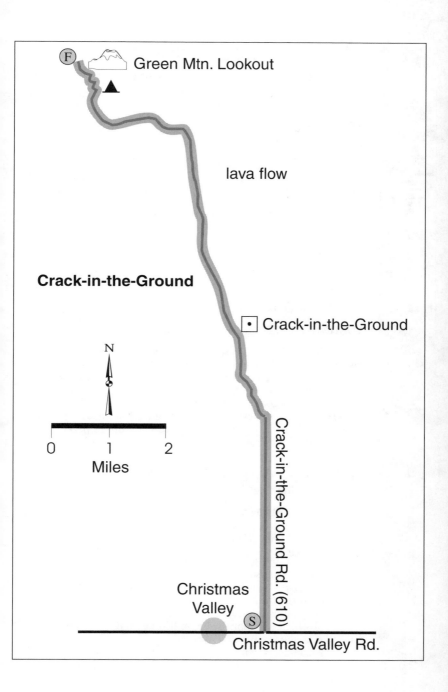

Lost Forest

LOCATION. Southeast of Bend, northeast of the town of Christmas Valley.

HIGHLIGHTS. An isolated ponderosa pine stand of great botanical interest. Some beautiful desert sand dunes.

DIFFICULTY. Easy level gravel road up to the dunes and Lost Forest. Once you arrive, the roads become moderate: narrow with lots of dips and a soft, sandy surface. These roads would be great fun for dune buggies, dirt bikes and 4WD vehicles, were it not for signs everywhere telling you to go slowly. It is very tempting, even for us respectful, cautious types.

DISTANCE. 16 miles from Christmas Valley Road to Lost Forest.

HIGH ELEVATION. 4,700 feet.

MAPS. Fossil Lake; Christmas Lake.

ADMINISTRATION: BLM Prineville District.

GETTING THERE. From the town of Christmas Valley, head east on the main highway, Christmas Valley Road, for 8 miles to a paved side road north (left), where a BLM sign says SAND DUNES—12, LOST FOREST—16 (Road 5-14-D). After 8 miles on 5-14-D, you come to an unmarked "T" junction. Go right (east) on the gravel. The dunes do indeed begin at mile 12 from the Christmas Valley Road turnoff, but the main dunes parking area lies 3 miles beyond, at mile 15, just before the Lost Forest parking area.

REST STOPS: Christmas Valley. Many people camp at Lost Forest but I didn't notice a restroom.

SPECIAL INFORMATION. A portion of the dunes have been set aside for dune buggies and dirt bikes. This is a pretty popular area in mid-summer. Many dune buggy people park at Lost Forest because the air isn't as gritty there from blowing sand.

THE DRIVE. The sand dunes come first on this short but fascinating trip. They can be seen in the distance, off to the right, almost from the turnoff from Christmas Valley Road to Road 5-14-D. Eight miles later, after you turn right onto the gravel, the sand dunes begin to loom large, still off to the right. Four miles after that, a sign warns that you are entering the dunes area and that the road may be a little rough (it isn't rough—at least not until you reach Lost Forest, 4 miles later). Most of the dunes near the road are covered with sagebrush, in contrast to the large naked sand hills off to the right.

At the sign announcing the beginning of the dunes area, the mysterious Lost Forest can be seen for the first time, dead ahead. The ponderosa pine forest clearly differs from the juniper forests surrounding it. According to a sign where you enter Lost Forest, the open, airy stand covers 8,960 acres and is the remnant of a

SOUTHEAST OREGON

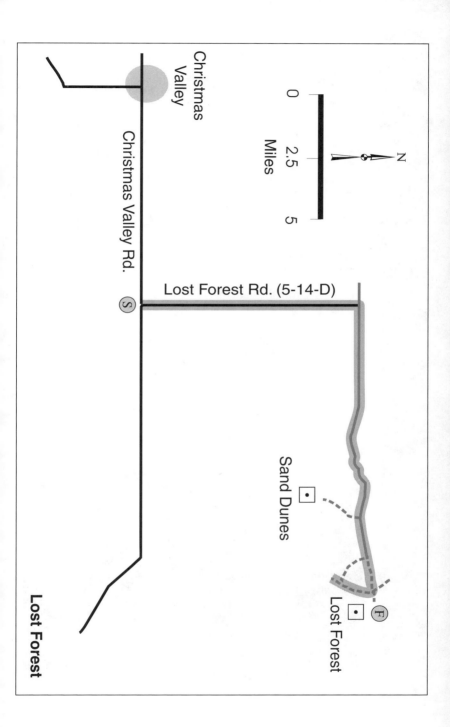

Lost Forest

much vaster ponderosa pine forest that once covered the entire valley before it became desert. The sign says that the nearest neighboring ponderosa pine forest is 40 miles away and that this isolated stand survives on much less annual rainfall than any other known ponderosa pine stand. Ponderosa pine, of course, is a fairly drought resistant and short lived species, albeit not as drought resistant as western juniper, which also occupies about half of this stand. And by the way, these are not the best looking ponderosa pines in the world. Most are quite small and many are dead or dying. Contrast them with the large, fat, straight, healthy ponderosa pines found on the Cascades' lower eastern slopes. A network of low-quality roads explores Lost Forest (go slowly).

Just before Lost Forest, a short side road left (south) leads to the parking area for the dune buggy area (go slowly again). It's an interesting road and parking lot, consisting entirely of sand with immense, gnarled junipers scattered about. The volcanic ash is much finer than beach sand, so the traction is better. But it also becomes airborne more easily than beach sand, which can be oppressive. To explore the barren dunes away from the dune buggy area, take the unmarked side road to the right, just past the ENTERING DUNES AREA sign. Drive as far as is reasonable, then get out and walk.

SIDE TRIP: While in the vicinity Crack-in-the-Ground and Green Mountain Lookout (Drive 62) should not be missed.

Dunes parking area

Abert Rim

LOCATION. South-central Oregon, north of Lakeview.

HIGHLIGHTS. The Abert Rim is supposedly the longest exposed normal geologic fault in North America, rising directly above Lake Abert, Oregon's third largest natural lake. A challenging 4WD route leads to the top.

DIFFICULTY. Difficult. There are no signs and there is a maze of primitive, bumpy dirt tracks with grass in the middle. The final "side road" to the rim overlook is barely a road at all.

DISTANCE. 9.75 miles from Highway 395 to the rim overlook.

HIGH ELEVATION. 5,800 feet.

MAPS. Coleman Hills; Commodore Ridge; Lake Abert North.

ADMINISTRATION. BLM Lakeview District.

GETTING THERE. From Lakeview, go north on Highway 395 for 55 miles to the turnoff right (east) to Plush. Another sign at the Plush turnoff says SUNSTONE AREA. After 4 miles on the gravel road to Plush, you'll come to a cattle grate, a small corral, and a couple side roads. You want the side road on the right (south) that begins just *before* the cattle grate. It's a little wider than the other side roads, with a bit of white gravel. This is theoretically the Mule Lake Road, but there are no signs. Follow this road for 5 miles, past the powerline (beyond which the road gets much worse). Continue to a little island of green, which may in fact be covered by a pond during rainy periods. Just before the green island (or pond), a narrow dirt track takes off right (west). It's 0.75 miles on this side road to the rim. You may have to stop and scout out this last segment, which gets very faint in spots, but it does lead to the rim.

REST STOPS. Lakeview.

SPECIAL INFORMATION. In addition to the described route, there is also a mostly gravel Fremont National Forest road leading to an official, designated vista point atop Abert Rim. This official route is 20 miles long, begins 50 miles from the lake, and leads to an area of the rim well south of Lake Abert. See Side Trips. The route described here gets you there in 10 miles, is a lot more fun, and emerges 1,500 feet directly above the lake.

THE DRIVE. I've read that the Abert Rim is the longest exposed "normal fault" (see below) in North America, being 30 miles long and rising 2,500 feet above Lake Abert. I'm not 100 percent convinced of this, though. The Chinese Wall in Montana's Bob Marshall Wilderness looked longer to me. I'm not convinced about the 2,500 feet, either. Still, the rim is awfully impressive, especially with the huge lake at the bottom. The rim's highest spot, it turns out, rises a few miles south of the lake, where a 600-foot vertical cliff drops down to a slope of debris, scree, and gravel. You see the entire rim from the bottom as you drive along Highway 395.

After you've explored the lakeshore from Highway 395, including the wildlife viewing turnout, continue beyond the lake to the Plush turnoff, which is atop a mountain pass. On the gravel road to Plush, be sure to drive a couple of miles beyond the unmarked Mule Lake Road junction, to the Plush Road summit. There you will be treated to an awesome panorama of the Warner Valley, with the Hart Mountain escarpment rising opposite (see Drive 65). The cluster of high peaks to the left (south) are the North Warner Mountains, whose Oregon segment rises to 8,400 feet at Drake's Peak. The South Warners, in California, top out at 9,800 feet (see Drive 66).

The geology confirms that this is basin-and-range country, formed by tension (pulling apart of the land) rather than compression (pushing together). Tension ranges and valleys are typically elongated and often run north–south, with major fault lines, like the Abert Rim, which defines the edge of the North Warner uplift, separating them. The Abert Rim is a "normal fault," typical of tension ranges, in which the high side of the fault does not overhang the low side, as opposed to a "thrust fault," where the high side does overhang the low side. The San Andreas Fault is a "slip fault," where the movement is mostly horizontal rather than vertical. The San Andreas Fault is over 1,000 miles long.

From the Plush Road, the Mule Lake Road goes over a hill and out onto a nearly flat, absolutely treeless expanse of sagebrush with continuing views of the North Warners and the Hart Mountain escarpment. The good news is that you can see for miles across the plateau top along which the road runs for miles so you don't need to worry about getting lost. The road is fairly rough to the powerline and a lot rougher beyond. But go slow and be careful in the rockiest spots and you should be fine. You'll pass what looks like a large crater 1 mile beyond the powerline.

The little side road to the rim, just before the "green-spot-sometimes-pond," is about 0.75 miles long and very faint. But the view at the end is fantastic. You come out directly above the lake's north end, with a terrific vista of the sand dunes and lake. This is one of the better places in the world.

SIDE TRIPS. According to the BLM map, Mule Lake Road leads to Mule Lake (about 2 acres) after 15 miles. I came to a major junction at mile 8 (no signs and the roads are not shown on the BLM map). My guess is that the right fork leads to another rim overlook and the left fork ends up at Mule Lake. Since I'd already found a good route to the rim, I didn't stop to explore every unmarked side road. (There were too many.)

Back on Highway 395 I passed a little side road at mile 82 that might also take you to the top of the rim. It's very steep and of even poorer quality than the Mule Lake Road. Check it out if you're feeling adventurous. Look for a large, unmarked gravel turnout on the east side of the highway, with a cow-path road taking off on the right, up a little canyon.

To visit the established Abert Rim View Point in Fremont National Forest, take Highway 395 north from Lakeview for 6 miles to the Highway 140 and Adel turnoff. At mile 8 on Highway 140, turn left (north) where the sign says MUD CREEK GUARD STA-

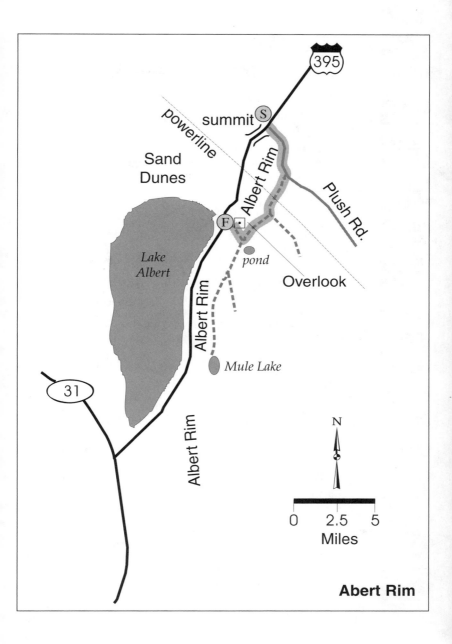

Abert Rim

TION. Follow this road (FR 3615) for 20 miles to a 0.5-mile dirt turnout, leading to the overlook on the left (west). FR 3615 and Fremont National Forest both end 1 mile past the view point turnoff. A couple of other side roads in the vicinity also access rim vista points. The highly scenic Plush Road is a marvelous way to combine this trip with Drives 65 and 66.

Hart Mountain
Antelope Refuge

LOCATION. In the desert mountains of south-central Oregon, east of Lakeview.

HIGHLIGHTS. Deer and antelope playing (but no buffalo roaming) on a desert plateau surrounded by high peaks, with a hot springs and a huge cliff that has an unbelievably beautiful chain of lakes along the base.

DIFFICULTY. Mostly easy, one-lane gravel road. The road up the escarpment to Refuge Headquarters is a little steep, and some of the side roads are fairly primitive.

DISTANCE. 27 miles from Plush to Refuge Headquarters.

HIGH ELEVATION. 6,000 feet.

MAPS. Plush; Hart Lake; Flagstaff Lake; Campbell Lake.

ADMINISTRATION. U.S. Fish and Wildlife Service and Hart Mountain National Antelope Refuge.

GETTING THERE. From Lakeview, take Highway 395 north for 5 miles to the junction with Highway 140, then go left (east) towards Adel. At mile 16 on Highway 140, in the Warner Canyon, turn left on the road to Plush and the Hart Mountain Refuge. It's 19 paved miles to Plush. From Plush, follow the signs, which take you through many turns, to the refuge, past Hart Lake, and along the base of the Warner Mountain escarpment. You run out of pavement after 14 miles, just before climbing the escarpment. Refuge Headquarters is at the top, 27 miles from Plush.

REST STOPS. Plush; Hart Lake Wildlife Viewing Area; Refuge Headquarters.

THE DRIVE. In this particular corner of Oregon, everything is named Warner. The drive on Highway 140 takes you through Warner Canyon in the Warner Mountains. You end up in the Warner Valley. And the highest point in the Hart Mountain refuge is not Hart Mountain but Warner Peak (8,017 feet). Warner Peak, however, is not in the Warner Mountains. This is all basin-and-range country, which means that the mountains were formed by the land pulling apart, as opposed to pushing together, as with the Siskiyous, or exploding, as with the Cascades. The results are long, narrow valleys alternating with long, narrow mountain ranges. The mountain ranges tend to have steep cliffs on both sides and fairly level, even tops.

Pronghorn antelope, the centerpiece of Hart Mountain refuge, require a lot of room so you're not likely to see more than three or four on any given trip. And you're just as likely to see them on the drive from Highway 140 to Plush as in the refuge, because the terrain, sage-brush desert, is identical. While not true antelopes,

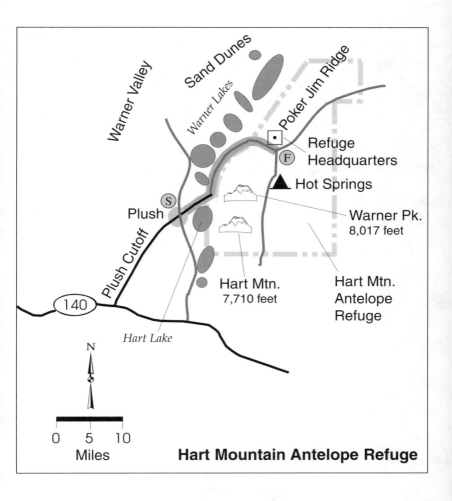

Hart Mountain Antelope Refuge

pronghorns may be North American's most beautiful large mammal.

The waterfowl viewing area, with a short trail, at Hart Lake, is also worth a stop.

Surprisingly, the most remarkable thing about this trip is not the pronghorns but the Warner Lakes, one of the most unusual and thrilling scenic wonders I have ever seen. Imagine: The state map of Oregon shows eleven large lakes lined up in the Warner Valley, along the base of the immense Hart Mountain (Poker Jim) escarpment. There are actually dozens of lakes, not just eleven, and at certain times of year there are hundreds, many with crescent or lunette shapes that reflect the contours of the intermingled sand dunes. The base of the escarpment reveals a dramatic rise, from 4,500 feet to 8,000 feet, up a barren rock face with many canyons cutting into the mountainside. They say you can sometimes see bighorn sheep high up in the crags.

By all means stop at Refuge Headquarters, on the desert plateau atop the escarpment, which has a small museum and some good information. Then you can either drive northeast, atop the plateau, in quest of mule deer and pronghorn, or you can head south and treat yourself to still more views of the magnificent desert mountains.

Hot Springs Campground lies 8 miles south of Refuge Headquarters, in the shadow of Warner Peak, near some aspen groves. The hot spring has a cinderblock wall around it. This is one of the most magically romantic spots one could hope for.

SIDE TRIPS. The refuge is full of side roads, all spectacular, many with views of the Steens (Drive 67) in the distance to the east. The narrow, primitive 10-mile road to Poker Jim Lake takes off just before Refuge Headquarters and is excellent for viewing mule deer. The road beyond Hot Springs Campground to Spanish Lake and Long Lake is scenic and challenging. If you turn left at Refuge Headquarters, it's 37 miles over the easy, mostly deserted gravel road to Road 205, 10 miles south of Frenchglen.

Hart Mountain escarpment

Surprise Valley

LOCATION. South-central Oregon, near Lakeview, including the extreme northeast corner of California along the Nevada line.

HIGHLIGHTS. This road explores the desert canyons, valleys, dry lakes, and foothills of the remote east side of the North Warner Mountains, dropping down to Upper Lake, Middle Alkalai Lake, and Lower Lake. Views of the 9,892-foot South Warners (Eagle Peak). Access to Nevada's Sheldon National Antelope Range.

DIFFICULTY. Easy, wide gravel road. Washboarded in spots.

DISTANCE. 33 miles from Adel to Fort Bidwell.

HIGH ELEVATION. 5,500 feet.

MAPS. Adel; May Lake.

ADMINISTRATION. BLM Lakeview District.

GETTING THERE. From Lakeview, head north on Highway 395. At mile 6, turn right (east) onto Highway 140, toward Adel and Denio. It's 28 miles from Lakeview to Adel. In Adel, turn right (south) on the road to Fort Bidwell, County Road 3-14, where the sign says FORT BIDWELL–35 (my odometer said 33).

REST STOPS. Adel; Fort Bidwell.

THE DRIVE. Like Oregon, California never seems to run out of scenic surprises. You have the High Sierra, with its string of 14,000-foot summits, forming the state's backbone. You have Mt. Shasta, a 14,000-foot volcano, standing guard over the state's far north. Tucked away west of Shasta, you have the Marble Mountains and Trinity Alps, two of the nation's largest, most rugged and most scenic wilderness areas. And down south, you have the desert mountain ranges, San Jacinto, and San Gorgonio, with peaks in excess of 10,000 feet.

Just when you're wondering how they can squeeze in all this magnificence, you learn about the Warner Mountains, in the remote Modoc region where hardly anyone lives and fewer visit. The Warners are a narrow, north–south range that, in California, parallels the Nevada line. They extend 60 miles south into California and 35 miles north into Oregon. The South Warners, south of Cedarville, California, reach a height of 9,892 feet. North of Cedarville, the North Warners rise to only 8,452 feet (Crane Mountain, in Oregon southwest of Adel).

Perhaps California's biggest scenic surprise is Surprise Valley, immediately east of the Warner Mountains. The Warners form a true rainshadow, blocking weather movement from the west. East of the Warners, you have desert. At the eastern base of the Warners, you have the towns and dry lakes of Surprise Valley. The towns are Fort Bidwell, Lake City, Cedarville, and Eagleville. Residents make their living by grazing cattle and growing irrigated hay. The towns all look eastward onto a string of three immense, usually dry lakes, Upper Lake, Middle Alkali Lake, and

Lower Lake. Middle Alkali, the lowest of the three, is alkaline in this internally-drained Great Basin valley. The other two lakes are not alkaline. East of the lakes lie a series of desert hills, much of which are encompassed by the Sheldon National Antelope Range.

To reach the Surprise Valley from Oregon, take the road south from Adel. The first 8 miles are paved, then the route goes to gravel as it winds into and over a narrow rock canyon with a pretty creek at the bottom. Crossing the state line at mile 18, the road drops down into the valley of Cowhead Lake, which is mostly hayfields. After that, it's up and over more hills, then down into the valley of Upper Lake. There's a terrific vista of the lake bed here, and of the town, and the high South Warners in the distance.

Four miles before Fort Bidwell, the pavement starts again. There's not much to the town, which is adjacent to an Indian reservation and a hot springs. It is tiny and cute, and lined with cottonwoods.

SIDE TRIPS. Four miles south of Fort Bidwell, the Fandango Pass Road leads northwest, back over the Warners to 395, south of New Pine Creek, which is on Goose Lake. Goose Lake is the immense lake that straddles the state line. It is the lake that is viewed from Lakeview, Oregon. New Pine Creek is 15 miles south of Lakeview. Fandango Pass Road (Country Road 9), is gravel and fairly straight and wide. It's rather high, though, topping off at 6,332 feet.

Cedarville, 15 miles south of Fort Bidwell, is the area's largest town. The paved highway west from Cedarville to Alturas crosses Cedar Pass, with access to the South Warner Wilderness. The gravel road east from Cedarville cuts across the Sheldon National Antelope Range and comes out on Highway 140 near Denio.

The remote, lengthy gravel road from Cedarville to Denio made national news a few years ago when a young couple, with their baby, tried in a blizzard to find a Christmas shortcut from Oakland to Boise, since Donner Summit was closed. They got stuck here and the young man trudged for miles in the snow to get help while his wife huddled in a cave with the baby. It was made into a TV movie. The road from Cedarville to Denio across the antelope range is not a safe road even in summer, even in the daytime. It's easy to get lost and you always need to be prepared. Driving the road at night in a blizzard is foolish.

Bullard Creek on road to Surprise Valley

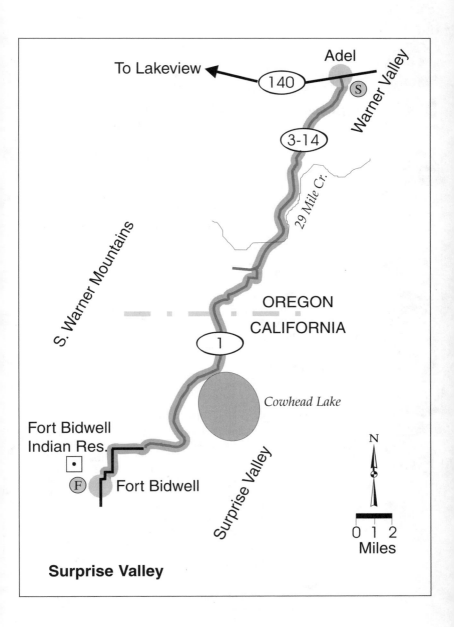

Surprise Valley

Steens Mountain Loop

LOCATION. Southeast Oregon desert, south of Burns.

HIGHLIGHTS. Oregon's highest road, cresting at 9,773 feet. Arguably Oregon's most scenic drive, paved or unpaved.

DIFFICULTY. Easy. Mostly one-lane gravel with turnouts.

DISTANCE. 49 miles from Highway 205 to the summit and back.

HIGH ELEVATION. 9,700 feet (not quite the summit).

MAPS. Frenchglen; Page Springs; McCoy Ridge; Fish Lake; Wildhorse Lake; Ankle Creek; Tombstone Canyon; Roaring Springs.

ADMINISTRATION. BLM Burns District.

GETTING THERE. From Burns take Highway 205 south for 61 miles to the village of Frenchglen. Go left on North Steens Mountain Road (Steens Mountain Loop). It's 24 miles to the summit, then 25 miles on South Steens Mountain Road back to Highway 205, emerging 10 miles south of Frenchglen.

REST STOPS. Fish Lake Campground; Jackman Creek Campground; Kiger Gorge overlook; Indian Creek overlook; Wildhorse Lake overlook (summit).

SPECIAL INFORMATION. They open this road in stages every spring as the snow melts. The spot that retains snow longest is located well beyond the summit, so even if the loop isn't opened all the way, you can often still make it to the top. Note: Several BLM Wilderness Study Areas in the Steens were converted to Wilderness in 1999. This does not affect the road.

THE DRIVE. Steens Mountain can be seen from just about everywhere in southwest Oregon, and vice versa. After rising from 4,200 feet to 9,733 feet in 24 miles, the tilted, 15-mile-long fault-block range then plummets in 3 miles down to 4,600 feet at the Alvord Desert. Understandably, there are no roads up that side.

The entire drive on Steens Mountain Loop is gorgeous, beginning with the historic village and state park of Frenchglen, on the Donner and Blitzen (German for "thunder and lightning") River, and continuing past Fish Lake and Jackman Creek. The scenery takes on world-class proportions at Kiger Gorge, 2 miles before the road crest. Kiger Gorge is a treeless, "U" shaped glacial basin that abruptly drops 2,500 feet from the cliff-top down to Kiger Creek. The notch on the ridge to the right is called The Gunsight, where two glaciers met back-to-back. Kiger Gorge is the best of the Steens' glacial valleys, although Indian Creek and Wildhorse Canyon are also spectacular.

At the road crest, a short spur road leads to the Wildhorse Canyon trailhead, and the long, gated, 0.25-mile road to the antenna-festooned summit. Wildhorse Canyon starts out as a tree-

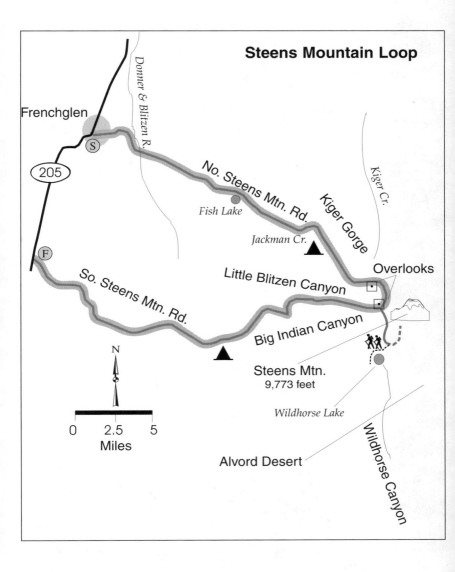

Steens Mountain Loop

Frenchglen

Donner & Blitzen R.

205

No. Steens Mtn. Rd.

Fish Lake

Kiger Cr.

Kiger Gorge

Jackman Cr.

Overlooks

Little Blitzen Canyon

So. Steens Mtn. Rd.

Big Indian Canyon

N

Steens Mtn.
9,773 feet

0   2.5   5
Miles

Wildhorse Lake

Wildhorse Canyon

Alvord Desert

less, semicircular, steep-sided, flat-bottomed glacial cirque, with the emerald gem of Wildhorse Lake in the center. Below the lake the canyon takes on a rocky, "V" profile. The glacier ended where the flat, "U" shaped bottom becomes a "V" shaped bottom.

From the summit, an aerie on top of the world, you can see the Alvord Desert and a vast expanse of Oregon. (A confession: There was a fog bank at the summit the day I visited, so I missed a large chunk of the view. I'm told it's impressive.)

The road beyond the crest is much like the road up, except a little curvier. A big switchback 8 miles beyond the crest tends to retain snow and usually keeps the South Steens Road closed much later in the year than the North Steens Road. The bottom 5 miles of the South Steens Road are home to a couple of wild mustang herds and are well worth a visit, even if the loop is not completely opened and you have to drive around from Frenchglen to see them. There are few sights in this world more breathtaking than wild mustang herds.

SIDE TRIPS. Many excellent backcountry drives may be found in the vicinity of the Steens, most of which have their own chapters in this book. The Alvord Desert (Drive 68) and Malheur Wildlife Refuge (Drive 70) should not be missed. The road through the Hart Mountain Antelope Refuge (Drive 65) comes out on Road 205 10 miles south of Frenchglen, just before the South Steens Road.

The Steens, Wildhorse Canyon

Alvord Desert

LOCATION. Southeast Oregon desert, south of Burns.

HIGHLIGHTS. Low desert along the base of the steep side of the Steens Mountains, with a close-up view of the dramatic 3-mile rise of the Steens from 4,600 feet to 9,773 feet.

DIFFICULTY. Easy, mostly level. Long roads, no services.

DISTANCE. 64 miles from Highway 78 to Highway 205.

HIGH ELEVATION. 5,200 feet.

MAPS. Folly Farm; Juniper Lake; Mann Lake; Miranda Flat; Alvord Hot Springs; Andrews; Fields.

ADMINISTRATION. BLM Burns District.

GETTING THERE. From Burns take Highway 78 east, then southeast, for 68 miles. The Fields-Denio Road to Alvord Ranch is on the right. Sixty-four miles from Highway 78, the Fields-Denio Road emerges, one mile north of the town of Fields on Highway 205, 57 miles south of Frenchglen and 21 miles north of Denio, Nevada.

REST STOPS. New Princeton; Alvord Desert.

THE DRIVE. This trip takes you along the base of the Steens Mountains for a close-up view of Oregon's steepest and most dramatic mountain rise. It's 35 miles of flat, occasionally marshy desert before you reach the base of Steens Mountain, although the range has been gradually building to this sudden crescendo since shortly after the turnoff from Highway 78. Directly opposite Steens Mountain lies the Alvord Desert, an immense dry lake bed and sink covered with sand dunes (this is part of the Great Basin and none of the creeks go anywhere).

Past the Alvord Desert, near the Alvord Ranch headquarters, just below the main summit, the road crosses Wildhorse Creek, which flows down a spectacular glacial canyon from Wildhorse Lake. But creek and canyon look fairly mundane by the time they reach the desert. Wildhorse Creek empties into Alvord Lake, which is passed on this drive at mile 58. The lake is sometimes a big, dry, alkali flat and sink, and sometimes a genuine lake.

The nicest thing about this drive is not the scenery, which is ample, but the lonely remoteness and the distance, both physical and spiritual, from civilization.

SIDE TRIPS. As long as you're in the area, don't miss the Steens Mountain Loop drive (Drive 67), the tour of the Malheur National Wildlife Refuge (Drive 70), Diamond Craters (Drive 71), and Duck Creek Valley (Drive 72). Also described as a separate trip is the Whitehorse Ranch Road (Drive 69), which parallels the Fields-Denio Road 20 miles to the south. For connoisseurs of solitude, Whitehorse Ranch Road is even more lonely and remote than the Fields-Denio Road, offering a slightly shorter route but an equally dramatic view of the Steens.

SOUTHEAST OREGON

In the BLM literature, Malheur Cave, just off Highway 78 halfway between New Princeton and the Fields-Denio turnoff, sounds like a "do not miss." To visit the cave, according to the BLM, turn east onto Malheur Cave Road, which is in the middle of a small lava flow, and drive 3 miles. The cave is on the left (north), just before a small reservoir. The formation is an extremely large lava tube, which means there are no stalactites or stalagmites. The tube is 3,000 feet long, with a ceiling ranging in height from 8 to 20 feet. The hikeable part of the tube ends at a large, underground lake. The tube slopes downward at the lake, with the ceiling disappearing into the water. One slight problem: I did not see Malheur Cave Road, or any other side road, on the east side of that stretch of Highway 78. That doesn't mean it wasn't there, of course.

Diamond Craters

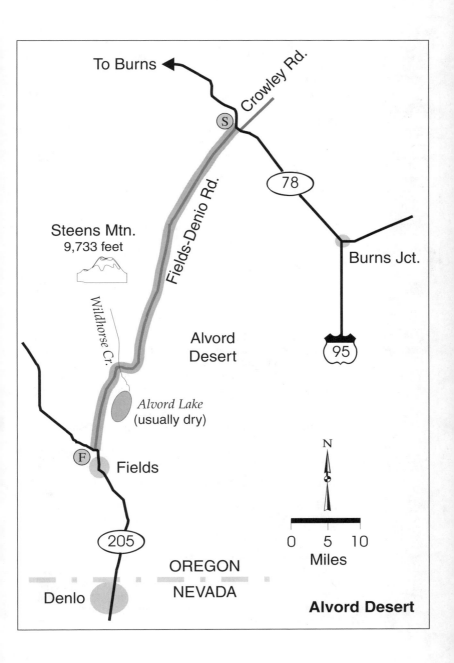

To Burns

Crowley Rd.

S

78

Burns Jct.

Fields-Denio Rd.

Steens Mtn.
9,733 feet

Wildhorse Cr.

95

Alvord
Desert

Alvord Lake
(usually dry)

F

Fields

N

205

0   5   10
Miles

OREGON

NEVADA

Denlo

Alvord Desert

Whitehorse Ranch

LOCATION. Extreme southeast Oregon, south of Burns and west of Jordan Valley.

HIGHLIGHTS. Spectacular view, from 20 miles away on one of the state's least-used roads, of the steep side of the Steens Mountains, Oregon's steepest mountain rise (5,173 feet in three miles, to 9,773 feet).

DIFFICULTY. Incredibly easy and fun. Mostly sand and gravel, almost perfectly level, and nearly straight.

DISTANCE. 49 miles from Highway 95 to Highway 205.

HIGH ELEVATION. 5,200 feet.

MAPS. Three Man Butte Well; Twelvemile Ridge; Whitehorse Ranch; Red Mountain; Pole Canyon; Trout Creek Canyon; Colony Ranch.

ADMINISTRATION. BLM Burns District.

GETTING THERE. Find your way to Jordan Valley, the picturesque Basque village that is Oregon's most southeastern, and most isolated, community. From Jordan Valley, take Highway 95 west and south for 66 miles, to the junction with Whitehorse Ranch Road, which goes to Whitehorse Ranch and Denio, Nevada. Turn right (west) and follow the dirt and gravel road 49 miles to the junction with Highway 205. The Highway 205 junction is 8 miles south of Fields and 12 miles north of Denio.

REST STOPS. The whole drive is a rest stop, but there are no actual rest areas, picnic sites, or established vista points.

SPECIAL INFORMATION. Either direction will suffice.

THE DRIVE. I love this trip! It's nearly identical to the Alvord Desert drive (Drive 68), except the Steens are a little farther away (20 miles), and the off-pavement segment isn't as long (49 versus 57 miles). What I like best is that unlike the Alvord Desert road, where you stood a remote chance of encountering another vehicle, the chances of that here are virtually zip. Think of it. Even though the road is unpaved, you could, if you were irresponsible enough, just point your car and hang on for the ride. You don't have to worry about oncoming traffic because (1) there isn't any and (2) you can see the road ahead of you for miles. Should your car veer off the road, you would be gently nudged back by a soft, curved bank at the road edge. And should your car go off the road, so what? It's all flat, barren desert occupied only by a few sagebrush plants.

I'm exaggerating, of course. I would *never* advocate less-than-cautious or off-road driving. For one thing, I have too much respect for the good people at Whitehorse Ranch, who would seriously, and correctly, object to visitors abusing their beautiful road.

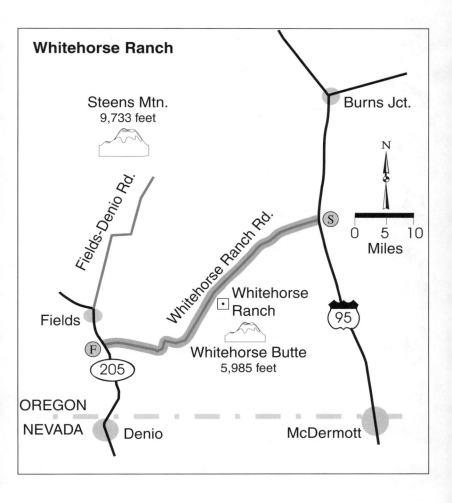

Whitehorse Ranch

Steens Mtn.
9,733 feet

Burns Jct.

N

Fields-Denio Rd.

Whitehorse Ranch Rd.

(S)

0   5   10
Miles

Whitehorse
Ranch

Fields

95

(F)

Whitehorse Butte
5,985 feet

205

OREGON

NEVADA   Denio   McDermott

SIDE TRIPS. Within a couple of hours of Whitehorse Ranch Road, you can explore the top of the Steens Mountains (Drive 67), the Malheur National Wildlife Refuge (Drive 70), the Alvord Desert (Drive 68), Diamond Craters (Drive 71), Succor Creek, Leslie Gulch (Drive 74), and basically the last 11 chapters of this book. Not all in one day, of course.

Malheur National Wildlife Refuge

LOCATION. Southeast of Burns in the southeast Oregon desert.

HIGHLIGHTS. One of the oldest, largest, and most productive federal wildlife refuges in the United States. The ultimate collecting pool for the vast, internally drained Harney Basin, which is the Oregon segment of the Great Basin.

DIFFICULTY. Wide, flat, and easy gravel and blacktop roads.

DISTANCE. 55 miles from New Princeton to Highway 20 (for OO Ranch, add 8 miles round trip).

HIGH ELEVATION. 4,000 feet.

MAPS. New Princeton; Malheur Lake East; Malheur Lake West; The Narrows; Northeast Harney Lake; Northwest Harney Lake; Stinking Lake; Moon Reservoir; Oakerman Lakes.

ADMINISTRATION. United States Fish and Wildlife Service and the Malheur National Wildlife Refuge.

GETTING THERE. New Princeton is located on Highway 78 and 47 miles southeast of Burns, near MP 38. A sign pointing west says MALHEUR REFUGE, DIAMOND CRATERS. The road west from New Princeton is paved for 2 miles to the beginning of the Diamond Craters loop (go left, south, for Diamond Craters). If you continue straight (west), you'll be on gravel Narrows-Princeton Road, which arrives at Refuge Headquarters 13 miles later. At the headquarters, go right, on the pavement, for another 7 miles to Highway 205, then turn right onto 205 for 2 miles, crossing The Narrows. Immediately beyond The Narrows, turn left (west), onto OO Ranch Road and continue for 14 miles to a junction. At the junction, go straight (4 more miles) for OO Ranch or right (17 more miles) for Highway 20. You'll emerge on Sage Hen Hill Road, near MP 115, west of Burns by 16 miles.

REST STOPS. Refuge Headquarters.

SPECIAL INFORMATION. Either direction works.

THE DRIVE. The Fish and Wildlife Service has some wonderful exhibits at Refuge Headquarters, mostly of stuffed birds, but they teach little about the geology of the two immense lakes that essentially make up the refuge. To understand the lakes' geological significance, you need to know that Harney Basin, covering one-fifth of Oregon, is part of the Great Basin, which occupies most of Nevada and parts of Oregon, Utah, and Idaho. As with the rest of the Great Basin, the Harney Basin has no external water drainage to the ocean (although the Owyhee River, which flows into the Snake River, cuts across the basin). Most of the basin's creeks end up in Harney Lake, including the water flowing out of Malheur Lake. Because it has an outlet, Malheur Lake contains fresh water, while Harney Lake, the ultimate receptacle, is alkali.

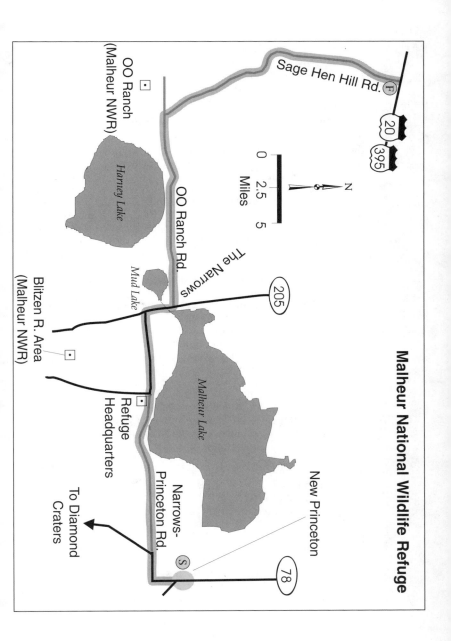

Malheur Lake is Oregon's second largest natural lake (after Upper Klamath Lake), while Harney Lake is the fourth largest, after Lake Abert (Drive 64). You catch glimpses of Malheur Lake from Highway 205 on the way to Frenchglen, and from the Princeton-Narrows Road. You catch glimpses of Harney Lake only from OO Ranch Road.

(If you've come to see wildlife rather than quest after glimpses of lakes, take the side trip from Refuge Headquarters through the Blitzen River marshes to the town of Frenchglen. See Side Trips. In fact, take that side trip regardless.)

For the first few miles, the Princeton-Narrows Road zooms across flat ranch country, eventually making its way onto a low desert rise that offers a fair view of Malheur Lake. You get a little closer to the lake as you approach the headquarters, but since the lake is surrounded by marsh and the water level fluctuates greatly, they wisely didn't build roads very close to it. Besides, it's a refuge. ("Malheur," by the way [such a pretty word], is French for "bad time.")

One feature of Refuge Headquarters is a hill with a lookout tower. You can't climb the tower but you can get a decent panorama from the base. Be sure to check out the little museum, which is full of stuffed birds.

After driving the rest of the way to Highway 205, heading north across The Narrows and turning left onto OO Ranch Road, you soon pass Mud Lake. About 5 miles later, Harney Lake appears far in the distance, surrounded by dunes and low hills. A couple of miles later, the road almost bumps the shore of Harney Lake. If you park at this point and climb the little hill, the lake is on the other side. This is the only good view of Harney Lake.

The OO Ranch Road quickly pulls away from the lake as it continues towards the junction with the road to Highway 20. The 4-mile (each way) trip from the junction to OO Ranch is probably worthwhile because of the marshes and wetlands on Silver Creek and Warm Springs Creek. The ranch features an interesting little historic cabin and a bunch of Fish and Wildlife Service buildings.

The road out to Highway 20 is straight and boring as it knifes across the almost featureless sagebrush desert.

SIDE TRIPS. The best place to view wildlife is from the Central Patrol Road, which follows the Blitzen River and adjacent marshes and ponds. Turn left instead of right when you hit the pavement just before Refuge Headquarters. It's 15 miles to the Diamond Craters cutoff and 15 more miles to Frenchglen. The road emerges 1 mile from Frenchglen on the Steens Mountain Loop, at P Ranch.

The stars of the wildlife show, which boasts a cast of 320 species, are the trumpeter swan, tundra swan, snow goose, snowy egret, white-faced ibis, double-crested cormorant, bald eagle, peregrine falcon, sandhill crane, mule deer, pronghorn, and mountain sheep. That's a pretty good show! And don't miss Diamond Craters (Drive 71) or the Steens Mountain Loop (Drive 67), which are described as separate drives.

Diamond Craters

LOCATION. Southeast of Burns, in the southeast Oregon desert.

HIGHLIGHTS. Small but spectacular volcanic area. Desert ranchland. Peter French Round Barn historic site.

DIFFICULTY. Easy, paved road to Diamond Craters. Narrow, unpaved side roads in Diamond Craters, some of which can be challenging. The second half of the loop road, through the town of Diamond, is unpaved.

DISTANCE. 50.5 miles from Highway 78 back to Highway 78.

HIGH ELEVATION. 4,800 feet.

MAPS. New Princeton; Barton Lake; Diamond; Adobe Flat.

ADMINISTRATION. BLM Burns District.

GETTING THERE. New Princeton is located on Highway 78 and is 47 miles southeast of Burns, near MP 38. A sign pointing west on 78 says MALHEUR REFUGE, DIAMOND CRATERS. It's 3 paved miles on the side road west from New Princeton to the Diamond Craters turnoff, where you go left (south), remaining on the pavement. From there, it's 10.5 miles to the Pete French Round Barn Historical Site, with the far unpaved end of the loop coming in from the left (east) immediately after. Staying on the pavement, it's 5 miles to Diamond Craters and 5 more to the junction with the cutoff road, on the right, to Frenchglen (called Diamond Lane). Bearing left (west) at the Diamond Lane junction, the pavement ends 5.5 miles later, at the town of Diamond (no services). After that, on the gravel, it's 3.5 miles to the Kiger Mustang Viewing Area turnoff, then 9.5 more miles through Happy Valley back to the Round Barn, the pavement, and the road back to New Princeton.

REST STOPS. New Princeton; Malheur Wildlife Refuge Headquarters.

THE DRIVE. According to a brochure put out by the BLM, Diamond Craters has "the best and most diverse basaltic volcanic features in the United States, all within a comparatively small and accessible area." It is a nifty place, I must admit. And there are some fun side roads up into the formation.

Your first stop will be the Peter French Round Barn, built by Peter French, a local cattle baron, in the early 1880s. Frenchglen is also named for Peter French, as is French Pete Reservoir, near Eugene. The man got around. And he was spectacular at designing round barns. Go through the closed gate to see the barn, or view it from the road.

Diamond Craters, as seen from the paved road, are incredible. Most noticeable are the ash and cinder craters, some with outpourings of black ropey ("pahoehoe") lava that appear as though the lava solidified maybe last week or the week before. Actually it all happened between 25,000 and 17,000 years ago. But in this arid country, things don't change very fast.

SOUTHEAST OREGON

At mile 21, in the middle of the crater complex, where a sign says DEAD END—4.5, turn right (west). The narrow dirt side road will take you past three spectacular craters in 1.5 miles before dropping off the volcanic upwelling, down to the desert, and indeed dead-ending in 4.5 miles. Look for a very narrow dirt road on the right, at about mile 1, that will take you around a crater and up to the top of the formation in about 2 miles. This is a fun little digression if you have high clearance and some power.

Beyond the craters, the pavement ends at the town of Diamond. If you're in a hurry, dispense with the unpaved half of the loop and take the cutoff to the Malheur National Wildlife Refuge and Frenchglen. Personally, I liked the far half of the loop. See Side Trips below for a description of the Kiger Mustang Viewing Area, whose turnoff is 3.5 miles beyond Diamond.

Past the mustang turnoff, the road climbs a little hill, with a view of the Happy Valley ranchlands, then drops back down to another view of the round barn. Then you hit pavement again and go back to New Princeton or wherever you're headed.

SIDE TRIPS. The Kiger mustang herd, which roams the lower slopes of the Steens Mountains, is one of the largest, purest, and most beautiful of the country's wild horse herds. The viewing area set up by the BLM begins 3.5 miles beyond the town of Diamond and is reached by an 11-mile, low-quality dirt road. The horses might not even be there but it's worth a shot because they're very impressive. I was struck by the difference in demeanor and expression between wild mustangs and "kept" horses when I saw the Kiger herd close-up on the South Steens Loop Road (Drive 67).

While you're in the neighborhood, the Malheur National Wildlife Refuge (Drive 70), and Steens Mountain Loop Road (Drive 67), described as separate drives, should not be missed.

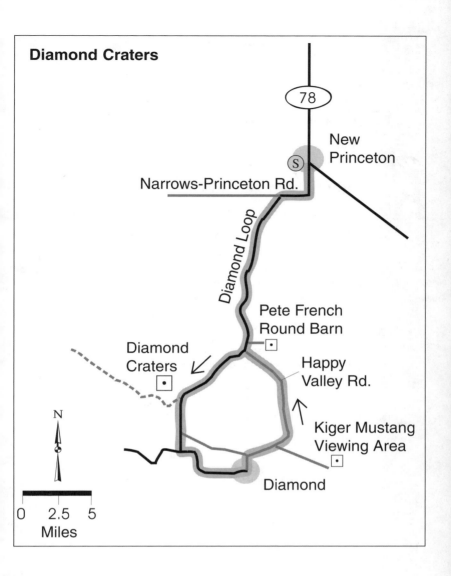

Diamond Craters

78

New
Princeton

S

Narrows-Princeton Rd.

Diamond Loop

Pete French
Round Barn

Diamond
Craters

Happy
Valley Rd.

Kiger Mustang
Viewing Area

N

Diamond

0   2.5   5
Miles

Duck Creek Valley

LOCATION. Southeast of Burns, in the southeast Oregon desert.

HIGHLIGHTS. A remote, isolated desert valley featuring a chain of dry lake beds and Duck Pond Ridge rising to the north.

DIFFICULTY. Easy, wide, mostly level gravel.

DISTANCE. 26 miles from Highway 78 to Crowley.

HIGH ELEVATION. 4,500 feet.

MAPS. Folly Farm; Dowell Butte.

ADMINISTRATION. BLM Vale District.

GETTING THERE. From MP 66 on Highway 78, north of Burns Junction by 26 miles, take Crowley Road northeast. The turnoff is located 0.25 miles south of the Fields-Denio turnoff, which is on the opposite side of the highway. Go as far up Crowley Road as the mood strikes you.

REST STOPS. None.

THE DRIVE. What can I say? I like desert backroads. Usually, you can speed along desert highways, cranking out the miles. But sometimes it's nice to get off the well-traveled tourist routes. This little road is about as rustically untraveled as you're going to get. It's not spectacular, like the nearby Fields-Denio Road (which, in fact, takes 25 miles to get spectacular), but it's awfully nice. The only other vehicles on the road will be driven by farmers, who will probably wave as you pass.

The road visits a string of dry lake beds along Duck Creek, unless you go in winter, or in spring of a particularly wet year. Then it visits a string of actual lakes. All of which demonstrate once again that this region is part of the Great Basin, with no external drainage to the ocean and where all streams end in either dry lakes, wet lakes, or sinks.

Initially, the road climbs a sagebrush hill dotted with juniper trees. It then descends to the edge of Duck Pond Lake, or what would be Duck Pond Lake if it had water. After 10 miles or so, the road goes over another hill. On the other side, the valley widens dramatically to accommodate the much larger Turnbull and Piute lake beds, with Duck Pond Ridge rising to the north. The lakes are beautiful when full and beautiful and green when they aren't. And yes, at the right time of year, you will see ducks.

It's 26 miles to Crowley, which is a cluster of farms. If you keep going for 40 or 50 more miles past Crowley, you'll emerge on Highway 20, between Burns and Ontario, Oregon.

SIDE TRIPS. As I said earlier, the Fields-Denio Road (see Drive 68), which goes through the Alvord Desert along the base of the Steens Mountains on their steep side, is spectacular.

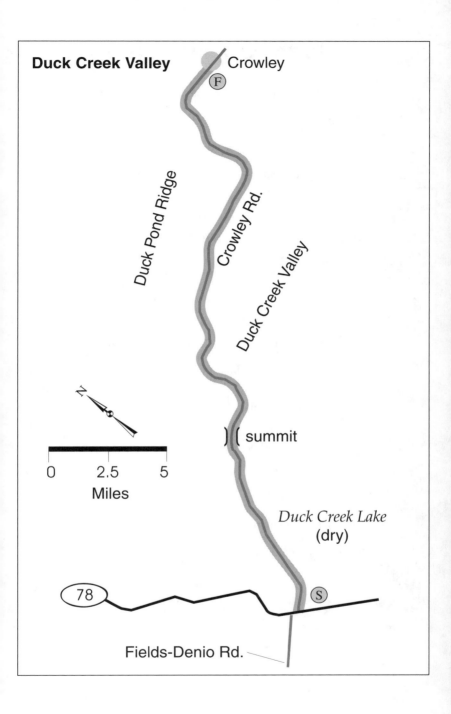
Duck Creek Valley

Crowley

Duck Pond Ridge

Crowley Rd.

Duck Creek Valley

N

0   2.5   5

Miles

) (summit

Duck Creek Lake
(dry)

S

78

Fields-Denio Rd.

North Fork Malheur River

LOCATION. Between Ontario and Burns in east-central Oregon.

HIGHLIGHTS. A beautiful little desert river and a charming reservoir, with a handsome mountain as a backdrop.

DIFFICULTY. Easy, wide, level gravel road.

DISTANCE. 15 miles from Highway 20 to Beulah Reservoir.

HIGH ELEVATION. 3,600 feet.

MAPS. Stemler Ridge; Petes Mountain; Beulah.

ADMINISTRATION. BLM Burns District.

GETTING THERE. Beulah Road begins just west of Juntura, off Highway 20. There are two signs at the turnoff. One says CHUKAR PARK CAMPGROUND—6. The other says BEULAH RESERVOIR—15. To reach these places, head north on Beulah Road.

REST STOPS. Chukar Park; Beulah Reservoir.

THE DRIVE. This exquisite little drive visits the North Fork of the beautiful Malheur River, which empties into the Snake River at Ontario. The first 56 miles of Highway 20 from Ontario follow the Malheur canyon and river. And a mighty handsome canyon and river they are. At Juntura, the Malheur divides into the North and South forks and the highway leaves them both behind.

The short, easy trip up the North Fork from Juntura follows a beautiful green valley with a large, clear, fast-flowing stream in the middle, hay fields on either side, and grassy, juniper-dotted hills lining the route. Beyond Chukar Park, at mile 6, the valley widens and the river slows a little, forming wide meanders and oxbow lakes.

Eventually, Castle Rock (6,837 feet) appears in the distance. This is a large, solitary peak with what appears to be a volcanic plug sticking out of one end (hence the name). The peak is exquisitely framed by the canyon for the last 8 miles of the drive. The prettiest part of the journey comes when you arrive at the little reservoir at mile 15, with the canyon still framing Castle Rock.

SIDE TRIPS. If you keep going beyond Beulah Reservoir, the road skirts the base of Castle Rock. After about 50 miles, it emerges on Highway 26 at the town of Ironside.

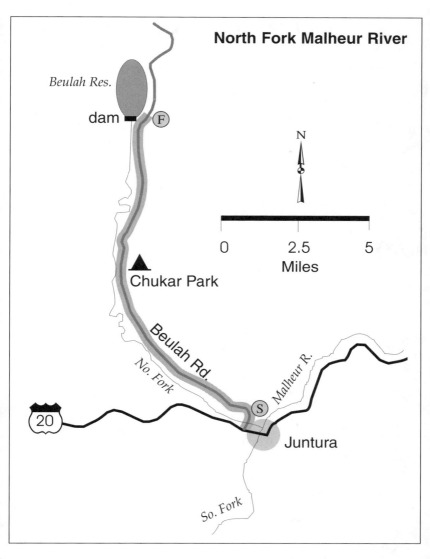

North Fork Malheur River

Beulah Res.

dam ▬ Ⓕ

N

0   2.5   5

Miles

▲ Chukar Park

Beulah Rd.

No. Fork

Malheur R.

20

Ⓢ

Juntura

So. Fork

Beulah Reservoir

Succor Creek, Leslie Gulch

LOCATION. Extreme eastern Oregon. Between Nyssa and Jordan Valley, near the Idaho line in the Owyhee River region.

HIGHLIGHTS. Succor Creek, a remote and beautiful desert canyon. Leslie Gulch, another canyon marked by towering red-rock spires. The upper end of Owyhee Reservoir, a spectacular rock gorge.

DIFFICULTY. Despite some washboarding, a couple of narrow spots along the creek, and a steep climb out of the canyon, the gravel road through Succor Creek Canyon to the hilltop above Leslie Gulch is wide, easy, and gravel. The road into Leslie Gulch is wide and gravel at the beginning and then steep and occasionally narrow for the last 3 miles, which run down the middle of a dry creek bed.

DISTANCE. 39 miles from Highway 201 to Leslie Gulch boat ramp.

HIGH ELEVATION. 4,000 feet.

MAPS. Adrian; Graveyard Point; Pole Creek Top; Rockville; Bannock Ridge; Pelican Point.

ADMINISTRATION. BLM Vale District.

GETTING THERE. From Ontario, take the combined Highway 201/20/26 south to Nyssa. In Nyssa, Highway 201 breaks off south (left) toward Adrian, 12 miles away. Six miles past Adrian, still on Highway 201, watch for a gravel road to the right (south), with a sign that says SUCCOR CREEK STATE PARK. (The Idaho state line is 2 miles beyond the Succor Creek turnoff on Highway 201.) It's 18 miles on the gravel road from the Highway 201 turnoff to Succor Creek State Park and 26 miles to the well-signed hilltop turnoff to Leslie Gulch. Go right at the hilltop for Leslie Gulch and straight for Jordan Valley. A final 13 miles take you through Leslie Gulch to the Slocum Creek Campground and boat ramp at Lake Owyhee.

REST STOPS. Adrian; Succor Creek Campground; Leslie Gulch landing.

SPECIAL INFORMATION. The lower portion of the road runs along a dry creek bed. Although the creek doesn't start very high up the mountain, this is an arid region and flash floods are a possibility, especially in summer when there are thunderhead buildups.

THE DRIVE. I first learned about Leslie Gulch in an Oregon guidebook, where it was listed under the heading "Geological Points of Interest." The book described a "10-mile long canyon" that "varied in width from 20 to 300 feet, with red spires over 2,000 feet high." It definitely sounded like a place to see. If the description was correct, not only should I have heard of it, but it

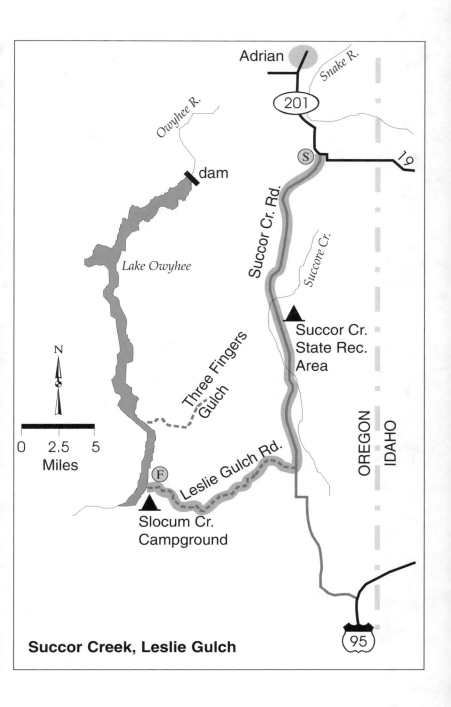

Adrian

Snake R.

201

Owyhee R.

dam

S

19

Succor Cr. Rd.

Lake Owyhee

Succore Cr.

Succor Cr.
State Rec.
Area

N

Three Fingers
Gulch

OREGON IDAHO

0   2.5   5
Miles

F

Leslie Gulch Rd.

Slocum Cr.
Campground

95

Succor Creek, Leslie Gulch

should have been a national park, like Utah's Bryce Canyon. Two-thousand foot spires?

To reach Leslie Gulch, I discovered, you have to go through Succor Creek Canyon on the gravel road out of Nyssa. I liked Succor Creek a lot. The road parallels a beautiful desert trout stream with huge yellow monoliths on either side of the creek. The drive culminates in a charming streamside campground full of cottonwoods. Just beyond the campground, the road climbs out of the canyon. The view back down to the campground from the climbout is especially pretty when the cottonwoods are changing color.

Eight miles beyond Succor Creek, amid a vast expanse of sagebrush, the road arrives at a hilltop junction and the turnoff right (west) to Leslie Gulch. From the hilltop, you can see Three Fingers Gulch, another canyon similar to Leslie Gulch. A much more adventurous and primitive road will take you there (see Side Trips below). You pass the turnoff on the way up from Succor Creek. The actual Leslie Gulch canyon starts 3 miles down the road from the Leslie Gulch hilltop.

As you may have guessed, the canyon was not quite as I'd imagined from the description in the guidebook. Nevertheless, it was impressive. I did not notice any place where the canyon was only 20 feet wide. And the tallest spires were 100 to 200 feet, which is still pretty tall. They were not red but a russet tan, formed from the shoreline wave action of a large inland lake, now long gone, against underwater lava. There is a 1,500-foot elevation drop between the Leslie Gulch hilltop and the Owyhee Lake boat ramp. A spire that tall would have been a sight to behold.

The last 10 miles of Leslie Gulch Road are narrow, curvy, and scenic. It appears that they ran the road down the middle of the dry creek bed for the last 3 miles because there was really no other place to put it, what with the spires and rock walls. Eventually, you end up at a little campground and boat ramp on the upper (southern) end of Owyhee Lake, which itself occupies an impressive yellow-rock canyon. I didn't run into any boats being towed down Leslie Gulch Road, but it is apparently common.

SIDE TRIPS. For a magnificent paved back road to Owyhee Dam and the lower portion of the reservoir, take the well-marked, 40-mile route south from Vale. The road along the Owyhee River below the dam is the best part. It makes many turns through flat farm country on the Snake River Plain.

The Three Fingers Gulch Road is on the right (west), 3 miles before the Leslie Gulch turnoff on the road from Succor Creek. It's longer than the Leslie Gulch Road, much rougher, and the canyon isn't quite as scenic.

The 9 miles from the Leslie Gulch hilltop to the junction with Highway 95, 18 miles from Jordan Valley, go through Basque country. You'll pass lots of sheep that are herded by colorfully dressed Basques on horseback. It's fascinating.

Owyhee Canyon, Three Forks

LOCATION. Extreme southeast corner of Oregon, near Jordan Valley

HIGHLIGHTS. The Owyhee Canyon and the confluence of the main, Middle, and North Forks of the Wild and Scenic Owyhee River.

DIFFICULTY. Easy-to-moderate for 32 miles, then moderate-to-difficult for 1.5 miles. Mostly narrow but level dirt road, with a few ruts and bumps. The last 1.5 miles are steep, narrow, and curvy, but not as bad as the warning sign suggests. The loop's return half is wide, level, gravel, and easy.

DISTANCE. 71 miles from Highway 95 to Three Forks to Jordan Valley.

HIGH ELEVATION. 5,000 feet.

MAPS. Danner; Little Grassy Mountain; Skull Creek; Whitehorse Butte; Three Forks; Juniper Point.

ADMINISTRATION. BLM Vale District.

GETTING THERE. From Highway 95, near MP 36, 16 miles west of Jordan Valley, turn south on Three Forks Road where signs say THREE FORKS and SOLDIER CREEK LOOP. It's 29 miles to a junction where you can either continue on to Three Forks (right, south) or loop back to Jordan Valley (left, east). From the junction, it's 4 more miles to Three Forks (the sign says 6). On the return leg, go right (east) for Jordan Valley, which is 34 miles away. The route is well signed.

REST STOPS. Three Forks; Jordan Valley.

SPECIAL INFORMATION. The sign at the Highway 95 turnoff says OWYHEE OVERLOOK—22, THREE FORKS—35. According to my odometer, however, the distances were 17 and 33. I liked the first (western) leg of the loop, from Highway 95, better than the second (eastern) leg to Jordan Valley because of the Owyhee overlook and the bleak desert atmosphere. The two legs are nearly equidistant.

THE DRIVE. The Owyhee River is one of Oregon's most beautiful and least visited Wild and Scenic rivers. Cutting through immense, steep-sided canyons for almost its entire length, the river runs through the state's most remote desert regions and provides rare external drainage to the ocean in what otherwise would be part of the Great Basin. The name "Owyhee," strangely enough, means "Hawaii," although the two places are as dissimilar as they could possibly be.

The trip's first 17 miles cross nearly flat desert whose only feature is an occasional cow. Despite the primitive road, the way is reasonably straight and level and you can get up a pretty good head of steam. At about mile 6, you cross Soldier Creek, which is a dry wash most of the year. Then you climb a hill on the far bank.

SOUTHEAST OREGON

At mile 12, the top of the Owyhee Canyon, a large black cleft, comes into view on the right.

At mile 17, you arrive at the overlook, which peers down the black, steep-sided gorge to the river, 300 feet below. After that, it's back across the desert, this time with the canyon popping up occasionally on the right. There are no more overlooks.

At the junction where you can either head toward Jordan Valley or continue to Three Forks, a sign announces that the latter is 6 miles away. After 2 miles, you come to another sign that warns that the route's final 1.5 miles are very steep, narrow, and rough (by my math, that comes to 3.5 miles, not 6).

Look for the three forks of the Owyhee River as you descend (the view is incredible). The main fork emerges from the deep, narrow gorge on the canyon's west side, the Middle Fork enters via the wide valley from the south, and the much smaller North Fork shows up via a smaller canyon to the southeast. After converging at a beautiful little green flat, they all disappear into the main canyon to the north. The flat is absolutely magical and well worth the drive.

The route back via Jordan Valley isn't as interesting as the route in but it's faster and wider, with a gravel road surface. Oddly enough, the return leg is a national scenic byway, whereas the Owyhee Overlook segment is not. After 18 miles on the return leg, you cross briefly into Idaho. A few miles later, you pick up pavement.

The route ends in the middle of Jordan Valley on Yturri Boulevard. It is not a boulevard, however, but a narrow country lane. Jordan Valley was founded by Basques and Yturri is a Basque name. So are the names on most of the stores. When I first visited Jordan Valley, in 1966, the main street looked like the set of an old Western movie, with wooden sidewalks and clapboard, false-front buildings. They've since modernized, which to me is a shame. It's still a nice little town, though.

SIDE TRIPS. Should you run out of things to do between Three Forks and Leslie Gulch (Drive 74), there are all manner of interesting places to visit around Jordan Valley. Start with the Charbonneau Grave Site. The turnoff is less than 1 mile west of the Owyhee Overlook turnoff on Highway 95 (MP 37), on the north side of the highway. It's 3 miles up a paved road to the site. You know how Sacajawea, on the Lewis and Clark expedition, is always depicted as carrying a baby? Jean Baptiste Charbonneau was that baby. He was born to Sacajawea and one of the other expedition members and lived from 1805 to 1866.

The Rome Pillars are also worth a look and involve another 3-mile side trip. Begin at the tiny village of Rome, 27 miles west of Jordan Valley, where Highway 95 crosses the Owyhee River in a green, picturesque farming valley. Turn north on one of the two gravel roads at Rome (the gravel roads converge after 0.25 miles), and continue for 1 mile or so until you come to a junction near the river. You can see the pillars, a series of white cliffs and columns, off to the left (west). Turn left at the junction, toward the pillars. The road goes up to the base, then heads up a side canyon, lights out over the desert, and drops down into another little side valley.

You might also try Jordan Craters. According to the map, you can get to Jordan Craters either from Danner, by continuing past

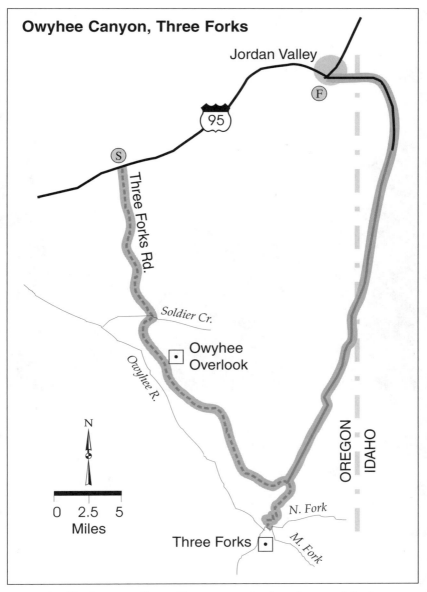

Owyhee Canyon, Three Forks

Jordan Valley

(F)

(95)

(S)

Three Forks Rd.

Soldier Cr.

Owyhee R.

Owyhee
Overlook

N

0   2.5   5
Miles

OREGON   IDAHO

N. Fork

Three Forks

M. Fork

the Charbonneau Grave Site, or on gravel roads out of Jordan Valley. These roads lead to a little reservoir (Cow Lake) on the east end of the lava flow. The highlight of Jordan Craters is supposed to be Coffeepot Crater, source of the lava, at the formation's northwest corner. You get there on the gravel road north from Rome, crossing the Owyhee River instead of turning left for the Pillars. It's a very long, complicated route.

Finally, just over the Idaho line on the return leg of the Three Forks loop, a sign at a side road says CLIFFS—6. I checked it out. The road does indeed lead to cliffs after 6 miles.

Road to Three Forks (Drive 75)

APPENDIX

A Simple Primer on Oregon Fire Ecology

Oregon's forests were "designed" to burn every 20 to 50 years. If you had visited the region a century ago, you would have seen many barren peaks that had been previously forested. In the ensuing years, fear and misunderstanding about forest fires led to massive efforts to stomp them out as quickly as they had started. In our more recent past, ecologists and forestry experts have contributed a more enlightened policy that accepts forest fires as part of a natural and necessary cycle. The lesson is: no matter what you do, the forest will eventually burn. Longer periods between fires mean the fires will be ever bigger, brighter, and hotter. When the forest has gone through many smaller and less intense fires, there are multiple openings and breaks and the fires will be more self-limiting.

So-called "ancient forests" of southern Oregon, whose trees rarely exceed 250 years of age, can withstand and benefit from cooler, smaller fires which scour out the underbrush and eliminate competition for limited resources of soil, sun, and water. They cannot withstand an intense crown fire, especially when the understory is choked with limitless unburnt fuel. There are tree species to which this philosophy does not apply precisely, and an example is the Douglas-fir, which grows in southwestern Oregon forests. These trees are somewhat unusual in that following fires or harvest, they tend to regenerate as "doghair" stands of closely spaced seedlings, saplings, and poles in which no single species of tree predominates. To grow better timber faster, and to lessen the fuel load in a forest fire, these stands should be artificially thinned.

When you drive through the Biscuit Fire, you quickly notice that not every square foot of every acre has burned to the ground. In fact, only 12% of the 499,570 acres that contained potentially valuable timber was burned, while 30% of the area wasn't burned at all, and 40% was only lightly burned.

2002 Biscuit Fire

2002 Biscuit Fire

Much of the area, particularly in the south, sits atop serpentinite, a rock that does not readily support dense forests or merchantable timber. Serpentinite-adapted vegetation consists mostly of manzanita brush and a few scattered Jeffrey and knobcone pines which typically burn every 10 to 20 years. However, many endangered shrub and wildflower species grow on serpentinite, including the rare and beautiful kalmiopsis plant (Drive 44), a kind of miniature rhododendron that reproduces mostly through natural cloning rather than by way of seed. I am unaware of any burned kalmiopsis sites.

At vista points, which are now more numerous and expansive, there are burned patches, some large and some small, and areas that were not burned at all. (This juxtaposition makes for excellent deer habitat, by the way.) Many burned zones were not entirely consumed and the evidence for that is that trees have survived, though their trunks are burned, and plants still grow, though their foliage has turned browned. In what seem to be unburned stands, closer examination reveals that the area was lightly underburned; this results in a natural thinning process which benefits the remaining trees. Occasionally, for no apparent reason, you see a green tree in the middle of a burned area.

The devastation was massive and total in a few drainages, including those of both Lawson and Little Todd creeks. No matter how you look at it, the fire was disastrous, even though in much of the area the burn was spotty and uneven. The edges of the burned areas reveal which tree species are the most flammable and which are the least. It turns out that the most shade-tolerant species are the least flammable and the most sun-loving are the most flammable. Knobcone pines flare in an instant, with Jeffrey and ponderosa pines being nearly as inflammable. Grand fir, Shasta red fir, and western hemlock are the most fire-resistant, with Douglas-fir close behind, and sugar pine and incense-cedar somewhere in the middle. Unfortunately, I saw some burned Port Orford cedar and Brewer spruce, which broke my heart since they are somewhat rare (especially Brewer spruce), and not particularly adapted to regeneration after a fire. On the other hand, Baker cypress is a tree that can only reproduce through fire.

Terminology

Here is a list of commonly used terms that are used in the text and may require elaboration.

4WD. Abbreviation for "four-wheel drive," where power from the engine goes to all four wheels instead of only two. The alternatives are "two-wheel drive," where power goes to the rear wheels only, and "front-wheel drive," where power goes to the front wheels only. For consistency, I have avoided the term "4x4."

Aggregate. The gravel used on road surfaces. Rated according to the diameter of the largest constituent rocks, for example "two-inch and less." The smaller the rock, the smoother the ride.

Association. An ecological term that refers to different plant species that grow in the same kinds of places. Pacific madrone, for example, is frequently found alongside Douglas-fir and ponderosa pine, but never alongside whitebark pine. There are all kinds of associations: geographic (such as Pacific Northwest, or Sierra Nevada), elevational, riverbank, north slope or south slope (aspect), desert, or coastal.

Boat launch. A road or ramp, usually paved, that leads into a lake, river, or bay and down which a boat trailer may be backed into the water.

Cattle grate. Instead of disrupting traffic by running fences or gates across public roads, ranchers have discovered that cattle will not cross a metal grate on the ground. Cattle grates turn up frequently on secondary roads, country lanes, and unpaved roads. Cattle also will not cross a series of parallel lines painted on the pavement to resemble a grate.

Forest Road. Often abbreviated as "FR." Refers only to roads on National Forest or BLM land. Two-digit forest road numbers indicate primary routes, four-digit numbers indicate secondary routes (with the first two digits matching the nearest primary route), and three digits indicate spur roads. The numbering system has little to do with the road surface, except that spur roads are almost never paved.

Glacial cirque. Mountain glaciers tend to cut amphitheater-shaped basins into the rock, with cliffs on three sides, a moraine (rock pile) on the outlet (creek) side, and often a beautiful lake in the middle. These basins, called "cirques," are very common in Oregon's high mountain areas. The glaciers, arising during the last Ice Age, which ended 10,000 years ago, are mostly gone.

Granite. A kind of rock formed when molten material (magma) solidifies deep underground. It can be recognized by the presence of large crystals. True granite has a specific constituent mineral content. "Granitic" rock forms the same way as does granite, but with different constituent minerals. Granitic rock types in Oregon include granite, quartz-diorite, gabbro, and serpentinite.

Great Basin. An area of the country, including most of Nevada and parts of Idaho, Utah, and Oregon, having no drainage to the ocean. The Great Basin is marked by "tension" or pulling apart of the land, which results in alternating narrow, lineal, mountain ranges and valleys.

Junction. A junction is a place where two or more roads come together.

Milepost. Often abbreviated as "MP." Most public highways in Oregon have a milepost every mile. So do many primary and secondary Forest Roads.

Prairie. In the Pacific Northwest, a "prairie" is a grassy opening on a mountainside and is usually caused by poor soils or repeated fires and grazing.

Rimrock. Much of central and eastern Oregon is marked by rimrock, which refers to a table-edged mesa with a flat top that drops off to a vertical, or mostly vertical cliff. Many rimrock formations are associated with the "lava plateau," an area of Oregon and Washington comprised of layer upon layer of lava that is mostly level and has no obvious source. Lava is fairly soft and erodes and cracks easily. Rimrock is often the result of river erosion or faulting of plateau lava or other layered rock materials.

Scenic Byway. The State of Oregon, United States Bureau of Land Management, and USDA Forest Service all have the power to designate roads as national scenic byways. Such roads may or may not be paved (most are). All the unpaved ones (except for a few really lousy ones) are included in this book. Personally, I would rather decide for myself which roads are scenic and which are not than have the government tell me.

Serpentinite. Serpentinite, often called "serpentine," is a type of rock found mainly on the ocean sub-floor. It is theorized that when serpentinite occurs on land, it was bulldozed up from the ocean by the advancing continent. Serpentinite nearly always occurs near the continent's advancing edge. Most common tree and plant species will not grow on serpentinite or are stunted by it. On the other hand, many rare and endangered species grow only on serpentinite.

SUV. Short for "sport-utility vehicle," a station-wagon type vehicle almost always equipped with either 4WD or AWD. They are ideal for the roads in this book because of their power, traction features, relatively high ground clearance, easy handling, and comfort.

Trailhead. The place where a trail begins. There are often road signs directing you to the trailhead. Trailheads usually feature parking and a prominent sign. They may have an interpretive display, pit toilets, picnic tables, and campsites. The fanciest, most popular ones will have a horse corral and loading ramp.

Washboarding. Occurs frequently on gravel roads, especially on uphill sections, where gravel accumulates into a series of narrow ridges a few inches high and wide and at right angles to the road axis, making the road resemble a washboard surface. The best solution to driving on washboarded roads is to go slowly to minimize vibration and impact on your car. Good shock absorbers help.

Waterbar. A ditch and berm (dirt pile) cut at right angles across a road to channel water off to the side so it doesn't create an erosion gully. They can be quite deep and will definitely slow you down. Cross them on the uphill side, at an angle, so that one wheel at a time goes over.

Wilderness Area. A wilderness area is an area of at least 5,000 acres, designated by an act of the U.S. Congress, where mechanized vehicles, forest management, and certain other human activities are prohibited. Obviously, no roads in this book go through wilderness areas, although several lead up to the edge of them. Three roads herein are bounded on both sides by federal wilderness for the last few miles: Badger Lake (Drive 3), Flag Point (Drive 6), and Fish Creek Valley (Drive 32).

References

Bernstein, A. *90 Best Day-Hikes, Southern Oregon and Far Northern California*. Grants Pass, OR: Cloudcap Books, 1994.

Bernstein, A. *Hiking the Southern Oregon Cascades and Siskiyous*. Helena, MT: Falcon Press, Globe Pequot, 2001.

Bernstein, A. *Native Trees of the Northwest*. Grants Pass, OR: Cloudcap Books, 1988.

Niehaus, T. *Pacific States Wildflowers*. Peterson's Field Guides. New York: Houghton Mifflin, 1976.

Oregon Atlas. Freeport, Maine: DeLorme Mapping, 1991.

Randall, W. *Manual of Oregon Trees and Shrubs*. Corvallis, OR: OSU Bookstores, 1981.

Approaching Dug Bar on Snake

Addresses

BUREAU OF LAND MANAGEMENT

Burns District Office
12533 Hwy 20 West
Hines, Oregon 97738
541-573-4400

Coos Bay District Office
1300 Airport Lane
North Bend, OR 97459
541-756-0100

Lakeview District Office
P.O. Box 337
1300 S. G St
Lakeview, OR 97630
541-947-2177

Medford District Office
3040 Biddle Road
Medford, OR 97501
541-770-2200

Prineville District Office
3050 NE Third Street
(P.O. Box 550)
Prineville, OR 97754
541-416-6700

Roseburg District Office
700 NW Garden Valley Blvd.
Roseburg, OR 97470
541-440-4930
www.or.blm.gov/roseburg

Salem District Office
1717 Fabry Rd. SE,
Salem, OR 97306
503-375-5646

Vale District Office
100 Oregon Street
Vale, OR 97918
541-473-3144
www.or.blm.gov/vale

FISH AND WILDLIFE SERVICE

Hart Mountain National Antelope
    Refuge
P.O. Box 111
Lakeview, OR 97630
541-947-3315

Malheur National Wildlife Refuge
P.O. Box 245
Princeton, Oregon 97721
541-493-2612
www.r1.fws.gov/malheur/

FOREST SERVICE

Deschutes National Forest
1645 E. Highway 20
Bend, OR 97701
541-388-2715
www.fs.fed.us/r6/centraloregon/

Fremont National Forest
Box 337
1300 S. G St
Lakeview, OR 97630
541-947-2151
Fax 541-947-6399
www.fs.fed.us/r6/fremont/

Mt. Hood National Forest
2955 NW Division St.
Gresham, OR 97030
503-467-2291

Ochoco National Forest
3000 E. Third
P.O. Box 490
Prineville, OR 97544
541-447-6247

Rogue River National Forest
333 W. 8th St. / P.O. Box 520
Medford, OR 97501-0209
541-858-2200
Fax 541-858-2220
www.fs.fed.us/r6/rogue/

FOREST SERVICE (cont.)

Siskiyou National Forest
200 NE Greenfield Rd.
P.O. Box 440
Grants Pass, OR 97526
541-471-6500

Siuslaw National Forest
4077 S.W. Research Way
P.O. Box 1148
Corvallis, OR 97339
541-750-7000
Fax 541-750-7234
www.fs.fed.us/r6/siuslaw/

Umpqua National Forest
P.O. Box 1008
2900 NW Stewart Parkway
Roseburg, OR 97470
541-672-6601

Winema National Forest
2819 Dahlia Street
Klamath Falls, OR 97601
541-883-6714
Fax 541-883-6709
www.fs.fed.us/r6/winema/

Wallowa-Whitman National Forest
P.O. Box 907
Baker City, OR 97814
541-523-6391
www.fs.fed.us/r6/w-w/

Willamette National Forest
Federal Building
211 East Seventh Ave.
P.O. Box 10607
Eugene, OR 97440
541-465-6521
www.fs.fed.us/r6/willamette/

STATE OF OREGON

Oregon Department of
    Transportation
355 Capitol St. NE
Salem, OR 97301
888-ASK-ODOT (275-0308)
www.odot.state.or.us

Index

About the Author

Art Bernstein has explored the trails and backroads of Oregon for over 30 years. He earned an MS in Natural Resources Management in 1970 from the University of Michigan, and celebrated by moving to Grants Pass, Oregon. Since then, he has worked as a County Forester, a national park Ranger/ Naturalist at Oregon Caves, and as an Instructor of Forestry and Outdoor Recreation at Rogue Community College. He has published numerous hiking books and books about the backroads and natural history of Northern California and the Pacific Northwest. *Oregon Byways* is Art's first book with Wilderness Press.

Art Bernstein at Klamath Canyon

"I want more!"

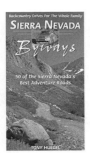

Let Tony Huegel's exciting series, *Backcountry Drives For The Whole Family,* guide you to even more off-highway adventure.

- ❑ **California Coastal Byways**
  ____ Copies ($18.95* each)

- ❑ **California Desert Byways**
  ____ Copies ($19.95* each)

- ❑ **Sierra Nevada Byways**
  ____ Copies ($16.95* each)

- ❑ **Colorado Byways**
  ____ Copies ($18.95* each)

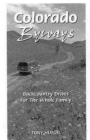

- ❑ **Idaho Byways**
  ____ Copies ($14.95* each)

- ❑ **Utah Byways**
  ____ Copies ($16.95* each)

- ❑ **Washington Byways**
  (Available November 2003)
  ____ Copies ($18.95* each)

- ❑ **Oregon Byways**
  by Art Bernstein
  ____ Copies ($16.95* each)

California residents add 7.25% sales tax. Please include $3 for the first book ordered, and 50¢ for each additional book to cover postage and handling.

$_____ Total

**Make a check out to Wilderness Press
or complete the credit card information below and mail it to:**

Wilderness Press, 1200 5th Street, Berkeley, CA 94710

Name: _____

Street: _____

City: _____ State: _____

Zip: _____

VISA ☐   MasterCard ☐

card number:

☐☐☐☐ ☐☐☐☐ ☐☐☐☐ ☐☐☐☐

Expiration date:

☐☐☐☐

Signature: _____

PHONE ORDERS: (800) 443-7227

*Prices may change without notice.

Notes

Notes

Notes